D0893253

Supplier Management Handbook

Supplier Management Handbook

James L. Bossert, Editor

Sponsored by the ASQC
Customer–Supplier Division

ASQC Quality Press
Milwaukee, Wisconsin

Supplier Management Handbook
James L. Bossert, editor

Library of Congress Cataloging-in-Publication Data

Supplier management handbook / James L. Bossert, editor; sponsored by
the ASQC Customer-Supplier Division.
 p. cm.
Rev. ed. of: Procurement quality control. 4th ed. ©1988.
Includes bibliographical references and index.
ISBN 0-87389-284-4
1. Industrial procurement—United States—Quality control—
Handbooks, manuals, etc. 2. Quality control—United States—
Handbooks, manuals, etc. I. Bossert, James L.
II. American Society for Quality Control. Customer-Supplier
Division. III. Procurement quality control.
HD39.5.S87 1994
658.7'2—dc20   93-41960
              CIP

10 9 8 7 6 5 4 3 2

ISBN 0-87389-284-4

Acquisitions Editor: Susan Westergard
Project Editor: Kelley Cardinal
Production Editor: Annette Wall
Marketing Administrator: Mark Olson
Set in Times and Helvetica Condensed by Montgomery Media, Inc.
Cover design by Montgomery Media, Inc.
Printed and bound by BookCrafters, Inc.

ASQC Mission: To facilitate continuous improvement and increase customer satisfaction by
identifying, communicating, and promoting the use of quality principles, concepts, and technologies; and thereby be recognized throughout the world as the leading authority on, and
champion for, quality.

For a free copy of the ASQC Quality Press Publications Catalog, including ASQC membership
information, call 800-248-1946.

Printed in the United States of America

  Printed on acid-free recycled paper

 ASQC
Quality Press
611 East Wisconsin Avenue
Milwaukee, Wisconsin 53202

Contents

Foreword

There are many reasons for the importance of a work such as this fifth edition of *Procurement Quality Control.* We are more living in a truly shrinking world, where the exchange of goods and services has no borders. As practitioners of the quality sciences, we recognize that in the chained series of exchanges, the weakest link defines the strength of the chain. Therefore, we are dependent on the levels of excellence we can attain from our suppliers. If we do not pursue strengthening the entire chain, it will break.

The expansion of the practices described in this text has been explosive from the time of the fourth edition. The practices that once were thought to apply only to the military-industrial high-volume manufacturing plants now can be applied to almost any exchange of goods or services. The only defining or controlling factor to use of the tools is the ability to describe clearly what is to be exchanged.

This fifth edition also formally marks the watershed events where the Vendor–Vendee Technical Committee completes its transition to the Customer–Supplier Division. Many of our division charter members have helped this transition. James Bossert, ASQC Fellow, has led us in the area of publications. Not only was he the fourth edition editor, but also the first division publications chair and a co-instructor of the ASQC professional development class Supplier Certification Processes (based in part on the teaching of this text).

We hope this text aids in your pursuit of excellence.

John O. Brown
Division Chair

Acknowledgments

Many people contributed to the writing of this handbook. The efforts of some deserve special recognition. Numerous people responded to the call for examples of supplier rating schemes. Although not all were used, I have tried to show some representative examples of what is being done across many industries. Each contributor is recognized with his or her rating scheme.

My wife, Nancy, patiently assisted me in the typing of this manuscript. She labored on in what seemed to be an endless task. Thank you, Nan, I could not have done it without you.

I was constantly reminded of my responsibilities by John O. Brown. Whenever things slowed down, there was a note or a phone call from John asking how things were coming. His gentle reminders kept me going. He contributed support as well in chapter 11.

Janet Raddatz contributed chapter 15 on the food industry, a welcome addition, and coauthored the rewrite of chapters 1, 3, 6, 8, and 10. She also offered some editing comments for the other chapters in an effort to help clarify things. Her comments challenged some ideas, which led to a collaboration; this helped to make this edition superior to the prior editions.

Finally, my daughters Lindsay and Ashley deserve recognition. Without their patience and support, I never could have completed this. Many an afternoon and evening were given up so that this text could be completed on time. Thank you all.

Why Procurement Quality?

Chapter 1

Key words: customer, distributors, inspection, integrity, ISO 9000, long-term commitments, objectivity, partnership, procurement quality, proprietary information, quality, quality systems, respect, strategy, supplier.

Summary
- The evolution of procurement quality
- The new role of procurement
- The basic requirements of a procurement system
- The consideration of primary business goals
- The development of a supplier strategy
- The benefits attained from a sound supplier system

Today the word *quality* appears on almost every product we come across—food, appliances, automobiles, and software. No matter where you turn, you see or hear about quality. In fact, we demand a certain level of quality in everything that we buy. This is evident in the increase of consumer complaint features in newspapers and on television.

What is meant by the word *quality?* The American Society for Quality Control (ASQC) defines quality as "the totality of features and characteristics of a product or service that bear on its ability to satisfy given needs."[1]

The features and characteristics of any product are how we as consumers evaluate how *good* that product or service is. For example, in a restaurant, the amount we leave as a tip is a direct reflection of the quality of the service that we have received. Satisfying given needs can include the quantity, price, or purity of something. It is what we as consumers have defined as our minimum acceptable standard. If, for example, there is a need for a chemical with a 99.9 percent purity level, but that level cannot be obtained unless we pay an exorbitant amount, that need may have to be redefined to a level that is more cost effective. So, the need for good specifications is established. These specifications will give the supplier the performance features that the customer requires.

ASQC states that

> Specifications for the manufacture of a product or the delivery of a service are a translation of these features and characteristics into manufacturing or performance terms. The features and characteristics often are considered in relationship to the *design* and *specification* of the product or service; to the *conformance* of the product or service to specifications and to the *compliance* of the supplier of the product or service to requirements.[2]

This approach serves as a reminder of the distinction between the functional and implemented aspects inherent in the design concept and specifications and in the conformance and compliance aspects of the product and implementation process.

So, now our definition of quality has expanded beyond the traditional designing and conformance aspects to the implementation and delivery of the product. Where does the product fit? How do we perceive it? How can we buy it? How do we know what we are buying? We need to answer these questions before manufacturing the product in the design reviews. Then and only then should we have confidence in the components we are purchasing.

The Changing/Transitional Role of Purchasing

Years ago, before the industrial revolution, products were made by skilled craftspeople. Only the highest quality was made and sold to those who could afford those products. The feedback to manufacturers was immediate because they could see if the quality was unacceptable by the expression on the consumers' faces. Only when Eli Whitney developed the concept of interchangeability of parts did the need for procurement quality begin.

As the complexity of products has increased, so has the need for quality. With this, purchasing agents have assumed the added responsibility of quality assurance. Traditionally, the role of the purchasing agent has been one of getting the product at the lowest cost. Potential suppliers were evaluated in terms of their ability to provide the following:

1. The desired quality defined as the suitability of product or service of use as intended
2. The total number of products required, including the schedule by which the product or service is required
3. Tangible and intangible services that are benefits over and above quality and price
4. Price, which is a measure of value

Purchasing agents also took into account additional factors that supplemented these four requirements. These included such things as geographic location, labor relations, the supplier's internal facilities, the supplier's reserve or backup facilities, capability of the supplier's management services, supplier's service capability, and supplier's financial status.

After this information was compiled, the purchasing manager might conduct plant visits for the prospective suppliers. This would be done only after the number of suppliers had been reduced to a manageable number. This on-site visitation might be used to appraise factors such as production control, cost control, morale, and the quality of the materials management activities.

Purchasing agents also might be asked to evaluate or rate suppliers. Supplier rating can take many forms, some simple and some complex. In chapter 7, supplier rating will be examined more closely.

When analyzing supplier performance, a purchasing agent evaluates how a supplier measures up to a defined set of performance standards that the purchasing agent applies to all suppliers. This enables a differentiation between good and marginal suppliers. A good system has guidelines that provide assistance in scoring all areas of resource selection. Any past experience with a supplier's quality and delivery performance is important because it is quantifiable data. Any past experience with technical, financial, and managerial services also can help in making an assessment. Price is not considered at this time. In fact, any quoted prices must be referred back to quality and delivery performance to have any validity. We need to know what to expect to determine the total cost of a purchased product accurately.

Performance standards reflect the cost that purchasing agents must incur in the satisfying of user requirements. For example, suppliers may be rated on quality in terms of three categories: cost of defect prevention, defect detection, and defect prevention. The sum of these costs for each supplier can then be expressed as a percent of the total value of materials purchased from that supplier.

Delivery performance may be expressed in terms of acquisition and availability costs. These costs may represent follow-up time, expediting time, telephone expenses, field surveillance costs, and premium transportation costs, in addition to manufacturing losses due to late deliveries.

Traditionally, this kind of information is then put into each supplier's overall rating. This composite score is made available to all purchasing agents in the organization. The rating can increase or decrease the amount of business a supplier receives, so the evaluation must be done carefully. The purchasing agent has fulfilled the traditional role. The times, however, are changing and now there is more emphasis on quality. The amount of technical knowledge needed to assess the adequacy of each manufacturing operation has caused a move toward the team approach for supplier rating. This will be discussed further in chapter 7.

What is procurement quality? There has been a brief discussion of the traditional role of procurement and the changes occurring in this area. Is procurement quality a measure of how well the procurement organization performs? Is it a measure of the quality of the products purchased? Is it somewhere in between? The true answer lies somewhere between the two extremes.

There is a need to purchase high-quality materials, but there also is a need for a high-quality organization to purchase the products. Procurement quality includes any and all aspects that deal with the purchasing of products. It sounds simple, but it really is a complex definition.

The definition assumes that there are well-defined specifications for the design and manufacture of the product being purchased. This implies that we have defined what conformance means in the product, that the measurement requirements are identified, that the reliability and maintainability of the product has been determined, that the delivery and packaging requirements are met, and that liability and environmental concerns are addressed. The communication that takes place among purchasing agents is critical in maintaining a favorable outcome.

There is a series of required steps to ensure good communication.

1. Learn as much as you can about sources.
2. Use site inspections.
3. Develop a process that ensures objective supplier evaluation system.
4. Make the selection based on all factors—not just cost.

First, purchasing agents need to develop good sources of information. There are many ways to obtain information: purchasing directories in magazines, industrial journals, catalogs, books, advertisements, handbooks, and purchasing bibliographies. These show the purchasing agent what is out there, and what suppliers are trying to sell. Another way is to interview sales personnel. Sales personnel can tell you what the competition is doing and can supply leads to other potential suppliers. Some sales personnel may have examples of comparative studies that have been conducted by their company or other independent concerns.

It also is time to look at establishing productive relationships with our suppliers. Through site visits and design reviews, the purchasing agent can obtain information on the acceptability and capability of potential suppliers. As the process progresses, the purchasing agent will be able to develop a relationship with the supplier in which both the customer and the supplier work together to solve problems.

Second, site inspections allow the purchasing agent to determine the capability of the supplier to provide the material and to convey the seriousness of the potential of doing business with the supplier. The site visit also serves as a means to impress on the supplier that the customer expects the supplier to provide exactly what the customer wants.

Third, the purchasing agent needs to evaluate the supplier in an objective manner. The intent of any evaluation system is to examine all suppliers according to criteria important to the customers. The purchasing agent will then take the top three or four suppliers to evaluate more closely. This is intended to determine the strengths and weaknesses of each candidate. It allows the purchasing agent and the customer to decide which supplier has the most promise for providing the required product.

The fourth step is the selection of the best candidate to provide the product. This involves more than determining the lowest bidder. All the information collected must be reexamined. All references must be contacted to obtain other viewpoints: technical competence, delivery performance, goodwill practices, statistical process control implementation, laboratory/measurement capabilities, financial outlook, service availability, and capacity. The intent is to obtain a supplier that will provide the specified quality, at the prescribed time, at a reasonable price. The supplier will provide good service when changes are necessary, take the initiative for technical innovations, provide advance notice for process changes, and work for the mutual customer–supplier benefit.

This is a lot of work for the purchasing agent to do alone. The purchasing agent's new role is to be a facilitator who obtains the necessary experts to evaluate and decide as a group which supplier has the best potential. There are a number of combinations of people that can comprise this team. It can include people from the development community who have developed product from an idea; it can include people from the manufacturing area who have to use the product as it comes in the door; it can include people from laboratories who have developed testing methods and need to determine the capability of the supplier; and it can include a person from the quality profession to evaluate the level of process control in a supplier.

This team is pulled together when the product is ready to go from the design phase to manufacturing. In the initial meeting, the team will cover what the product is, its intended use, and the timeframe within which they have to work. At subsequent meetings, the team can examine the preliminary list of potential suppliers and the initial quantities needed for scaleup.

After the evaluations have been made, and the supplier is selected, the team must document the reason for the selection in a report kept on file for future reference. This team will continue to meet for up to one year to review the supplier's performance. If any problems arise, it is up to the team to work with and assist the supplier in providing the product. At the end of the year, the team will either disband or continue to audit the supplier semiannually. A copy of any reports written at this time should be given to the supplier to keep the supplier informed. It is encouraged that, where possible, the supplier participate in these meetings either through conference calls or by visits to the user.

Use of the team format is encouraged due to the success that has been attained by companies that have tried it. A team can be as small as two people, so any size company should consider this format.

There are circumstances where a company does not deal directly with a manufacturer, but with a distributor. This issue requires a slightly different supplier management approach.

What Is a Distributor?

A distributor is a nonmanufacturing source of product. In some industries, distributors are called brokers. Generally, the distributor does not change the product itself. The distributor may change the packaging to meet the customer's needs, but only in rare cases does the product change. The chemical industry is one example where some distributors may mix chemicals together to form a new product. Basically, the three types of distributors are (1) a surrogate sales force for a manufacturer, (2) a repackager, and (3) a surrogate sales force and a manufactuer/distributor.

A surrogate sales force for the manufacturer serves as the marketing function for the manufacturer. It takes a product from the manufacturer as is. The manufacturer has the responsibility for product quality because the user receives the package in the original condition from the manufacturer. When necessary, the distributor is trained by the manufacturer in the proper handling and storage needed to maintain the quality of the product while it is in the distributor's possession.

The repackager and surrogate sales force receive the product in large quantities and repackage the product to sell in the customer's desired quantities. Here the distributor and manufacturer work together to ensure that nothing compromises product quality in the repackaging phase. The manufacturer/distributor performs a similar function to that of the repackager. However, the manufacturer/distributor also produces a new product by the addition of other ingredients.

Supplier programs with a distributor tend to be more difficult to set up because the distributor has no control of the manufacturing process. The most common way to set up a supplier program is to have distributors work only with certified manufacturers for the products they handle. This can be accomplished in the following two ways: Distributors can get their manufacturers together and work with users to certify the manufacturers, or users can recommend suppliers that already have been certified so distributors can establish contracts with those manufacturers.

A distributor supplier program has five basic components: (1) a manufacturer audit system, (2) a shipping/packaging control system, (3) a storage control system, (4) a specification program, and (5) a quality information system. The manufacturer audit system is a systematic way of assessing the quality program at the manufacturer. The purpose of this is to evaluate, document, and ensure that the product produced is of the quality level the customer desires. The shipping/packaging control system is a way of ensuring traceability and lot integrity from various suppliers and that the quality is not compromised in the repackaging operation. The storage control ensures that the product maintains the quality while in the distributor's possession. The specification program is the maintenance of up-to-date specifications for all the distributor's customers and, when necessary, documentation of who at the manufacturer's facility has a copy of the specification. The quality information system maintains information from the supplier on the user's most requested quality characteristics. This would be sent with every shipment containing that lot/batch of materials.

In addition, distributors may be evaluated on the technical support and service they provide. There are times when distributors will be contacted for quality problems that occur in the products they supplied. The technical expertise distributors possess or have access to can be critical in the resolution of the problem. The level of satisfaction with a distributor is directly related to the quality of the response and the time taken to respond.

Strategic Considerations
When trying to decide how to work with suppliers, it is imperative that company directions and goals be taken into account. The bottom line is simple—the main goal of any business is to make money. The way to get there can take many forms. The best way for long-term stability and profitability is to produce the highest quality product at the

lowest possible cost. The procurement organization is given the task of developing a supplier base that allows this to happen.

There is a trend in many companies to strive for what is known as world-class quality. *World-class quality* is defined as the ability to buy and sell products of such conformity to specification that it will enable both the supplier and the customer to compete successfully with the quality of anyone marketing a similar product or service in the world.

The first step in this journey is the recognition that you are a supplier to your customer. What are the things that you must do to meet your customer's needs? Is your management committed? Do you perform the necessary steps to produce the highest quality product at the lowest possible cost? If someone was considering you, how would you measure up as a supplier? Would someone want to do business with you, or would they look elsewhere?

Supplier Strategy

Strategy means many things to different people. In its simplest form, it is a way of maximizing the actions you have control over and minimizing those you do not. This means that for any business, there has to be a set of guidelines that dictates where we want to be at a given point and that this is clearly understood by everyone. For example, if it is stated that the business wants the highest quality available then there must be a definition of *highest quality*. It could mean that certain physical characteristics are met consistently; it could mean that the product is recognized by others as being the best in the field; it could mean that the product attains an increase in the market for your product.

There is another aspect to this that directly impacts the business. If the supplier consistently provides the highest quality, there will be gains in productivity of the manufacturing operation resulting in reduced internal costs. The business can control the quality of the product entering the plant. The business can influence the communication between it and the supplier so that mutually beneficial policies provide incentive to the supplier to provide the highest quality. This is the foundation for the development of a supplier partnership strategy.

Today there is an increased need to develop a consistent supplier strategy. With the increase in technology, there are many small shops that provide highly specialized services/products that can answer a specific need in the marketplace. These shops can be considered the new guilds. These are the craftspeople of today who provide a high-quality product for a select customer. They work hard to maintain their status in being on the cutting edge of their technology.

Many companies are studying ways to shorten the development cycle to introduce new products to the marketplace sooner. One way to achieve this is to bring in the critical suppliers during the development process and enlist their assistance. A critical supplier is one whose product is necessary for the production of a new product. Many times suppliers are aware of new technologies in their field. They also are aware of the capabilities and limitations of the current products they provide. As they learn what the expectations are for the product they are providing, they can recommend changes in the product that will enhance its performance. For example, a certain plastic part was to go into a copier. The supplier was brought in and found out that the part was to be located near a heating element that could cause the plastic part to warp over time. The supplier recommended a different composition of resins with a higher heat resistance. This resulted in an improved product and a significant savings in potential redesign and service costs.

Many businesses are examining ways to reduce inventories. Traditionally, inventories have been maintained to provide against unforeseen incidents. This gave the customer a constant supply source. A supplier program can reduce the risk involved because there is routine communication between the supplier and the customer. Some of the communications can include revised forecasts covering long- and short-term needs, and updates on the present performance of the supplier. This allows the supplier to provide the product on a just-in-time (JIT) basis if that is how the business is operating.

When suppliers know what is expected of them and how they are evaluated, they can focus on reductions of variation and costs. The cost reductions resulting from the variation reduction will enable suppliers to enter into longer-term contracts without threatening their goal of making money for their company. At the same time, suppliers are assured of a longer-term partnership with the customer, a benefit to both parties. Many companies have reduced costs through the implementation of statistical process control (SPC) techniques. These techniques are simple to use and place the responsibility for quality on the worker. The purpose of SPC is to prevent poor quality from occurring by controlling the process. This is different from the traditional concepts of inspection and sorting to maintain the desired quality level.

The implementation of SPC is an evolutionary process. The supplier and the customer must establish a timeline to measure the progress of the SPC implementation. This allows both the supplier and the customer to be fully aware of each organization's expectations. It also gives the customer an opportunity to assist the supplier with resources to accomplish the agreed upon goals. As the supplier attains SPC on the processes, the customer initially can reduce any incoming inspection with the intent of eliminating all inspection when the supplier achieves statistical control.

There are various strategies that have been used by businesses. The most common is that of giving the supplier increased responsibility in terms of product. The strategy here is that the supplier is certified, which means that no incoming inspection is performed on a product or grouping of products. The certified supplier may be entitled to a variety of benefits: increased opportunities for new business, long-term contracts for products, cost rebates for consistently meeting requirements, and so forth. However, there also are some risks involved: the supplier commits to an SPC program as a way to keep costs down, the price is fixed for the duration of the contract, and the raw materials may be required to be purchased from another certified supplier. These things must be considered because in many cases the supplier will be held accountable for any loss incurred through the shipment of out-of-spec products.

Another strategy is where the supplier is made part of the design team developing new products. Here the supplier is expected to lend expertise to a new design. It is a mutual commitment because both the customer and supplier will benefit from the results. The customer gets the latest technology in the supplier's specialized area, and the supplier gets an opportunity to increase business and improve relations with the customer. Here the supplier is expected to participate in design reviews, specification development, prototype products, measurement assurance, and life testing. The supplier is given unique opportunities to have some control in new products.

Another strategy is the practice of improved forecasts for products. This means that the supplier receives updates of the production schedule. Thus, the supplier is continually updated on both the short- and long-term schedules. This enables the supplier to adjust the schedule and maintain as little inventory as possible. With the advent of computerized telecommunications, this is becoming a preferred way of doing business.

The most popular strategy today is to work only with suppliers who are registered to a particular quality system, such as ISO 9000. The logic is that the supplier is working within an accepted system and has the potential for improvement. Utilizing a system demonstrates that the supplier has the management support that will enhance the partnership process.

The various strategies discussed here work well with all types of suppliers: those who manufacture a product; those who supply such common items as desks and office supplies; and distributors. The strategies have been developed with the manufactured product suppliers in mind, but with a little modification the others can be brought under the supplier program umbrella.

The Psychology of Supplier Relationships

When dealing with suppliers, the most important thing people must remember is, "What would I be doing if I was in the supplier's place?" This type of thinking will assist the procurement team members in conducting themselves in a manner beneficial to both companies' interests.

This has not always been the case. Traditionally, the customer/supplier relationship has not been one of consideration, but of dictation. The customer dictated to the supplier exactly what the customer wanted. No deviations were accepted. If the supplier did not want to do business, there were plenty of other suppliers who were interested. Consequently, supplier relationships were one-sided. The suppliers also quickly learned how to get deviations from the specifications. The simplest way was to announce a price increase shortly after obtaining the contract. The customer would call to tell the supplier that the price increase was out of the question. Then, the supplier would tell the customer that the order could not be met. The customer would inquire why and the supplier would tell the customer that under the current specification, a certain dimension could not be met consistently. To ensure that the specification could be met, a price increase was necessary. Then, the customer would ask the question that the supplier had been waiting for, "What if we could get you a deviation from the specification?"

This is exactly what the supplier wanted. The supplier knew from the beginning that the specification was unrealistic. The supplier also knew that if a deviation or change in the specification had been requested at the beginning, the supplier would have been eliminated from getting the contract. So, the supplier waited until the contract was obtained before making a move.

The traditional relationships were based on a carefully executed program of moves similar to a chess game. Neither side was willing to be completely open. The difficult dimension was recognized by the supplier (the expert in the field), but the customer's company recognized no experts other than its own. If the design engineer put the dimension on the specification, it was considered correct. Supplier expertise was viewed as inferior when it may have been just the opposite. The supplier understood that the best way to get the change made was to speak in terms that the customer would understand—dollars. If the customer accepted the price change, the supplier had enough money to either improve the process or to hire more inspectors. In either case, the supplier won.

On the other hand, the customer had a problem. A specification deviation or change was necessary if the parts were to be delivered on time. If the change or deviation was not possible, then the customer's company would pay more for the product than was originally contracted. Either way, the customer looks bad, as if enough research was not done during the supplier search. The idea that the design was wrong never occurred to anyone.

So, here is the classic situation of mistrust on both parties' accounts. This has resulted in increased product costs, high waste, and, in some cases, field failures. The customer's company lost its reputation for providing high-quality product that took years to reestablish, because the customer's company did not acknowledge that there were any experts except its own.

Today's competition has forced this situation to change. As major companies shrink both their employees and their supplier bases, the concept of partnerships has grown. A partnership grows with time. The development can be compared to an interpersonal relationship resulting in marriage.

When first meeting with a potential supplier, it is like going on a blind date. Both parties try to put their best foot forward. As the selection process ends (if all goes well), the supplier is given the initial contract. This begins the dating phase. If all continues to go well, more contracts are awarded. This evolves into the going steady phase. Both parties are now making a limited commitment to determine if the initial impressions are true. This can lead to the engagement phase where longer-term contracts are considered and awarded based on performance. Marriage occurs with the long-term contract and a request to the supplier for assistance in new product development. All new product development is confidential and both parties agree not to divulge any information to their companies. The honeymoon phase occurs when everything is rosy between the customer and the supplier. This can last a long time (up to one year) or be very brief (one week). Once the honeymoon is over, the true partnership begins. This is when both parties work toward mutual benefits.

When a problem occurs, both parties work together to solve it. This may mean traveling to each facility to discover possible solutions. It may mean a redesign of the part/process to correct some unanticipated defect, or a mutually agreed upon absorbance of costs to alleviate short-term setbacks. Whatever the problem is, it is worked on and solved together. There is no assigning of blame.

The key elements of a partnership can be summarized into an informal code of ethics. This code was originally developed by the ASQC Vendor–Vendee Technical Committee. The motivation behind it was the understanding that both the customer and supplier have an interest in obtaining the same objectives. The 12 elements of the code follow:

1. *Personal behavior*–All dealings between both quality control/quality assurance functions should be conducted in a manner to credit the companies and the individuals involved. In contacts between the quality functions of both the customer and supplier, it is necessary to avoid compromising relationships.

2. *Objectivity*–Both the customer and the supplier should address the fulfillment of all contractual requirements and objectives. The legal aspects of a contract cannot be ignored, but there also is a moral obligation to achieve a satisfactory end product. It is to the mutual advantage of both parties that the objective attained is accompanied by a fair and equitable cost distribution.

   In this case, the customer and the supplier need to focus on what is required by each to achieve the desired outcome. If the customer is requesting some requirements that incur additional expense, that customer should expect to pick up part of those expenses.

3. *Product definition*–The customer should furnish a complete description of the quality characteristics in writing for the procured item, including minimum workmanship standards. The customer's quality organization is morally obligated to ensure that all requirements are clear, complete, nonconflicting, and correct. Assistance in the interpretation of requirements should be readily available to the supplier.

Simply stated, all specifications should be understood by everyone, and any additional information to help clarify the specifications should be freely given.

4. *Mutual understanding*–Direct communications between quality functions should be implemented at the initiation of all contracts and continue through the life of the contract. Direct communication assures professional maintenance of the mutual obligation by the respective quality managements. To allow quality functions to be handled through default by others will result in product quality degradation and a loss of reputation for the profession.

    Allow the quality people to talk to quality people. Let the operators talk to operators. Keep the communications as direct as possible; avoid all intermediaries.

5. *Quality evaluation*–It is the customer's responsibility to appraise the supplier's quality performance fairly and it is the supplier's right to be aware of this appraisal. The supplier has the benefit of knowing what the comparative quality position is with the customer, because this factor predicts the supplier's future. Common benefits are derived by working together. It is important to commend a supplier when consistent, satisfactory performance is achieved.

    Evaluate the supplier with a consistent rating system. Let the supplier know the rating. Discuss possible areas of improvement and, where applicable, ways to achieve improvements.

6. *Product quality*–Suppliers should honestly and fairly inform customers of the quality status of delivered items. Delivery implies that contractual objectives have been met. Certifications that fail to indicate deviations or commissions are misleading and demonstrate poor practice or lack of good faith. Unintentional discrepancies that could jeopardize a customer's program should be clearly communicated to responsible individuals to assure maintenance of the supplier's quality and ethical reputation.

When there is a problem with a shipment, notify the customer. Data should be sent with every shipment if that is part of the contract. If a deviation has been granted, it should be noted on the data sheet.

7. *Corrective action*–Corrective action should be actively pursued and implemented by both customer and supplier. The acceptance of this responsibility by both demonstrates good faith in the contractual relationship as well as quality discipline and technical competence.

   Working together to solve problems when they occur saves time and money. It also fosters the partnership between the two companies.

8. *Technical aid*–Technical support should be provided by the customer when requested by the supplier. Care must be exercised because such efforts may confuse the question of responsibility. Technical support activities must be conducted by mutual respect for the competence of both the supplier and the customer, in their respective specialties.

   When there is a request for technical support, the customer's two options are to provide someone from their company, or recommend an independent source. This does not mean that the customer assumes responsibility for the product that the supplier provides. It simply means that the customer is willing to help the supplier on a specific problem.

9. *Integrity*–Facilities and services should be used by the visiting party only to the degree of the contractual obligation, or as volunteered by the supplier or customer. Inspection, laboratory facilities, and equipment must be provided to the extent specified in the contract. The supplier must permit the customer access to the facilities where the customer can perform source inspection and/or other associated functions involved with the assurance of contractual obligations. The supplier should normally permit the customer to observe inspections or tests and to review the resultant data. The visitor must not accept

gifts, entertainment, or other preferred treatment of any nature, thus eliminating any unethical behavior by which the level of quality may be compromised. Do not do anything that could embarrass you or your company.

10. *Rewards*–Supplier quality management should encourage its purchasing agent to use only qualified suppliers. Quality management should compile and maintain a current list of qualified suppliers based on performance. The use of the most qualified suppliers from a quality control viewpoint should be considered when selecting suppliers, rewarding those suppliers that consistently produce conforming products.

   Establish a list and use it when selecting suppliers.

11. *Proprietary information*–Both parties should refrain from divulging proprietary information obtained in confidence. Divulging privileged information violates ethical and moral standards and is not in the best interest of either party.

   Betraying a trust is destructive to business relationships.

12. *Safeguard of reputation*–Both parties should avoid making false, unsupported, or misleading statements. Integrity and professionalism are paramount in every business relationship.

   There must be an open, honest relationship established if a partnership is to grow and develop. Anything less than that works against everything you are trying to accomplish.

Notes

1. *Glossary and Tables for Statistical Quality Control.* Milwaukee, Wis.: American Society for Quality Control, 1983, p. 4.

2. See note 1, p. 5.

How Do You Appear to Your Supplier?

Chapter 2

Summary
- The old way of working with suppliers
- The way we would like to work with our suppliers

In this chapter, two scenarios will be presented. The first scenario is the way that many companies operated when the dictation method of working with suppliers was popular. The second scenario is the approach that many companies are using today. As you read the scenarios, consider where you would be placed by your suppliers.

Scenario 1

The place is a Midwest manufacturing plant. There are four people seated in a conference room. The purchasing agent is running the meeting. No agenda has been set. The meeting is about a supplier evaluation that is going to take place the following week. The QA manager and the design engineer are looking forward to seeing the tourist sights. The incoming inspection engineer is wondering why they are going to this supplier because the scrap rate is so high. The purchasing person explains that the trip is going to take three days. On the first day, the team will arrive in the afternoon and will pick up the passes for the golf game that will take place after they arrive. Then the supplier will take them to dinner and a night on the town. The next day, they will arrive at the supplier's plant and meet with the management. They will explain what they want and the price that they will pay. Then they will go to lunch on the supplier. After lunch, they will have a quick tour of the plant and go play another round of golf. They will celebrate a successful trip at the supplier's expense and return home the next day. The question is raised about what to do if the supplier asks about data. The response is that another trip will have to be made.

At the supplier's plant, the team finds out that the specifications being used are six years old. The new specifications were never sent, so the nonconformities are understandable. The secretary is blamed for the error. A new spec is given on the spot and the supplier is asked if the part can be made. Before an answer is given, the vice president enters and talks about the supplier's commitment to quality. During the discussion, the fact comes out that the QA department reports to production. A question is raised about a conflict of interests. The reply is that it has never been a problem before, so why should it be a problem now. The group breaks for lunch.

Following a three-hour lunch, and plenty of war stories, the group goes on a plant tour. In the receiving area, they observe that products are not segregated or labeled, so there is no way of knowing what is good or bad. In the production area, they look for some inspection sheets. The only ones that could be found are three days old because the inspector is on sick leave and no one has acted as a replacement. The employees are not empowered and do not use statistical quality control techniques because they consider it quality's job. Measurement assurance is nonexistent.

The exit meeting was a lesson in patience. The design engineer was called out of town for an emergency. The supplier was told that the plant was in trouble. The recommended independent testing facility was not used because they rejected everything, so another local place was found. Unfortunately, their methods are not traceable to any national standards, but they do pass the product. It was discovered that the product was not made in the plant visited, but in another location. After telling the supplier how bad they were, the customer requested a price reduction. The supplier's vice president made a point of quickly turning things around by promising all corrections would be in place by the following week.

Six months later, in a follow-up call, the situation has deteriorated. The quality is worse, only a few of the corrections have been done. The customer is threatening the supplier because of excessive costs due to poor quality. Obviously, this supplier will not be used again.

One year later, the team is pulled together again. The team is tasked with the problem of getting the supplier out of its quality problems. The team is to use any means available to accomplish the task—threats, increased inspection, site inspection, looking over their shoulders, whatever it takes. The team would rather drop the supplier, but that option is not available because the supplier is the lowest cost supplier.

Prior to visiting the supplier, the team decides to examine the product and specifications. The first thing that is noticed is how tight the specs are. When asked, engineering simply states that they do not need them that tight, but it is the only way to ensure that the supplier will conform. When asked to clarify what *clean* means, the reply is that everyone knows what that is. The team notices that there has not been a change in raw material for more than 15 years. No change is considered necessary because there is no idea of what newer product is available and if it is even needed.

At the supplier's plant, the team talks to the supplier (*dictates* is probably a better term). No more dirty products are required. The problem rests with the distributor that sends whatever is available. The quality is supposed to be equivalent, but no one knows for sure. No widening of the specifications is being allowed, even though the data show that the supplier cannot make the part to the spec routinely. However, the supplier has a legitimate concern in that no notification of nonconforming product has been sent.

One month later a follow-up call is made. The team leader insults the supplier's QA manager because nothing has changed. Product is still being rejected at incoming inspection. Nothing has been returned because the part is still usable, but no widening of the specifications is being considered. This further degrades in a dictation of how the QA manager should run the plant. At that point, the QA manager hangs up.

Contrast this situation with the following.

Scenario 2

In a different Midwest company, another meeting is taking place. The purchasing agent is conducting the meeting with three other members of the team. They are talking about bringing a new supplier on board. The first item of business is some background on the supplier, why it is being looked after, and the game plan that the team is going to follow. This is done so that the team buys into the process. At the meeting, the quality of the products is discussed, as well as some items that need to be addressed when the team meets with the supplier. The team prepares an agenda for the supplier visit and makes the appropriate plans. They break up with the agreement that they will meet on the night before to review what they want to cover at the supplier's plant.

At the opening conference, the vice president kicks off the session welcoming the group. Then the meeting is handed over to the sales and QA people so they can work on things. The QA people talk to the customer team about the specifications. The team listens to the presentation on the process capability study that was run and what the supplier thinks they can hold based on the study. Although they do not like what they hear, they are willing to investigate whether or not they can do something on their end to widen the specs. They also are willing to work with the supplier in an effort to determine whether some in-plant help might be available based on some of the customer's expertise. Prior to the plant tour, the supplier mentions that only one area of the plant will be closed, but that no parts are made there. They hope that the customer understands.

In the plant tour, the group goes from receiving to the shipping department. At each step, the team talks to the operators to determine what is done and what is standard practice. There is some question over some nonapparent items, such as calibration stickers, but that is resolved when the operator shows how the system works and explains the frequency of checking. Questions on sampling and control charting are fielded in a similar manner. The type of records and retention times also are discussed and an agreement is made on how to handle it. While looking at the procedures, a comment is offered as to how to keep the procedures clean so that they will not have to be replaced as often.

In the exit conference the team reviews what is being done well, and what needs corrective action. The conference was handled in a professional manner. No accusations were made; everything was based on data. People were assigned tasks with deadlines, and the expectation was that if the deadline could not be met, there would be communication between the appropriate parties. Finally, there was a time set defining when the official report would be sent. Both parties left the meeting feeling good about what had taken place.

Three months later a follow-up call was made. During that call, the team reviews what has occurred since the evaluation meeting, including the performance of the product, the status of the corrective action, and an overview of a follow-up visit to confirm the corrective action. Based on the visit, the supplier has decided to hire temporary help to perform capability studies. This is a sign of good faith to the customer that the supplier is committed to doing whatever is necessary to ensure that the customer's expectations are met.

One year later, the customer company has decided to consolidate its supplier base, based on some meetings with a famous quality guru. Instead of simply performing supplier evaluations, the purchasing QA group is going to work with suppliers in a certification program. The emphasis is on continuous improvement and formation of a solid partnership. A team is comprised to study potential candidates for the initial group of supplier partners. The customer team is brought together to set up a visit with the supplier to inform the supplier of the new directions and the plan for partnership.

When examining the current records, the supplier has had some problem with the parts being clean and meeting some tolerances. At close inspection, the designer concedes that the part tolerances may be unrealistic and loosening of them could be acceptable. The clean part arises from the fact that only one source of raw materials has been identified and that another source should be found. This will ensure that the supplier has an ample supply of raw materials and will not have to accept nonconforming materials in order to meet the customer's requirements. It also was felt that if the supplier understood how the part was used, some of the specification requirements would become self evident.

When at the supplier's plant, the team first goes through the change in philosophy in working with suppliers. As a sign of the new era, the team addresses the specifications. Two critical specs are opened up, which make it easier for the supplier to meet the third spec. The clean requirement is made more understandable by showing how the part is used and by putting some quantifiable characteristics in the explanation. All in all, the supplier is happy to have a better understanding of what the customer wants and the customer is happy because the supplier is willing to work on the path toward the partnership.

The follow-up meeting results in a review of the incoming materials' quality. There has been some difficulty in getting a clean product. After the overall quality report, the supplier requests assistance from the customer. The customer responds positively and sends some specialists to work with the supplier. The partnership is growing.

How do your suppliers see you? Are you a good customer, or do your suppliers cringe when they hear you are coming?

Lessons Learned

This chapter showed two different ways how a customer can interact with a supplier. The way the customer acts will invoke a similar reaction by the supplier. Always remember that as a customer, you first act as a supplier of information. The better and more consistent the communications, the more honest the reaction. The development of a partnership is a slow process that can be damaged by the customer saying one thing and acting in another way. Once mistrust has developed, it is difficult to get rid of it. Suppliers have long memories (as do some customers). Consistency of behavior is the key to success. This was why the second scenario had a happy ending. The supplier felt that the customer did value what the supplier had to contribute to the partnership. Always ask yourself, How would I react if I was the supplier?

Basic Issues: Specifications
Chapter 3

Key words: analytical specification, ISO 9000, Malcolm Baldrige National Quality Award, process capability index (PCI), process specification, product specification, properties, raw material specification, sampling, specifications, standard terms, test capability index (TCI).

Summary
- What is a specification?
- What are the types of specifications?
- What are the components of a specification?
- How should specifications be determined?
- The impact of ISO 9000 and Baldrige on specifications

A specification is a grouping of specific parameters that are required to ensure the success of a product to perform as designed. This is sometimes a difficult set of expectations. Many times the capability of the manufacturing process is the critical factor that results in deviations from specifications. In fact, industry recognizes that changes are necessary in the development and implementation of specification change and deviation procedures. It is the challenge to the design/development community to develop specifications that are meaningful and within the manufacturing process capability.

The five basic types of specifications follow:

1. *Product specifications*–This is the most common specification. It defines what is required for a product to perform as expected by the consumer.

2. *Process specifications*–This type of specification defines the parameters of the manufacturing process that must be controlled in order to produce a product.

3. *Analytical specifications*–Where applicable, this type of specification defines the analytical methodologies to measure a required level of accuracy.

4. *Raw material specifications*–This type of specification defines what is acceptable as raw material entering a manufacturing process.

5. *Quality management*–This type of specification defines the management practices under which you wish to have products produced.

These specifications follow a hierarchy. Generally, the product specifications are determined first. They are the driver for the process, analytical, and raw material specifications. These specifications enable the design and manufacturing people to communicate in common terms, which are the requirements at every level of the manufacturing process. Specifications provide checkpoints in manufacturing that ensure quality of the product.

There are common components to all specifications. First, there is a description of the product. It can be narrative or, if a manufactured part, a profile. After the description, list the required characteristics. These characteristics include the upper (and lower) tolerance limits. Whenever a tolerance is established, a measurement should be referenced with the units of measurement, and in the case of chemical, physical, and microbiological tests, the test method procedure. The test method describes the instrument, the exact procedure for sampling, the sample preparation, and the limit of detection, as well as desired precision and accuracy.

The third component includes the handling and packaging requirements. These identify how the product is to be packaged and handled. To a specification, different industries attach various addenda, such as test method descriptions, test method and sampling procedures, environmental testing requirements, certificate of analysis information, product identification elements, codes, expiration date, process control requirements, safety requirements, and various governmental regulatory requirements.

In addition to these common elements, product specifications should contain the following:

1. Reliability, serviceability, shelf life, and maintainability requirements
2. Permissible tolerances and comparisons with process capabilities
3. Product accept/reject criteria
4. User instructions, such as installability, ease of assembly, storage needs, shelf life, and disposability
5. Benign failure and fail-safe characteristics
6. Aesthetic and other qualitative specifications and acceptance criteria
7. Failure modes and effects analysis, and fault tree analysis
8. Ability to diagnose and correct problems
9. Labeling, warning, identification, traceability, risk management, and recall requirements
10. Review and use of standard parts[1]

By containing these components, product specifications will contain the information necessary to minimize liability issues.

Process and analytical specifications also have some unique components which follow:

1. Manufacturability of the design, including special process/analytical needs, mechanization, automation, assembly, and installation of components
2. Capability to inspect and test the design/prototype, including special inspection and test requirements
3. Specification of materials, components, and subassemblies (including approved supplies and suppliers), as well as availability
4. Packaging, handling, storage, and shelf life requirements, especially safety factors relating to incoming and outgoing items[2]

The completeness and clarity of the specifications are particularly important in the procurement process. There appears to be no limit to how nonconformities can occur or to the questions concerning the characteristics of purchased material. Certain areas (such as visual requirements and workmanship) are subjective. These can be troublesome unless some discussion between the customer and the supplier results in agreement on objective standards to clearly define requirements.

The pertinent specifications and drawings should clearly define the characteristics of the material so that the supplier fully understands what is required, measured, and reinforced. Specifications should be free of ambiguities that could lead to differences in interpretation by the supplier and the customer.

Material specifications should specify the end requirements that must be met. In some instances, the customer may specify raw materials and methods of manufacture, but must then assume responsibility for the resultant product. This manner of specification excludes the supplier's technical knowledge and should be avoided whenever possible.

There are many ways to develop specifications. Everyone has an opinion on how specifications should be developed. Some people work on hunches, some simply trust their instincts, and others use statistics.

Obviously, the best specifications come from the utilization of statistics. Now, another potential problem occurs—which statistical tool should be used? Are histograms OK? Should one conduct designed experiments? What about just using a mean and standard deviation? Is one *more* correct than another? In many cases, the answer is no. The only difference in using statistical tools is how fast one can get to the final specification. Is there any final specification? A specification can be thought of as an evolutionary document that provides checkpoints at parts of a continuing cycle. The popular phrase today is *continuing improvement.* This means that all products can be improved, and that if your company is to remain competitive, you must find ways to improve. A specification is a plateau where the evolutionary climb has established a base. This base remains until there is enough information to establish a new base. So, you can consider specifications as both a stabilizing influence and a dynamic document.

In developing specifications, simple tools such as histograms, averages, ranges, and standard deviations can provide great insight with small amounts of data. One of the most common ways is to calculate an index known as the process capability index (PCI). This statistic informs the development and procurement people how much of the specification range is taken up by the manufacturing process variation. The formula used is

$$PCI = \frac{\text{upper spec} - \text{lower spec}}{6 \text{ standard deviations}}$$

This is sometimes written as C_p. The inverse of this index tells the percentage of specification.

$$\frac{1}{PCI} \times 100 = \text{percentage of specification taken up by the process.}$$

There are variations of this calculation which can further refine the use of these indices. *Defect Prevention* by Victor Kane devotes a chapter to this material.

Recently, another statistic has been utilized for analytical testing. This is known as the test capability index (TCI), which is used in a similar manner as the PCI. The TCI is calculated as follows:

$$TCI = \frac{\text{upper spec} - \text{lower spec}}{6 \text{ standard deviations of testing method}}$$

This provides information as to the adequacy of the testing methods on the product being developed. The inverse of this provides the information as to how much analytical variability takes up the specification range. As a rule of thumb, at least 25 data points are needed to determine the standard deviation.

These two indices, PCI and TCI, enable the design/development and procurement personnel to effectively develop estimates that can evolve into specifications. One assumption is essential if the indices are to have any meaning. The process is assumed to be stable and therefore predictable over time. This is called being *in control.* This is important because if the process shows a lack of control, there is no predictability in the process.

The specification team consists of development people, the material supplier, the procurement person, and the manufacturer. This team examines the data that the design people have utilized, the data on the manufacturing capability, the data from the supplier's capability, and develops a specification over a period of time. This team can utilize other people as appropriate, such as an analytical representative if there is lab testing involved. This team works to develop specifications that are realistic and meet the customer's needs.

Quality Management Specifications

There has been an explosion of consensus standards that define management practices under which we may desire to have our products or services produced. They range from the ISO 9000 series of standards and the government military procurement standards (such as

MIL-Q-9858A) to the advanced total quality management model such as the Malcolm Baldrige National Quality Award (MBNQA) criteria.

The ISO 9000 series standards, specifically ISO 9001 and ISO 9002, require that you specify the title number and issue of the quality system standard under which you wish to have your product or service produced. If you are working within a registered system, the issue of passing on quality management expectations is moot. You must then set quality management expectations for your suppliers. You do not have to require registration or certification of your suppliers; simply list the standard they are to use.

The growth of competitive recognition systems, such as the MBNQA, provides another set of criteria. These can be used to set in place expectations of both the quality management practices you expect to see in place at the supplier, and speak to the cultural style of management you can expect to see in place.

This is a two-edged sword. The first edge is one of positive reinforcement if you have success in the adoption of the culture that these type of criteria have reflected within them. We may be most successful with this strategy if the supplier is like us in culture and wants to partner with us. The other edge raises the questions whether you really wish or need to dictate a management style to your supplier. Think of the push back you will get in asking for a Baldrige culture to be adopted in one of the remaining communist countries or in a theory X culture down the street, or at the small mom-and-pop shop that only has three to five employees that you use for their quick turnaround. One of the former Baldrige winners found more trouble pushing their suppliers to apply for Baldrige. Much time was spent in having to defend their position.

Government Quality Specifications and Standards

Those working with governmental agencies have another set of criteria that is contained in the Government Quality Specifications and

Standards. Government quality documents normally begin with a specification of quality program requirements. This requires a documented program for all activities necessary to attain continuous control of product quality during manufacturing. Usually this program will be reviewed and accepted by the customer after he or she is satisfied that the necessary activities do exist and are being performed effectively. The quality program specification or the contract typically will refer to other government documents to which compliance also is required. These secondary documents may refer to still other applicable documents that establish the requirements of additional program and product details. The second level of quality documents may specify equipment calibration systems, sampling procedures, product detail requirements, and analysis of all raw material.

Government documents are obtainable through the procuring activity, the government contracting officer, or directly from the U.S. Government Printing Office. Those documents which pertain to other governments must be obtained from the appropriate governmental agencies.

A few of the basic government quality program specifications are

- DOD MIL-Q-9858A Quality Program Requirements
- DOD QRC-82 Quality Program Requirements Supplement to MIL-Q-9858A
- DOD MIL-I-45208A Inspection System Requirements
- DOD ISR-1 Inspection System Requirements Supplement to MIL-I-45208A

The local government contract administrating offices will aid suppliers in setting up procedures that comply to government requirements. In addition to their responsibility for surveying/auditing facilities to determine quality program compliance, they advise on how to comply. Specialists in a wide variety of technical subjects are available to aid in interpreting details and in establishing procedures that will provide the control required.

Government quality requirements currently are more detailed than most commercial requirements. The extensive details included in government documents have evolved from quality experience in the past. It is mandatory to the success of aerospace projects, military endeavors, and the preservation of human life that a deficient level of conformance be eliminated. Therefore, government documents have become concerned with both program concepts and product details, so that quality is thoroughly defined. Product specifications and standards also are necessary to provide interchangeability of products from more than one source.

Continuous source inspection, surveys, and audits are frequently used. In order to ensure that end items have incorporated the requirements specified at all levels of procurement, government contracts rely on source inspections, quality program audits, and surveys. Resident government representatives are assigned when the frequency of shipments, the complexity of the product, and the criticality of performance requires constant surveillance at the manufacturing facility. Their primary responsibility is to ensure the product conformance when shipped. In addition to outgoing inspection, they also perform continuous audits of control procedures to ensure that quality programs are maintained.

The supplier should become acquainted with all requirements included in the specifications and standards. The total performance and documentation requirements are not apparent from a single or a few specifications listed in a contract. The supplier should also thoroughly review and be informed of all program requirements, product specifications, and documentation details that apply in the referenced documents before committing to a government contract. If suppliers do not become familiar with the specifications imposed, they may learn too late that costs were greater than expected and the product cannot be shipped because of standards that were not met.

Modifications to government documents may be included in contract conditions. Changes to the pertinent specifications and standards are not possible for individual procurement. Hence, justified changes must be made as additions or exceptions in the contractual agreement. Identification and clarification of questionable details must be completed before the contract is signed. This ensures performance on schedule and avoids delays that can be costly to both supplier and customer.

The supplier and customer should be aware of added cost factors resulting from the conformance requirements to government documents. Some may not be apparent unless all specifications are reviewed in detail. The additional work required can affect costs significantly and should be considered in pricing.

Some of the cost factors are certifications from subcontractors, inspections to approve quality programs, certification of specific processes, additional documentation required to provide objective evidence of compliance to details, changeovers to military-type materials and finishes, additional environmental testing, and time required by program reviews.

A critical aspect of the customer–supplier relationship is acquisition of realistic specifications. The customer is responsible for clearly defining the requirements; the supplier is responsible for accurately determining whether it has the capability to meet those specifications. Some up-front planning is necessary to develop plans to meet the agreed upon specifications. Failure to do so will only result in unwanted cost to both customer and supplier. Realistic specifications meet the needs of both sides.

Registration or certification of the supplier's quality management system by other than your company is becoming a viable option in many industries. The true third-party registration system offered by many under the ISO standards is rapidly becoming the most popular. Within an industry such as the automotive industry, acceptable quality systems audits are becoming acceptable to competitors as a cost and consistency factor. You need to decide what it will really tell you. Registration or acceptance of a quality management system by some other party is just that. A recognition of the system, this will not replace detailed discussions about product, process, materials, and analysis discussed previously. You still need to gain agreement on those specifications and work at the product and service delivery level in order to continue to satisfy the ultimate customer of the product or service.

Notes

1. ANSI/ASQC Standard Q94-1987, "Quality Management and Quality Systems Elements—Guidelines," p. 9.
2. See note 1.

Basic Issues: Record Keeping
Chapter 4

Key words: attribute data, *c* charts, control charts, mainframe, nonconforming materials, *np* charts, part number, PC, *p* charts, *u* charts, variables data.

Summary
- What types of data are important?
- What types of reports can be set up?
- What types of system concerns need to be addressed?

One of the first questions that the customer must ask is What information do I want from this supplier? From this a series of secondary questions can arise, but the primary question that remains is What is to be addressed here? When trying to decide what information to receive from the supplier, the customer must determine how to use that information. For example, if a particular dimension is critical, the customer may want the supplier to control chart that dimension. This accomplishes the following:

1. The supplier will establish some long-term information about the critical dimension.
2. If the supplier is not using SPC techniques, it will have to begin to be able to supply the data to you.

This type of data where some characteristic can be measured is called *variables data*. Variables data easily lends itself to control charts and histograms. The collection of this data can be time-consuming, but is useful in development of specifications.

Another type of data is *attributes data*. Attributes are counting data. Attributes data also can be control charted. Generally, it is obtained from go/no-go gages or appearance defects. The number of rejects are counted and compared to the total number of pieces in either the lot or those inspected. Attributes data is relatively quick to obtain.

There is a third group of data that, in some respects, is the most important—lot traceability information. This grouping includes part number or characteristic identification, supplier identification, number of parts shipped, and so on.

From this information, the customer decides how to track the characteristics of interest. The best way to accomplish this is through the use of control charts. ASQC defines control charts as "a graphical method for evaluating whether a process is or is not in a 'state of statistical control.'"[1]

"A process is considered to be in a 'state of statistical control' if the variations among the observed sampling results from it can be attributed to a constant system of chance causes."[2] All this simply means is that data is plotted on a graph and decisions are made based on that graph.

There are six types of control charts that are commonly used from this information; two types for variables charts, and four for attributes charts. The two variables charts are

1. $\bar{X}$ and range/standard deviation charts
2. Individual with a moving range charts

The four attribute charts are

1. p charts (percent defective charts)
2. c charts (defect charts)*
3. np charts (number of rejects charts)*
4. u charts (defects per unit charts)

$\overline{X}$ and range/standard deviation charts are used when there are subgroups of data that are collected. This is the most sensitive of all the control charts listed herein. Sensitive means that any unusual occurrences that can cause an out-of-control condition will be picked up quickly on the chart.

An individual chart is used when subgrouping of data is not feasible. This can be due to restriction in time, excessive costs to obtain the data, or a lack of materials. In this case, a moving range chart is used to artificially create subgroups to estimate control limits and determine the state of control.

The p chart is used to estimate the percent defective of all lots shipped. It is not as sensitive as the prior two charts, but it does enable the customer to make some determination of consistency.

The c chart measures the number of defects in a sample. There is a restriction of a constant subgroup size for this type of chart. The np chart serves a similar function and has the same restriction on subgroup size.

The u chart measures the number of nonconformities per unit. This can be extremely useful in products that can have multiple defects in the same unit, ranging from complex machinery (copiers) to sensitive, complex products (film/food) where destructive testing takes place.

Certificates of analysis are another source of data, which are sent by the supplier to the customer for each lot. This data usually includes laboratory-tested results, which cover the characteristics of interest. This information can be sent by the supplier to the customer, who then places the data into an overall reporting form.

* Must have constant subgroup size.

There are many ways to report data. Generally, a graph works best if it is kept simple. Only data that is necessary for a clear interpretation of information should be included. The report should be in a logical sequence of information. Present summary trend reports first, followed by detail reports. The summary trend reports should indicate supplier quality levels for a given period. The detail reports allow the operating personnel to select product that needs some corrective action. This selection can be based on volume, frequency, or cost of nonconforming parts.

There are four basic types of reports.

- Percentage reports
- Cost reports
- Significant problem reports
- Personnel or gage control records

1. *Percentage reports*–This type of report is designed to show supplier or in-house quality as a percentage relationship of nonconformities to inspections, operations, or work hours expended. For example,

Supplier or department	Parts inspected	Nonconformities	% Nonconforming
WXY	10,000	10	.1
XYZ	50,000	100	.2

Advantages: Report is easy to prepare and comprehend.
Disadvantages: Percentage nonconforming may be inappropriate if used to compare supplier to supplier (or department to department) unless each is producing equally complex parts.

2. *Cost reports*–A cost report shows supplier and in-house costs incurred due to improper quality.

Supplier	Product cost	Quality cost	% Quality to product cost
WXY	$25,000	$5000	20.0
XYZ	$150,000	$5000	3.3

Advantages: Cost has greater impact on management and is a good criteria for determining when corrective action should be applied.

Disadvantages: Accurate dollar values are extremely difficult to obtain.

3. *Significant problem reports*–This technique points out the most significant problem or operations by listing items in rank order with the highest percentage listed first. Details are required on major items only.

Total nonconformities	1200
Total different supplier or operations	50

Part number	Supplier	Operation	Noncon-formities	% of Total nonconformity
1234	WYZ	10	500	41.7
4567	WXY	75	300	25.0
Remainder of problems			400	

Advantages: The most significant nonconformities are selected and efforts are directed toward attaining the most effective corrective action.

Disadvantages: Difficulty of establishing criterion for selection from among critical problems.

4. *Personnel or gage control records*–Generally, this technique is used to indicate requalification date of personnel or recalibration date and inventory data on gaging.

Name	Department or supplier	Type test	Due date
John Doe	123	XYZ	4-07-85
Jane Doe	234	WXY	4-12-85

Gage number	Department or supplier	Due date
123456	Dept. 12	4-08-85
234567	Dept. 15	4-09-85

When setting up an information system, the first question to answer is, Should this system be a PC or mainframe system? A PC system is most practical for low-volume, multiproduct operations and for high-volume, single-product operations. The amount of data to be collected is much less than for mid- to heavy-volume, multiproduct operations, which can be more efficiently collected on a mainframe. However, it is not the amount of data, but what you want to do with it that dictates what type of system to select. Some types of graphs and data reports require that a mainframe system be utilized from a time factor. If it takes one hour to generate a report on a PC (and you have to wait until it is done before you can do anything else) against 15 minutes on a mainframe system (where you can do other things while the report is being generated), then a mainframe may be more cost effective.

After selecting the type of system, you must determine how data is input. Years ago, keypunched cards were the only way to input data. Now a floppy disk can contain all the information already input into the desired format, or data can be transmitted over the phone lines directly into the data base, or stored in a data collection device and sent to the computer at regular time intervals, or punched in as it is received. The options are increasing every day, so ask the computer people about what is available.

The data that should be input depends on the types of reports you want to generate. At the minimum, the input should include supplier identification, part/product identification, lot number, quantity and the received, quantity rejected (if any), the nonconformity description, and the resultant corrective action. This information, along with any control chart data, will be the foundation for the routine reports for management.

So, in attempting to set up an information system, all anticipated and potential users must be contacted. Explain what you want to do and ask for suggestions. After this list of suggestions is developed, determine the most critical components. Design a system that is simple to use and adaptable. Generally, this is done by developing a system in a series of modules that are linked together through a series of menus. Each menu would be linked by common identification, such as the part ID and the supplier ID. This allows the system to start out small and grow as necessary.

In summary, three types of information are important for any system: variables, attributes, and traceability data. From this, the types of reports desired from the supplier (mainly control charts and/or certificates of analysis) enable the customer to design a system that meets present and future needs.

Notes

1. *Glossary and Tables for Statistical Quality Control.* Milwaukee, Wis.: American Society for Quality Control, 1983, p. 30.
2. See note 1, p. 35.

Basic Issues: Site Inspection
Chapter 5

Key words: acceptance, ANSI/ASQC Q90 series, design, economy of resources, metrology, process evaluation, procurement, product evaluation, program evaluation, quality management, surveillance.

Summary
- Why evaluate?
- Types of surveillance
- Basic principles
- How to conduct an evaluation

Whenever a customer is ready to place a contract with a new supplier, it is a common practice to make a site inspection to evaluate the extent to which the supplier's quality program conforms to the ANSI/ASQC Q90 series. This series defines the "Guidelines for the selection and use of a series of standards on quality systems that can be used for external quality assurance purposes."[1]

The primary reason for evaluation of a quality program is to make sure that the program is accomplishing its intended function effectively and economically. This evaluation can be useful internally, as well as externally. Management can rapidly determine inefficient operations when using an evaluation as a self-audit.

This is critical because every organization relies on a quality program to some extent. An intolerable situation would quickly develop if each customer insisted on specifying the supplier's quality program in detail. Conflicting requirements would make compliance virtually impossible. So, the quality program evaluation needs to focus on basic principles and leave the details to the supplier. This means that the quality program evaluation is concerned with the control by management of the factors that can affect the quality of product. The simplicity or complexity of controls and the specific methods of operation are the supplier's management prerogatives. The function of the evaluation is to ascertain that an adequate quality program has been established and that it is effectively operated. This is a strategy that considers the supplier's quality program as an extension of the customer's program in order to minimize or omit all receiving inspection of products that have been certified by the supplier. This does not mean that the customer does not perform periodic audits to verify the incoming product.

There are three types of evaluation that are commonly used.

1. *Program*–This judges the effectiveness of a program on the basis of conditions in which it operates. This is used primarily in supplier selection. It entails consideration of such things as space, facilities, and the number and type of employees. Program evaluation assumes that at least a satisfactory level of quality is present if the facilities, personnel, and the program itself are operating effectively.

2. *Product*–This consists of gathering evidence that indicates the degree of conformance of the product to the stated design. This is useful for nonproduction involving a large volume of identical products over a long period of time.

3. *Process*–This emphasizes things that the manufacturer, worker, and machine do in arriving at an end product. It involves assumptions that

certain methods of operation will lead to desirable results, and that such results can be most effectively obtained when activities are directly related to goals and objectives. A process evaluation requires the examination of the overall program for evidence relating to (a) the setting of process performance goals, (b) the existence of adequate procedures for attaining the goals, (c) the implementation of control procedures, (d) the determination of the extent to which the goals are achieved, and (e) the improvement of the procedures when a need is indicated.

It must be remembered that evaluation is the systematic gathering of evidence concerning selected parameters of the quality program and arriving at a decision on the basis of the evidence collected. This involves three distinct steps.

1. Selecting and defining parameters to be evaluated
2. Developing and applying measurement to those parameters
3. Assigning appropriate values to the evidence obtained to achieve a sound basis for decision making

In order to carry out these steps, the objectives of the program must be known. These are compared to the results of that program. Explicit statements of objectives are essential because they are the basis for formulating, operating, and evaluating the program.

A simple example is baking a pie. The objective is to make the pie. The formulation phase is where all the ingredients are put together on a table where the manufacturing will be done. All the components are put together and placed in the oven in the operating phase. The evaluation phase is where the result is tested and compared to the objectives. How well was the objective met?

The program evaluation is a joint supplier–customer activity. When the evaluation is properly accomplished, it is mutually beneficial for all parties. It is essential that the evaluation recognize and encourage continuation of those activities that are done well, and that it specifically identify the ways in which improvements may be realized in areas of less than optimum performance.

Simply stated, the best way to control and improve quality is to prevent nonconformity. The successful prevention of defects is not a chance occurrence, but the result of an aggressive, tough-minded insistence that the product be manufactured correctly the first time.

Realistically, no single program can accomplish this for all products in all types of organizations. There are eight basic principles that are the foundation for every successful program. It is in the effectiveness with which these principles are applied that determines the success of a program.

1. *Control of quality management*–There must be adequate planning, forceful direction, and control in how the operators measure and evaluate product. The quality organization must be equal in authority to other organizations with direct responsibility and accountability to top management. Quality begins with planning and continues through product delivery.

2. *Control of design improvement*–A system that ensures that all specifications are current is essential to the control of the product. This also is known as *document control.*

3. *Control of procurement*–The end product is only as good as the raw materials that go into it. Suppliers should look into establishing their own supplier program.

4. *Control of material*–It is not enough that the correct material has been specified and purchased. It also must be properly identified, stored, issued, and used.

5. *Control of manufacture*–The control of processes is necessary for the production of a conforming product. Uncontrolled processes result in waste and excessive variability. With some products, the only time particular characteristics can be verified is when the product is made. This is common with sealed or black box devices, or with prod-

ucts like film, food, or light bulbs where evaluation after it is made destroys the product.

6. *Control of acceptance*–Verification that the finished product meets the design intent. This is sometimes called the inspection and testing component.

7. *Control of measuring instruments*–Inspection and testing are only as good as the precision, accuracy, and reliability of the measuring instruments.

8. *Use of quality information*–All quality-oriented information should be directed toward the product and process. This means placing it where it has the most impact—on the production floor.

There are many techniques for conducting quality program evaluations. The simplest is to walk through the plant and allow general impressions to accumulate into an opinion of the quality program. The dangers of this method are obvious. For example, superficial and showy examples may oversell the entire program, or some small deficiency may disproportionately reflect on an otherwise satisfactory program. Generally, more reliable results are obtained if a more formal technique is employed to compile objective information in an orderly manner.

Questionnaires, checklists, survey forms, rating systems, and other tools of the trade vary widely. Much has been written about the merits and demerits of these tools, and the interest in such systems often is far greater than merited. More important is a basic understanding of the fundamental principles that must be applied in order to consistently manufacture conforming products. Successful quality program evaluation systems invariably utilize professionals as evaluators, and major reliance is placed on the evaluator's judgment rather than on a stereotyped technique. No two quality programs are the same. Each is the product of different environments, personalities, and problems. A model program in one plant might not work in another. Thus, the evaluation of a quality program is a review of a one-of-a-kind set of policies, procedures, and operating practices. Effective application of the eight basic principles set forth is what should be measured. The particular administrative method used in applying these principles is not of concern as long as the principles are applied in a manner that will ensure conformity. Evaluating is a viable means to ensure that supplier and customer program, process, and product requirements are satisfactorily achieved and maintained.

Professional societies, industry associations, and various international governments have long sought ways of standardizing methods of maintaining surveillance over quality programs. The goals have been to make such surveillance more effective and to minimize replication costs by both customer and supplier. One factor that has tended to defeat efforts at standardization is the fact that virtually every customer has attempted to impose his or her own unique program requirements. These unique requirements have given rise to the development of lengthy and detailed questionnaires and checklists,which tend to oversimplify actual situations. Finally, wide differences in the professional and technical competence of evaluators, and variations to their ethical standards have made customers reluctant to rely on evaluations by others. With the advent of ANSI/ASQC Standard Q90 series, *Quality Management and Quality Systems Guidelines*, some of the benefits of standardization may be realized.

Before conducting an evaluation, considerable effort should be made by the evaluator to become familiar with the products involved. Drawings and specifications should be studied to determine which requirements are critical, major, and minor. Inspection records, reliability test results, and, if available, customer service history should be perused for possible items of particular concern.

Prior to any evaluation, there will be communication of intent made to the supplier identifying the specific nature of the visit. This communication will advise the supplier as to the purpose of the evaluation, specifically what is to be evaluated, and an acceptable date to both the supplier and customer. No attempt to evaluate any supplier should be made before an agreement is obtained and an invitation has been extended.

The evaluation should begin at the supplier's facility with the contact organization and other supplier-selected representatives in attendance. The scope of the evaluation should enumerate the specific area(s) that will be observed. At this time, all questions should be answered. After the conclusion of this preliminary conference, the evaluation will be conducted. It is suggested that a representative of the supplier accompany the evaluator or evaluating team at all times during an evaluation.

Much time should be spent during an evaluation observing normal operations to obtain objective evidence that must support subsequent ratings, evaluations, and conclusions. It is important that the value decisions of the evaluator be based on actual observations of operations, rather than implied examples of performance or procedures. Throughout the observation of operations, the evaluator should be accompanied by a supplier management representative. Comments and questions directed to management personnel and other employees must be carefully considered and clearly stated so they do not create any impression of disagreement with or disparagement of operations. It is equally important that any differences of opinion among visiting evaluators should be kept objective and inconspicuous.

An evaluation represents a best judgment after all evidence has been considered. The results of operations' observations, discussions with supplier personnel, and considerations of data provided by the supplier should be included as evidence. Individual value decisions should be reviewed by the evaluator and the management representative in preparation for a report to management. Ordinarily, there should be agreement between the individuals concerned, but if such cannot be reached, the respective positions should be clearly and objectively defined.

It should not be assumed that the need for knowledge, experience, and associated good judgment can be overruled by technique. Invariably, a competent evaluator must utilize a checklist or evaluative criteria to ensure the completeness and objectivity of the evaluation.

As the evaluator observes performance, the questions included in applicable sections of the objectives should be kept in mind. The objectives' documents should neither be in constant evidence as though they were absolute references, nor should they be used conspicuously in order to create an impression of being used to evaluate individual job performances. The important considerations relate to the nature of the quality program, as it is compared with the statement of principles that precedes each set of objectives. Sufficient notes should be made during the course of the evaluation to provide information for rating purposes and composing statements describing explanatory or supporting evidence.

An evaluator is expected to verify to his or her own satisfaction, by direct observation, the degree of conformity of the supplier's practice to the general principles stated in the criteria, relying on his or her own experience and knowledge to determine the adequacy of actual operations. From this information, the evaluator can prepare a written report for the closing conference including pertinent commendations and recommendations.

A closing conference, conducted in the same cooperative spirit that has characterized the entire evaluation, should provide an immediate basis for growth and improvement of the quality program and for bettering the relationship between supplier and customer. Participation in the closing conference should include management and any experts, consultants, or other advisory personnel who have participated in the evaluation. The evaluator should present a written report and orally discuss activities, areas covered, procedures used, findings in particular areas, and the considered conclusions. Any member of the closing conference should be allowed an opportunity to present evidence appropriate to items being discussed and to question any evaluation. The results of the final review should represent the evaluator's best judgment. If areas of disagreement exist and a common understanding cannot be obtained, a clear explanation of the factual basis for divergent opinions and conclusions should be recorded and appended to the report. If the evaluation concludes that areas of deficiency are present in the program, recommendations should be presented.

The most important part of an evaluation is the action taken upon its completion. If unsatisfactory conditions are not corrected, both the evaluator and the group evaluated have wasted a lot of time and money. No action may give an indication of what to expect in future dealings with this. The recommendations of the evaluator should provide a good starting point for revising and improving the overall quality plan. Proper application of this revised plan should result in more effective control.

The customer should expect some benefits from an evaluation of a supplier quality program. If the evaluation has been conducted and concluded in a professional, objective manner, it should be expected that improvement in quality of delivered products or services would be realized. Such a result cannot be anticipated, however, if the closing conference and final report of the evaluation are an end point or termination of the supplier/customer relationship. The customer must maintain communication with the supplier, especially when recommended changes require action on the supplier's part.

When a supplier exhibits a satisfactory quality program, as concluded by the evaluation, the customer may reduce receiving inspection or other verification activities without significantly increasing practical risks. When deficiencies are noted, the customer possesses sufficient evidence to strengthen inspection requirements of products received from this supplier. Occasionally, an entire quality program may be deemed unsatisfactory. This may prompt immediate action by the customer, which includes such actions as rejection of product, management meetings, and possible contract cancellation.

Over the years, various types of supplier survey evaluations have been developed, among which are those concerned with program, product or service, and process. This chapter has been devoted primarily to a discussion of evaluation. Emphasis was placed on the importance of developing basic parameters common to quality programs, as well as appropriate evaluative criteria. Recommended techniques for the performance of an on-site evaluation included self-evaluation on the supplier's part, initial and closing conferences, systematic compilation of data, and preparation of oral and formal written reports. Finally, attention was called to a number of benefits that may be expected to accrue from the evaluation of supplier quality programs.

Note

1. ANSI/ASQC Standard Q90-1987, p. 1.

Basic Issues: Measurement Assurance

Chapter 6

Key words: accuracy, error, precision, repeatability, reproducibility, special processes, test capability index (TCI), testing.

Summary
- Testing considerations
- Data concerns

Analytical Data Accuracy

When receiving any type of analytical data, the data receiver should wonder, How good are these numbers? Critical decisions will be made based on the data, so there should be some concern about the test's accuracy. Traditionally, what occurred was a quick once-over of the data to determine if any points were out of specification. If none were, then the lot was accepted and the material was either put into production or stored for later use. This practice seemed to be acceptable most of the time. On occasion, the product did not come out as expected and the test data for the suspected raw material would be reexamined. In some cases, the material might be analyzed again. Only if the data were different, would a question be raised about accuracy of the testing.

Today, many industries are aggressively studying all types of test method correlation in order to reduce the cost associated with testing and to meet the demands of consumers. Some industries do it simply because of various types of regulatory requirements (U.S. Department of Agriculture, Environmental Protection Agency, Health Care Financing Administration, and the Organization for Economic Cooperation and Development). Others do it to gain a competitive advantage in the marketplace. Regardless of the motivation, there is greater interest in test method capability than ever before. Different industries refer to test method capability studies by different names; for example, the automotive industry calls them *repeatability and reproducibility* (R&R) studies while chemical, food, drug, and process industries call them *correlation* studies. What is being looked at fundamentally is how accurate the data is and how confident the receiver of the data can be.

The desire is to minimize the amount of variation in a test method so that results between the customer and supplier are identical. This also minimizes the contribution the test method introduces to overall product variation. Usually, this variation is measured by the two parameters of precision and accuracy. The definitions around these parameters are so important that it is worthwhile to explain each one.

Precision is the closeness of agreement between repeated measurements made under the same conditions.

Accuracy is the closeness of agreement between an observed value and an accepted reference value; how close the value is to the real answer.

Other definitions are helpful when considering measurement performance issues. These definitions are random error, systematic error, repeatability, reproducibility, and TCI.

Random error is the variability between independent tests by the same laboratory on the same material for the same property. These variations tend to be small and normally expected. These are called *common causes.* Traditionally, duplicates or triplicates are tested and averaged to minimize the random error.

Systematic error is the variability due to assignable causes. These causes may be a result of different equipment, techniques, technicians, environmental conditions, and so on. Often this is referred to as the *bias.*

Repeatability is the ability to get the same answer when the same sample is tested by the same method by the same analyst in the same lab. Sometimes this is called the *within-lab precision.*

Reproducibility is the ability to obtain the same answer with the same sample tested by the same method, but by a different analyst in a different lab. Sometimes this is called the *between-lab precision.*

TCI is a measure similar to the PCI, which gives an indication of how good a test method is in relation to your interest.

When developing specifications for a product (discussed further in chapter 4), the use of these parameters can enhance the communications between the customer and the supplier because the requirements and measurement system are established up front. This is not to imply that these items are routinely known; in many cases, they are not. So, this presents the opportunity for the customer and the supplier to initiate internal and external studies.

Internal studies focus on what the capability of the test method is in both the customer's and the supplier's facility, respectively. This is called repeatability.

The external study determines how well a method relates so that the customer can, if the customer so desires, rely on the supplier's data and minimize internal testing. This is called reproducibility. The customer assumes responsibility for conducting periodic audits to ensure that the data remains in agreement between the customer and the supplier.

The four primary techniques used in auditing the accuracy of data are proficiency testing, spiked samples, split samples, and repeat samples.

Proficiency testing–A proficiency test is a systematic testing program in which a sample is analyzed by a number of laboratories to assess continuing capability and relative performance of each lab.

Spiked samples–A known quantity of chemical is added to a sample and analysis is performed for that chemical.

Split samples–The same sample is split in half and analyzed by an accredited (referee) lab, or another independent lab. This also is known as companion samples.

Repeat samples–The same sample is used a second time for analysis and the results are compared. This applies for nondestructive testing.

Frequently a supplier is asked by its customer to provide data for some specific attribute that is not a routine test for the supplier. This creates a dilemma because the ability for this may not be available in the company. When this occurs, most companies rely on an outside source (such as an independent lab or its supplier) for a required service that is not available within its own facility. This stems mainly from economic or safety limitations rather than the lack of technical ability. Special testing examples are heat treatment, plating, sterilization, magnetic particle inspection, liquid penetrant inspection, X-ray inspection, chemical (inductively coupled plasma, gas chromatography) and microbiological testing (pathogen analysis).

In many cases, special testing is required by the customer because conformance to a specification cannot be verified through routine analytical methods. This is used to verify what is known as a *special process*. A special process is a method in which a material undergoes a physical, chemical, or metallurgical transformation. Traditional process control efforts tend to be concentrated on the operating conditions of the process or the finished product. These operating conditions are necessary for the product to be made, but they are no guarantee that the product is acceptable. Testing for these special attributes can take the following two forms.

1. Nondestructive testing such as radiographic (X ray), magnetic particle, penetrant, ultrasonic, and eddy current inspections

2. Destructive testing such as chemical analyses (atomic absorption spectrometry, high-performance liquid chromatography), salt spray analysis, tensile and shear strength analyses, and impact testing

These types of tests can be expensive, so when a customer requires this type of test, it is to eliminate doubt in the supplier's capability to provide accurate data. It is a common practice to rely on the supplier's integrity and accept a certificate of compliance that lists all critical characteristics which have been agreed upon. However, there are alternatives for attaining confidence in the supplier's data. A customer can certify the capability of the manufacturing equipment as measured by a specific test method as defined in the specification. In this way, the customer has some assurance that the equipment can consistently manufacture the product if properly set up.

A customer can request that the supplier certify the people who perform tasks and inspections in accordance with the requirements in the specification. The customer is now more confident that the supplier's people have the minimum skills necessary to produce the product.

A customer can certify the limit of nonconformity of major and/or minor characteristics. Frequently this is observed in automotive requirements where critical parts allow no nonconformance to the specifications and minor parts may allow one or two per lot. As a general trend, most companies are requiring 100 percent conformance to specifications. In a few years, all companies will require 100 percent conformance. Special process certification can be done on a lot-by-lot basis, but it also can be used for continuous production if agreement can be made on the start and finish dates.

After a standard operating procedure has been established by a company for special processes and the personnel is certified, an audit should be performed by a team from the customer's facility. This team has three purposes.

1. To provide for a periodic review of special processes to see that the special process instructions are available to the people running the process, that the instructions are current, and that the instructions comply with the quality and contractual requirements.
2. To verify that manufacturing and quality assurance practices are in accordance with the established procedures.
3. To audit a test method of the product to ensure the data's accuracy. At a minimum, this audit should be performed annually.

If the company conducts business with the government, there are contractually imposed government specifications for special processes. These special process specifications have been established by certain industries, commercial standards associations, and engineering associations, such as the American Society for Testing and Materials (ASTM), the American Society for Nondestructive Testing (ASNT), and the National Institute for Standards and Technology (NIST).

All military specifications are listed in the publication *Index of Specifications and Standards.* Part I is alphabetical; Part II is numerical. They both can be obtained by subscription. These and individual military standards, specifications, and handbooks may be purchased from The Naval Publications and Forms Center, 5801 Tabor Avenue, Philadelphia, PA 19120.

Routine Testing

Not all products require special testing. Many products can be monitored routinely with common and traditional tools such as go/no go gages, optical comparators, calipers, height gages, titrators, and so on. Periodic calibration of these instruments is essential. Generally, instrument calibration is one of the first items examined in an audit of the supplier's facility. Some companies have their own internal calibration group that performs maintenance on a scheduled basis. Some companies contract out this type of service. The logic behind this is simple: If the instrument cannot provide accurate data, it is of no value to the company. Calibration is done to help ensure accuracy of the data.

Many companies have some type of inspection performed to ensure conformity of purchased materials, parts, and assemblies. This is commonly referred to as receiving inspection, incoming inspection, or purchased parts inspection. Whereas the latter clearly refers to inspection of purchased parts and assemblies only, the terms receiving inspection and incoming inspection generally are used interchangeably to refer to inspection of all incoming material. In some companies, however, incoming inspection refers strictly to inspection performed on incoming raw materials such as strip, rod, tube, chemicals, and powders for casting or molding processes, and so forth. Usually this inspection consists of fairly simple checks with some possible sampling of the material for basic analysis. Sampling and testing may be performed by the same personnel who do the actual receiving and handling of material.

In other companies, receiving inspection means the inspection of purchased parts and assemblies that ordinarily require skilled personnel. These inspections may include any or all of the usual types of checks or tests—dimensional, visual, chemical, physical, electrical, organoleptic, and any special tests that may be devised.

The optimum organization of a receiving inspection department will vary depending on the volume, variety or mix, complexity, number of suppliers, quality and services supplied, as well as the scheduling requirements within the customer's plant and the caliber of the customer's quality assurance personnel. The usual and recommended practice is to establish a central receiving inspection department separate from other inspection functions within the company. There are several reasons for this, including the following:

1. Usually incoming material is physically received at one central station in the company due to special requirements,

such as receiving docks, traffic arrangements, and material handling equipment.

2. Documentation and routines associated with purchased material have unique features compared to those required in other inspection areas and must be uniform within the company.

3. Dealing with suppliers produces special and complex problems compared with those encountered within the customer's company. These differences become increasingly important because of the trend toward supplier certification.

There are companies whose receiving inspection consists merely of checking the package contents and packing slip for agreement between the material's identification and the purchase order. This may be adequate depending on the type of material purchased, the customer's subsequent manufacturing operations and inspection, the supplier's quality system, and the quality history of the supplier. Generally, the degree of inspection is directly related to the risk the customer assumes. If a supplier has a good history of conforming materials, the risk may be low and inspection reduced. If, however, the materials are critical or complex in nature, or the supplier's conformity history is substandard, 100 percent inspection may be required. These elements must be considered to yield an effective and efficient inspection program. One of the most critical elements of an inspection program is how large a sample is and the number of samples needed. Many industries have recommended practices that have been accepted over time. The question that needs to be addressed is whether enough data has been collected to make a prudent business decision. Such a decision is one where all the risks are accounted for and understood. Traditional practices may not be enough for the increased demands that are being placed on most companies by today's customers. Inspection is expensive, so companies should explore all options to determine the most viable and cost-effective means available.

If inspection is considered necessary, the most effective and economical inspection is attained through the use of statistical sampling plans. These plans provide the greatest assurance (over a lengthy period of time) of economically determining whether submitted material meets the customer's quality requirements. Sampling schemes, such as MIL-STD-105E, are commonly used for this purpose. These schemes describe systems of classifying nonconforming material as critical, major, or minor and provide sampling plans for a wide range of acceptance criteria that might be assigned to each class of defect. This standard provides routine procedures for shifting between normal, reduced, and tightened inspection in response to the quality of lots submitted.

In addition, the customer and supplier must examime the sampling methodology in order to minimize the sources of error that can be introduced by sampling. How is the sample to be taken? Where is it taken? What type of sampling tool is used? How is the sample to be stored before it is analyzed? How is the sample prepared for analysis? Are the technicians following the procedures exactly? Are the samples taken randomly or from the easiest place to obtain them? Are the samples collected and tested individually or are they blended together to form a composite sample? These and other questions help the customer and supplier address potential sources of error that can occur when sampling occurs.

Initial lots shipped by a new supplier, or initial lots of material manufactured to a new design/formulation by an established supplier, often are inspected to tighter levels than shipments received after the supplier's quality level has been determined. This is known as *first article inspection.* Inspection should be comprehensive in nature to determine conformity requirements.

In some instances, the customer furnishes raw material, parts, or assemblies for subsequent supplier operations or processes. It is important that the purchasing agreements establish the supplier's responsibilities to (1) receive, inspect, account for, and store such material, (2) contact the customer regarding disposition of any nonconforming material prior to using it, and (3) determine the total cost of such material that may be unacceptable after the supplier has performed work on it.

The amount of receiving inspection required for material purchased from another division of the same company depends on the degree of centralization and uniformity of policies and quality standards that prevail within the company. This situation provides an opportunity for improved efficiency and cost savings when applicable. In some industries it is a common practice to supply a certificate of certification along with the shipment. A certificate of certification is a document of supplier-generated data to demonstrate how the material complies with all areas in which the customer is concerned. These areas include not just conformance to specifications, but also safety, environmental, and other value-added items.

Certificates of certification come in various forms. The one that probably is most familiar is the certificate of measurement, which is issued by standards laboratories when they calibrate instruments and gages. Many companies have found it a wise practice to require that the supplier furnish certification of critical and major characteristics from an independent laboratory, particularly when the supplier's quality history is not established or well known.

The form of certification will vary depending on the material and its critical and major characteristics. Certificates of analysis, certificates of test, and certificates of compliance are commonly used. The customer may choose to furnish a form with blank spaces to be filled in by the supplier. Data required from the supplier may take many forms: control charts; batch-by-batch information; and frequency distributions, which indicate the data of the supplier's inspection of the lot shipped.

A critical component of the customer–supplier relationship is that the data is accurate. If there is enough confidence in the data that is supplied with the incoming materials, the customer can eliminate nonvalue-added testing.

This chapter has attempted to show what is important about data. Whenever a measurement is taken, whenever an audit is performed, data is gathered. In some cases, it is required by a government agency; in others, it is voluntary. In either case, it is essential that there is a comfort level around the numbers collected. Doing everything in this chapter will not make the data perfect, but it will enable the supplier to define the level of uncertainty associated with the data that is collected.

Basic Issues: Supplier Rating
Chapter 7

Key words: data analysis, performance measures, quality information systems, source selection, supplier reporting.

Summary
- Reasons for rating
- Objectives
- Data collection
- Elements of rating
- Reporting .
- Use of rating
- Potential rating problems

Reasons for Rating

Supplier rating has been a basic element of comprehensive quality programs for many years. Most major corporations have developed and implemented a form of supplier rating and as a need to know increases, many more organizations will be creating their own new systems.

As new programs emphasizing ship-to-stock, manufacturing resource planning II (MRP II), and JIT are implemented, there is an ever-increasing requirement for strong discipline in purchased material control operations. Information previously not considered significant has taken on new meaning and many elements of supplier performance previously ignored now are being monitored.

Maintaining satisfactory supplier performance is essential to all who purchase goods and services; therefore it is necessary to continuously monitor supplier activities. Data must be collected and analyzed to establish trends and identify areas requiring further action. In order to be effective, a supplier rating must be an operating function in an organization, not just another report to show, "Look what we did."

The basis for supplier rating is a quality information system that allows for the retrieval and analysis of data. It also is dependent on information from other operating systems to reach beyond the basic elements of scrap, rework, and deficiency reporting.

More often than not, the requirement for a rating evolves as a quality program matures and the need for more usable information relating to purchased materials is realized. This need is reinforced by various guidelines defining the elements of comprehensive quality programs; therefore, ratings typically are in use by major organizations that have developed sophisticated quality systems.

Governmental and regulatory agencies, as well as some industry groups, define requirements for control of purchase material, and a supplier rating program can serve to document trends in performance. The Automotive Industry Action Group's *Industry Guideline for Quality Certification* is one such document that applies to organizations desiring to attain certified supplier status. The guideline simply states

> The supplier will be responsible for assuring continuous quality improvement of materials, processes, supplies, parts, and services that are purchased for use in the supplier's products and must establish and maintain procedures related to this responsibility.

Although supplier rating is not mentioned, an effective rating system can be the basis for establishing and measuring supplier performance. Through planned data collection and analysis, a supplier rating can be an important function in ensuring that continuous quality improvement is achieved. Supplier rating is more than just a report or a measure of past performance. It is a major operating system essential to a disciplined purchase material control program.

Federal motor vehicle safety standards, military standards, good manufacturing practices, the aerospace industries association's *Guidelines for Supplier Performance Rating Systems,* and other source documents also dictate that strong control of supplier operations must be maintained. An integrated supplier rating system can be a real asset in the implementation of a comprehensive supplier assurance program.

Corporate requirements are one of the most common reasons cited for establishing a rating. In many instances, the edict will be general in nature and only state that suppliers are to be rated. The development and implementation of the rating is then left to the discretion of the operating staff.

This has not always been the case. The other extreme is the situation where a rating package is handed down with thou shalt do instructions. The user has little or no input to this type of program and operations have a tendency to become more busy work because, "Corporate said so."

Perhaps the best reason for implementing a supplier rating is that it allows a greater awareness of achieved supplier performance. When integrated with other operating functions, a supplier rating can serve many purposes ranging from monitoring quality costs to tracking the timeliness of incoming materials. A strong rating can provide information necessary to effect change and contribute to the profitability of an organization.

Other than contractual requirements, perhaps the most important reason for implementing a supplier rating is that it can be effectively used to optimize purchased material costs. Through analysis of past and current performance, it is possible to coordinate a planned supplier improvement program to reduce defect costs and advance toward the goal of on-time receipt of defect-free product.

Even if you have an operational rating, the information contained in this publication may yield some new insights and ideas for improvement. As data gathering technologies and capabilities increase, the opportunities for system upgrade must be recognized and a continued quest for improvement maintained.

A comprehensive supplier rating program will provide the information necessary to plan and achieve the discipline necessary for continuous quality improvement. The following segments will develop the various aspects of supplier rating and describe how the concepts may be applied to strengthen your supplier assurance program.

Objectives

The following objectives identify what can be achieved with a supplier rating.

Information system–A supplier rating is primarily an information system that permits the analysis of data to identify opportunities to effect change.

Measure performance–Before quality improvement can be demonstrated, it is essential to establish and document the baseline. Some commonly evaluated elements are quality, delivery, cost, service, and compliance.

Trend performance–Trending is an indicator of change in a supplier's performance. This can be beneficial in the identification of specific areas that need work.

Source selection–A supplier rating allows customers to make more intelligent decisions when sourcing new jobs or considering present jobs for resourcing.

Recognition–A supplier rating system provides an objective means to determine your outstanding suppliers.

Initiate action–When results do not meet expectations, a supplier rating provides data on what areas need work, and by whom. (The supplier is not always the reason for not meeting expectations.)

Plan activities–Audits, meetings, performance reviews, and improvement projects are all activities that can be assisted with a good supplier rating system.

Data collection–Effective utilization of data that is currently collected, as well as the integration of new data, is accomplished with a good system. You do not want to become a slave to your data system, you want it to work for you.

Elements

At a minimum, there are three elements for any supplier rating system.

- Quality
- Delivery
- Cost

Quality
Quality improvement and defect-free performance imply a relationship between quality and deficiencies. The absence of reported deficiencies equates with desirable quality performance, so that the measure of quality is directly associated with whatever deficiency reporting system you may have in place. Your rating can be only as good as the data that are available, so if you have incomplete or flawed data, your ability for an effective rating is hampered.

Some common measurements of quality relate rejections to receipts. Quality performance can be expressed in many ways: percent defective (for parts or lots), parts per million, defects per million, parts per billion, and defects per billion.

Delivery
Delivery is an item that is becoming more critical as companies move to decrease their inventories and look at becoming more JIT oriented. Some common considerations are percent of on-time delivery (as specified by the purchase order), percent of early deliveries, percent of late deliveries, percent of overorder quantity, and percent of underorder quantity.

Cost

A major criterion of supplier evaluation is the cost of doing business. If your company has a quality cost system in place, then the cost can be incorporated into the supplier rating and you can have a look at the true cost of each supplier to your business. This can include items such as scrap, inspection, rework, and return costs.

Other elements that can be included are compliance (how well does the supplier comply with the specifications?), service (what type of service does the supplier provide?), technical support (is any available?), response to schedule changes, and price-quoting accuracy.

Reporting

After the data base has been established, it is necessary to determine what should be reported, to whom, and how often. Computers can handle more data than most people could ever review, so care must be taken that the report is both meaningful and utilized. For example, to summarize a supplier's performance, the suppliers requiring detail might be sorted out, then trended. For a commodity, there might be a comparison of all the suppliers in a given commodity and what problems have occurred with each supplier. A purchasing manager may want to rank suppliers by each buyer, so that work loads may be more evenly distributed.

Management reporting generally is focused on the economic factors of supplier performance. Some of the elements that can be included in this are total supplier responsibility defect cost, total dollar value of purchased material, percent defect cost to dollar value purchased, total defect cost debited to suppliers (recovery), percent defect cost recovered, number of lots received, number of lots inspected, number of lots rejected, number of supplier detail performance meetings, trends of defect cost and recovery, and corrective action activity.

Use of Rating

A rating is only as good as the way it is used. In many cases, after the supplier rating is set up, the training program begins. All expected and potential users must be trained on what is available, what it means, and how it can be used. This not only includes the customer's facility, but also the supplier's. Lack of familiarity, or a negative outlook about the rating can create many roadblocks to current and future use. After this hurdle is overcome, the supplier rating can be used in the following ways:

Performance evaluation—ranking–Supplier performance should be ranked in terms of the category that is most important to you. This ranking can be done in two ways. First, report the suppliers that have the highest potential for improvement. When gains are made, they should drop off the list. A second method is to list the best suppliers in descending order. This allows the customer to quickly determine which suppliers should be getting more business and identifies candidates for partnerships.

Action planning–If a supplier is rated low, some efforts may be desirable to bring it up to expectations. Based on the data, the customer can determine if the low rating was due to an unusually bad lot, or a series of lots. What has been done and what still needs to be done?

Meeting with suppliers–Supplier rating is a means of communicating with your suppliers. It creates another vehicle for dialogue to take place. The sharing of information will be enhanced because the supplier understands how all suppliers are rated. Objective data is used as opposed to opinions.

Product and process audits–When problems occur, it becomes necessary to perform a special audit. The audits are functions above and beyond the routine operations and require the allocation of additional resources for a limited period of time. Actions will have to be prioritized to maximize the use of resources.

Corrective action program–As in any action-oriented program, the purpose of your rating is to effect change. When problems occur, many customers expect to identify what corrective action has taken place to ensure that the problem is fixed. Ideally, the fix is permanent, but if it is not, the customer can use the corrective action activities as a springboard to reevaluate the goals and expectations of the supplier partnership and what long-term activities must occur.

Supplier recognition–Suppliers that continually demonstrate outstanding overall performance can be identified and slated for special recognition.

Potential Rating Problems

As with any system, there are some potential problems that must be considered. The theory behind this segment is that if you are aware of the potential problems, you should be able to avoid them when developing your system. The seven most common problems follow.

System not documented–In many companies, one person is designated as the one to develop the supplier rating system. That person becomes an expert in the system and manages all aspects of it. Unfortunately, when that person moves on to another assignment, leaves, or retires the system falls apart. Little or no documentation was developed because it was not considered necessary. Total dependence on one or two people (who have all the information in their heads) is contradictory to the basics of sound operating systems. Instructions, guidelines, responsibilities, and procedures must be documented and kept up to date.

Cluttered reports–The format in which the information is presented plays an important role in determining the report's usability. Care must be taken to structure your reports for readability and ease of use. Your supplier rating is not the place to present all the information that has been accumulated to develop that rating.

Data base maintenance–In the quest to collect and save every tidbit of information, there is a tendency to require a significant amount of unique data to be collected for rating purposes alone. You have to fight the urge to make this data base the recipient of every piece of data even remotely related to suppliers. Keep only current and relevant data. If you have no use for certain elements of data, do not keep those elements in the data base.

Timeliness–Do not get locked into a time frame that prohibits the timely monitoring of supplier performance. The effectiveness of your rating is directly related to the timeliness and completeness of data. Guidelines must be established to achieve prompt data entry.

Lack of discrimination–Ratings that are too general are not effective in identifying areas for action. When only summary-type information is available, problems often are not identified by the rating. This can occur when supplier identity cannot be associated with the product, or when the identity is lost in processing because it is based on the item number and more than one supplier is supplying that item.

Operational problems–Implementation and maintenance of the supplier rating system has to be an integrated effort. All operating departments must be aware of each other's needs and share information. Failure to do so creates a situation in which systems changes can destroy data. The system has to be user friendly in all senses of the term, not user vicious.

Management support–If there is a lack of management commitment to the project, the utilization of the data may never be realized. Management plays a major role in the acceptance and use of a supplier rating.

Two Supplier Rating Schemes

Two examples of supplier rating schemes currently in use follow. The first one is a relatively simple system used by Hughes Missile Systems Company. Raymond Wittkop, the section head of the supplier product assurance engineering group obtained permission for inclusion of this system in this edition. This example not only shows how an easy to understand and use system can be initiated, but also how it can be documented and implemented. Anyone seeking further information should not hesitate to contact Ray Wittkop at 602-794-7402.

Example 1

Why We Need a Supplier Rating System

Hughes Missile Systems Company's (HMSC) Supplier Performance Rating System (SPRS) helps to ensure the reliability and performance of the products it supplies to its customers. HMSC depends on its suppliers to meet all of its cost, schedule, and technical requirements. HMSC's SPRS provides information needed to support selection of the best supplier for each job. The purchased price of material is only a part of what it costs HMSC to buy from a particular supplier. HMSC also incurs nonproductive costs (events), the cost of anything that HMSC has to do as a result of a supplier's reduced quality or delivery nonconformity. These nonproductive costs would not occur if each supplier routinely shipped conforming product. The SPRS uses a best value algorithm to evaluate performance. Receiving, inspection, and manufacturing floor data are used to develop a history of each supplier's performance in supplying a particular part. The total projected cost of buying a specific part from a particular supplier is used to determine the best value when analyzing bids for awards.

How the System Works

The best value algorithm determines each supplier's performance rating based on a performance index (PI), which is the relationship of nonconforming costs to purchased costs.

There are five indices developed by best value which a procurement uses for evaluating suppliers during the bid evaluation process.

1. *Part performance index (PPI)*–Best value data collected and expressed by part number/supplier. The PPI is the index that includes

both quality and delivery data and is used during the bid evaluation process to help determine the best value supplier.

2. *Supplier performance index (SPI)*–Best value data collected and expressed by the supplier's rated supply point. This is an overall performance index that includes both quality and delivery costs for *all* of a supplier's parts and is utilized for tracking and analyzing performance trends.

3. *Commodity performance index (CPI)*–Best value data collected and expressed by commodity grouping. This index identifies the performance of all parts/suppliers within a specific commodity group. This index is used for a supplier/part when no performance history is available.

4. *Quality performance index (QPI)*–Best value data collected and expressed by part number/supplier for quality events only. This index shows performance on quality-related events, such as floor failures, scrap, supplier corrective action reports, receiving inspection failures, and so forth.

5. *Delivery performance index (DPI)*–Best value data collected and expressed by part number/supplier for delivery events only. This index only looks at how suppliers perform in delivering parts against purchase order requirements. Are they on time, early, or late?

There are a variety of supplier-caused nonproductive events that incur costs. The most common are

1. Reject nonconforming material and return to supplier.
2. Reject nonconforming material at source and make second source inspection.
3. Accept nonconforming material after rework or repair by HMSC.
4. Accept nonconforming material by material review action.
5. Floor failures.
6. Material delivered early or late.

Each nonproductive event costs HMSC time and money. These costs have been evaluated and a standard cost has been assigned.

Only supplier-caused events are figured into the PI. Every week data is tallied for the preceding two years. HMSC isolates all records for each specific supplier/commodity/part number and determines the total purchased cost for the past two years. Then nonproductive costs for the same period are determined by multiplying the applicable standard cost per event by the number of recorded events. The total purchased cost and the total nonproductive costs for the two-year period are added together and divided by the total purchased cost to determine the PI.

$$PI = \frac{\text{purchased costs} + \text{nonproductive costs}}{\text{purchased costs}}$$

By isolating purchased and nonproductive costs, PIs can be reported by supplier (SPI), by supplier/part (PPI), by quality events for a supplier/part (QPI), by delivery events for a supplier/part (DPI), and by commodity (CPI). The commodity index shows the performance of all suppliers within a given commodity grouping. A supplier without any nonproductive event charges will have an index of one (1.0).

The equation on page 83 shows how an index is derived (fictitious costs given for purposes of illustration, only).

Total purchased cost		$100
Nonproductive costs		
Return to vendor	2 @ $4 =	$8
Material review	2 @ $2 =	$4
Material late	3 @ $3 =	$9
Material early	1 @ $1 =	$1
Nonproductive costs subtotal		$22
Purchased plus nonproductive costs		$122
PI ($122/$100)		1.22

A PI can go below one (1.0). A supplier credit can be applied which, when subtracted from zero (0) nonproductive costs, results in a performance rating of less than one (1.0).

Example certified supplier credit: $10

$$PI = \frac{\text{purchased costs (\$1000)} + \text{nonproductive costs (--\$10)}}{\text{purchased costs (\$1000)}}$$

$$PI = 0.99$$

Supplier credits are obtained through the application of HMSC's certified supplier program. Supplier credits will only allow a performance index to go below one (1.0) if credits exceed the nonproductive costs.

Certified Suppliers

Certified suppliers are those that consistently meet all of our requirements and with whom we have certified supplier agreements to reduce source and receiving inspection. We believe in rewarding good performance. HMSC's estimated savings from dealing with a certified supplier are factored into the PI. For information on certified supplier status, contact your buyer or supplier control in HMSC's materiel department.

Supplier Data Sources

HMSC's quality and acquisition data bases collect supplier performance information from various sources.

Initial inspection data–Each source surveillance or receiving inspection/test is documented in the SPRS. This data includes part number, lot size, number of parts accepted or rejected, reason for any rejections and the quality disposition. HMSC maintains data by supplier, part number, and commodity.

Floor failure events–Supplier-caused discrepancies found after a part closes to stores or has been installed in an assembly, can have serious impacts on HMSC's operations and on the quality of its products. HMSC adjusts the supplier's PI accordingly.

Conditionally accepted materials–Information is gathered on materials that do not conform to specification, but are accepted through the material review process.

Receipt vs. schedule–The SPRS system tracks the difference between purchase order schedule and actual receipt dates, identifies undelivered, past-due items and unauthorized early deliveries.

How HMSC Uses the System

Past performance is a good indicator of potential future performance. HMSC's intent is to use suppliers that have the best indices. Business with suppliers who have an unsatisfactory performance rating is discouraged. Past performance also is used to determine levels of inspection, to nominate candidates for certified supplier status, and to advise any supplier whose performance needs improvement.

The supplier/PPI allows HMSC to establish the total evaluated cost for buying a particular part from each supplier. The total evaluated cost becomes the best value price.

	Supplier A	**Supplier B**	**Supplier C**
Quoted price	$1000	$1065	$1025
(X) PPI	1.45	1.20	1.04
Total evaluated cost	$1450	$1278	$1066

Although Supplier C does not have the lowest quoted price, the history of reliable performance results in the lowest total evaluated cost, or the best value; therefore, Supplier C would be the recommended choice.

The average PI for all suppliers in each commodity is also calculated. Suppliers receive quarterly reports of their standing in relation to this average CPI. New supplier/parts are given the average commodity index until history is established.

Many of HMSC's customers are represented by the defense plant representative office (DPRO), which periodically reviews HMSC's subcontract management methods. HMSC is also frequently audited by other customers and government agencies. SPRS demonstrates to them that HMSC is choosing responsible suppliers, that it is working with suppliers to improve their performance where needed, and that it is reducing unnecessary costs.

How Suppliers Can Help

Like any other computerized system, the SPRS depends on human input. Data errors that cause inaccurate PIs are correctable. HMSC encourages its suppliers to join it in continually improving the system.

Specifically, HMSC appreciates supplier input in three areas.

Requirements–Suppliers should note on their quotation any requirement contained in the drawing or specification callouts that cannot be met, or where alternative equivalent methods would result in lower overall cost.

Responsibility for defects–Defects that cannot be substantiated as HMSC-caused will remain the responsibility of the supplier. If a supplier can show that a defect charged to them was caused by something HMSC did, the rejection will not affect the supplier's PI. HMSC makes every attempt to ensure that responsibility is properly assigned in the first place.

On-time delivery statistics–When HMSC-initiated changes on a part cause a delay, suppliers should request appropriate changes in the purchase order delivery date. Suppliers should also process outside receiving reports promptly. Material that has been sent back to the supplier will be tracked for return delivery status.

HMSC's system allows buyers to compare each supplier's overall performance against the requirements of the purchase order and the performance of other suppliers providing the same commodity. Suppliers are encouraged to inform the responsible buyer of potential problems.

Variability Reduction and Process Control

One of the most important things that you can do as an HMSC supplier is to understand, promote, and practice *variability reduction* on all of your operations. Integral to this is *process control*. The word *process* in process control means any activity that a company performs that takes an input and produces an output (products, services, or information) for a customer. This could mean everything from receiving parts and materials at your dock, to how you load and prioritize your work on the production floor, to how you market your products or services. A process should add value to a product. However, some processes are inefficient and add more costs than are required. This is where the *control* comes in. If a company can understand its processes and control them effectively, it can produce products that make it more competitive. This means looking at all facets of a business from an overall perspective with the result being a more competitive company. HMSC is reviewing all of its processes from *A* to *Z* to improve its position in its market. Suppliers that incorporate this example will naturally improve their position with HMSC. HMSC is offering to help its suppliers, through training, information, and support, to follow its lead in variability reduction. Please contact your HMSC buyer or supplier control for more information.

Supplier Report Card

For every quarter that a supplier has had activity within the last two years, a report that shows overall performance and the performance of part numbers supplied will be available. Supplier overall performance is identified by the SPI. The SPI is calculated from the purchased costs and the cost of nonproductive events over the previous two years. The SPI presents the supplier with performance trend data, in relation to SPIs from previous report cards. A reduction in the SPI indicates improvement.

The real story is individual part performance. The supplier report card shows four indices that help suppliers review their individual part number performance. These same indices are used by HMSC buyers when determining source selection.

The CPI is the performance index of all part numbers from all suppliers within a commodity grouping. This can tell the supplier and the HMSC buyer how a specific supplier/part has performed relative to the commodity average. The CPI is also the performance index applied to a new supplier/part number where no performance history exists.

The PPI is the performance index of a specific supplier/part. This is the overall performance for this particular part number for that supplier. Once the HMSC buyer has received bids from suppliers, those bids are factored by the specific supplier/part PPIs to determine the projected best value. The best value is what HMSC uses in source selection.

In the following example, we use the previous best value example and show the same scenario but this time the best value supplier, Supplier C, has no supplier/part history. The CPI for this part number will be 2.00. Remember, the CPI is the average of all supplier/parts within a given commodity classification.

	Supplier A	**Supplier B**	**Supplier C**
Quoted price	$1000	$1065	$1025
(x) PPI	1.45	1.20	2.00 (CPI)
Total evaluated cost	$1450	$1278	$2050

This time the best value price is from Supplier B. Even though Supplier B has the highest quoted price, its PPI makes its total evaluated cost the best value. This example shows the importance of supplier performance. In this case, it is likely that Supplier B would receive the award.

The QPI is the performance index of supplier/part events that pertain only to quality and have been determined to be the supplier's responsibility. Quality events include inspection, material review, return-to-vendor, floor failures, supplier corrective action requests, or any event based on quality-related issues. The only events that are not quality-related are delivery events.

The DPI is the performance index of supplier/part events that pertain only to delivery. The measurement criteria covers three delivery events: on time, late, and early. Delivery events are calculated by comparing the purchase order delivery date of a shipment to the actual receipt date of the shipment. Late deliveries cost HMSC in scheduling delays, external and internal expediting, and customer confidence. Early deliveries cost HMSC in working capital, excessive incoming-receiving inspection queues, and related priority management. Delivery performance is an important issue.

The supplier report card will show all of the performance factors affecting the supplier/part performance rating. Unsatisfactory events are listed, allowing the supplier to verify and identify any problem areas. HMSC requests that all suppliers identify, to the buyer, any event that seems to be incorrect. The supplier and HMSC, as a team, can investigate and correct any errors.

The following material illustrates the new supplier report card that incorporates these new measurements. For your information, the HMSC SPRS core development team consisted of Jim Benjamin,

Nancy Brydle, Chris Collins, Gail Dunlap, Dave Landesberg, Blake Lindstom, and Raymond Wittkop.

Supplier Report Card Example

The first part of the supplier report card is the introductory letter. This letter displays your SPI, the data cutoff date, and the total number of lots received during the two-year rating period.

August 3, 1992

Hughes
Missile Systems Company

ABC Corporation
Resistor Division
28 Carbon Street
Ohms Law, NY 12024

Attention: Contract, Quality, Materiel, and Manufacturing Management

The attached supplier report card details your performance as a Hughes supplier. The assessment is based both on your quality and delivery performance. The time period of this evaluation is a two-year period ending 28-Jul-1992.

The supplier report card consists of three sections:

Part number summary data: Provides basic performance data for each part delivered to Hughes over the past two years.

Nonproductive events for the current quarter: Supplier-caused events that cost Hughes money. All of the events are listed for the current quarter performance.

Documentation: The last page of this report briefly describes the performance indices and the nonproductive events that can appear on the report. Additional documentation can be obtained from your buyer or the supplier performance rating system handbook that has been provided to your company.

Please review the supplier report card data. If you have any questions, or if it does not agree with your assessment, please work with your buyer for resolution.

Sincerely,

Materiel Management
Hughes Missile Systems Company
P.O. Box 11337
Building 807 M/S A2
Tucson, AZ 85734-1337
602-794-7402

Report card—part 1.

The second part starts the listing of specific part number information for all part numbers that you supplied during the two-year rating
period. This listing has two sections. The first section is the supplier
information, and the second section, identified as *Part Number
Summary*, shows summarized data about all the part numbers you
have supplied.

As of date: 7/28/92	Supplier Report Card
	ABC Corporation
	Ohms Law, NY 12024

Lots presented:	44	Supplier code:	12345A
Two-year SPI:	1.30		

Part Number Summary   Page 1

	—Current Qtr—		—Two Year—		Lots in insp	—Two-year indices—			
Part number	Lots prsnt	Lots reject	Lots prsnt	Lots reject		CPI	PPI	QPI	DPI
6100500-2	0	0	18	2	1	1.08	1.31	1.01	1.29
6100500-4	3	3	12	2	0	1.08	1.31	1.06	1.25
6100197-1	3	0	9	0	0	1.08	1.58	1.02	1.56
650056-1	0	0	1	0	0	1.42	2.69	1.00	2.69

Report card–part 2.

The third part contains the section called *Nonproductive Events
for the Current Quarter*, lists all nonproductive events. These nonproductive events are a part of the current quarter indices calculated by
best value.

As of date: 7/28/92   Supplier Report Card
                                   ABC Corporation
                                   Ohms Law, NY 12024

Nonproductive Events for the Current Quarter							Page 1
Part number	Event date	Event code	PO number	PO line	Receiver	Qty	—Document— Sys number
6100500-2	7/28/92	LDLV	900001	0001		18	
6100500-2	7/28/92	LDLV	900002	0001		1	
6100500-4	7/09/92	PRB	900040	0002	292B001	6	RI 0000001234
6100500-4	7/09/92	PRB	900040	0002	332C001	32	RI 0000001235
6100500-4	7/09/92	PRB	900040	0002	337B001	19	RI 0000001238
6100500-4	7/09/92	RI	900040	0002	292B001	6	RI 0000001234
6100500-4	7/09/92	RI	900040	0002	332C001	32	RI 0000001235
6100500-4	7/09/92	RI	900040	0002	337B001	19	RI 0000001238
6100500-4	7/09/92	RTV	900040	0002	292B001	6	RI 0000001234
6100500-4	7/09/92	RTV	900040	0002	332C001	32	RI 0000001235
6100500-4	7/09/92	RTV	900040	0002	337B001	19	RI 0000001238
6100500-4	7/09/92	LDLV	900040	0002		64	
6100197-1	7/02/92	EDLV	900042	0003	424B002	4	
6100197-1	7/02/92	EDLV	900042	0003	424B008	4	
6100197-1	7/06/92	LDLV	900087	0005	428C012	2	

Report card—part 3.

This portion of the report card allows you to see where problems
have occurred and lists ample information for discussing any problems with your buyer.

The last page of the report card is a glossary of terms used in the
report card and the SPRS system.

Explanation of Indices

All indices represent a ratio of the total cost of ownership compared to the price of the product. For example, an index of 1.85 means that for every dollar Hughes spends with you, it costs Hughes a total of $1.85. The lower the index, the better. Indices are summarized in five different ways as described below:

PPI–part performance index	Summarized by supplier/part for all quality and delivery nonproductive events
QPI–quality performance index	Summarized by supplier/part for all quality nonproductive events
DPI–delivery performance index	Summarized by supplier/part for all delivery nonproductive events
SPI–supplier performance index	Summarized by supplier/part for all quality and delivery nonproductive events
CPI–commodity performance index	Summarized by commodity code for all quality and delivery nonproductive events

Legend of Event Types

Event code	Description
EDLV	Early delivery against PO contract schedule
LDLV	Late delivery against PO contract schedule
RI	Receiving inspection failure
SI	Source inspection failure
PRB	Item processed through Hughes Preliminary Review Board
MRB	Item processed through Hughes Materiel Review Board
RTV	Item returned to vendor
RWK	Item requires rework
SCRAP	Item scrapped
FF	Item failed on the shop floor
GIDEP	Processing of a government industry data exchange program action
SCAR	Processing of a supplier corrective action request issued by Hughes
XORD	Hughes Incurs costs beyond the scope of normal supplier relations

Report card–part 4.

Extraordinary Costs

Extraordinary costs are costs incurred from tasks performed beyond the normal scope of work and not tracked/recorded within the existing systems. An example of this would be actions taken to resolve supplier problems or the monitoring of the supplier's progress. These actions may involve personnel from procurement, engineering, quality, production control, or management.

Data Security

All information in SPRS is considered Hughes-proprietary and is provided only to those involved. Suppliers have access only to data on their own performance.

Conclusion

Working as a team, HMSC and its suppliers can develop a significant competitive edge. In addition, HMSC is committed to treating all of its suppliers fairly, equally, and ethically. The SPRS assists the process by identifying the best performers, as well as those that need improvement.

HMSC enjoys working with its suppliers to implement concepts and techniques that improve quality and productivity, and reduce costs. Working together in long-term relationships to build quality products, delivered on time, is mutually beneficial.

If you have any questions, or would like further information, please contact your buyer or supplier control in HMSC's materiel department.

Materiel Department
Hughes Missile Systems Company
P.O. Box 11337
Building 807 M/S A2
Tucson, AZ 85734-1337
602-794-7402

The second system is one that is at the other end of the supplier rating spectrum. This is a sophisticated supplier rating system which has evolved into what is presented here. This system is used by Western Foundry Company Limited. Harry Schiestel, the manager of corporate quality, submitted a complete supplier rating scheme. This is an excellent example of what can be developed if a company is willing to devote resources to it. What impressed me the most is not just the completeness of the system, but the simplicity. Everything is contained on the forms so no further paperwork is needed. (The forms are reprinted with permission by Harry F. Schiestel, CET, Manager Corporate Quality, Western Foundry Co. Ltd., Wingham, Ontario, Canada.

The first form is the full business assessment, which looks at the supplier from a business aspect incorporating leadership, quality, delivery, cost, and technology into the overall rating. This is an annual rating that looks at long-term growth. The second form is a quality system survey, which looks at the supplier's quality system, on an as-needed basis. The third form is a quarterly assessment for quality and delivery. This is a nice interlocking system which complements all pertinent supplier information. It has value in that both Western Foundry and the supplier know exactly where they stand at any point in time. Harry is willing to talk to anyone who is interested in more information about the system that he uses. His phone number is 519-357-3450.

Example 2

Western Foundry Company Limited
Box 460, Wingham, Ontario, Canada NOG 2W0
519-357-3450   Fax: 519-357-2486

Supplier Rating
Full Business Assessment

Supplier Information

Name: Auto Supply Ltd.
Location: Smalltown, U.S.A.
Contact: Ed R. Haines
Phone (111) 555-4444   Fax (111) 555-9999
Commodity: OEM automotive parts for passenger cars and light trucks

Rating period: 01/01/92 — 12/31/92
DUNS code: Donegood
Annual Sales: $50 M
Sales to WF: $5 M   10 %

Legend

		Percent	Code	
9	Excellent	☐ 100–85	☐ E	
6	Satisfactory			
4	Deficiency		S	■ 84–70
2				
3	Unacceptable	☐ 69–0	☐ U	
0				

Supplier status
Code E ☐ Preferred
Code S ■ Approved
Code U ☐ Unapproved

Supplier Rating

Requirement
- Excellent/low risk: Minimum 85%. Quality system score and each of the five assessment categories rated 70% or higher.
- Satisfactory/medium risk: Minimum 70%. Quality system score and each of the five assessment categories rated 50% or higher.
- Unacceptable/high risk: Below 50% or fails to meet the minimum requirements for overall rating of satisfactory.

Supplemental Remarks and Overall Assessment

Item	

Signatures

WF lead assessor: _____
Supplier acknowledgment: _____

Distribute copies to
☐ Supplier
☐ WF director sales
☐ WF materials mgr
☐ WF mgr corp qlty
☐ WF supplier—file

Director sales   Date 12/31/92
Materials mgr   Date 01/05/93
Mgr corp qlty   President & COO

Route original for WF acknowledgment

Note: Return original copy to WF manager corporate quality

	Previous 12/31/91	Current 12/31/92
Leadership	13·21 62%	16·21 76%
1. Companywide continuous improvement	6	6 2 0
2. Responsiveness to customer needs	4	4 2 0
3. Changing management philosophies	6	6 2 0
4. Human resource utilization	3	3 2 1
Quality	27·31 68%	25·31 81%
		10·13
1. Quality system score 76 %	9	9 3 0
2. Demonstrated product capability	6	6 3 0
3. Quality products, zero defects	6	6 3 0
Delivery	8·18 44%	10·18 56%
1. Product delivered on time	6	6 2 0
2. Delivered product quantity	4	4 2 0
3. Packaging, labels, and documents	6	6 2 0
Cost	12·18 67%	14·18 78%
1. Competitiveness, achieves contract	6	6 2 0
2. Cost reduction efforts shared	4	4 2 0
3. Profitability long term	6	6 2 0
Technology	10·12 83%	10·12 83%
1. Facilities effectiveness	6	6 4 2
2. Technical support, research & development	4	4 2 0
Supplier Rating	66 U	75 S
• Overall percent		
• Supplier code	Previous	Current

Revision: A   Date: 06-15-92   \FWFSOARATE.FRP

Western Foundry Company Limited

April 01, 1993

Auto Supply Ltd.
17 Maple Street, P.O. Box 142
Smalltown, Michigan 99999-5555
U.S.A.

Attention: Mr. Ed R. Haines
            Director of Operations

Dear Ed:

Please find enclosed two copies of the Supplier Quality System Survey dated March 19, 1993 and the Supplier Quarterly Assessment Quality and Delivery 1st Quarter 1993.

The Quality System Category was assessed as "Satisfactory" having achieved a system score of 81%. The Supplier Quarterly Assessment was assessed an overall score of 78%.

To aid our mutual efforts in pursuit of continuous improvement, please forward by April 30, 1993 the System Survey Improvement Plan with timing for each question/item rated below "Satisfactory." The System Survey Improvement Plan must document a planned response to correct each discrepancy per the Quality System Survey and the Quarterly Assessment.

Please sign and date the Supplier Acknowledgment section of the System Survey and the Quarterly Assessment. Return as soon as possible the Original Copies to my attention in the envelope provided. Retain photocopies for your records.

Western Foundry is available to assist its suppliers in achieving continual improvements in quality and costs. Please feel free to contact me if I can be of further assistance.

Yours truly,

WESTERN FOUNDRY COMPANY LIMITED

Harry F. Schiestel, CET
Manager Corporate Quality

HFS:mrl
Enclosures
Copy to: John Leitch
             Larry Cerson

Wingham:
  P.O. Box 460
  454 Industrial Rd.
  Wingham, Ontario, Canada
  N0G 2W0

  Phone (519) 357-3450
  Fax (519) 357-2486

Brantford:
  P.O. Box 1930
  Powerline Road West
  Brantford, Ontario, Canada
  N3T 5W5

  Phone (519) 759-0452
  Fax (519) 759-8535

Western Foundry
Company Limited
Box 460, Wingham, Ontario, Canada NOG 2W0
519-357-3450   Fax: 519-357-2486

Supplier Quality System Survey

Supplier
Auto Supply Ltd.

Address
17 Maple Street, P.O. Box 142

City, Prov./State
Smalltown, Michigan 99999-5555

Phone   **Telefax**
(111) 555-4444   (111) 555-9999

Survey Type

☐ Potential source
☐ Initial evaluation
■ Routine evaluation   03 / 27 / 92
                        M   D   Y
                            Previous

System Survey Results

Quality system score
Current   Previous
  81 %   76 %

Part Description and Service

OEM automotive parts for passenger
cars and light trucks

Quality System Category

☐	Excellent	☐
■	Satisfactory	■
☐	Minor Deficiencies	☐
☐	Major Deficiencies	☐
☐	Unacceptable	☐

Yes ■   System survey improvement plan required   ■ Yes
No ☐   By date   04 / 30 / 93   ☐ No
                        M   D   Y

Remarks _____

Survey Participants

	Name	Title
Supplier	Ed Haines	Director of Operations
	William Levan	Technical Director
	Claude Beghetto	Materials Manager
	Ross Wilhelm	Quality Assurance Manager
	Blair Alton	Sales and Service Representative
Western Foundry	John Leitch	Materials Manager
	Doug Merkley	Customer Service Representative
	Carl Mowbray	Manufacturing Manager
	Harry Schiestel	Manager Corporate Quality

Signatures

WF lead assessor _____   Date 03 / 19 / 93
                                                M   D   Y
Supplier
acknowledgment _____   Date 04 / 10 / 93
                                                M   D   Y

Distribute copies to

☐ Supplier
☐ WF director sales
☐ WF materials mgr
☐ WF mgr corp qlty
☐ WF supplier—file
Revision: D   Date: 06-15-92
\F\WF\SUPQLTYS.FRP
Page 1 of 6

Route original for WF acknowledgment

Director sales   Materials mgr   Mgr corp qlty   President & COO

Note: Supplier to return original copy to WF manager corporate quality

\\�загⱽ⸗ **Supplier Quality System Survey**   Page: 2 of _6_

```
Unacceptable  ───────────────────────────┐
Major deficiency  ───────────────────────┐│
Minor deficiency  ─────────────────────┐ ││
Satisfactory  ───────────────────────┐ │ ││
Excellent  ────────────────────────┐ │ │ ││
```

General
                                        1 2 3 4 5

1. Does an organizational chart exist outlining quality relationships relative to
    production and other departments?   ■ □ □ □ □
    • Who does the quality manager report to?
    • Have job descriptions been developed for all employees?

2. Is there a quality manual containing procedures defining the organization,
    functions, and operations of the quality system?   ■ □ □ □ □
    • Is the manual updated as changes occur?
    • Does it contain procedures pertaining to this survey?

3. Does a control plan exist to summarize the quality planning for products
    supplied to Western Foundry, from receiving to shipping?   ■ □ □ □ □
    • Does it contain the necessary information?
    • Has a process flowchart been developed to assist the control plan?

4. Is there a documented system for ensuring that only the latest applicable
    drawings and specifications are in effect?   □ □ ■ □ □
    • Is there a log maintained to record latest ECL dates and revision levels?
    • Is all obsolete information removed from all points of use?
    • Is review of drawings and specifications to latest date and level verified annually?

5. Are documented internal system audits performed periodically that assess
    compliance to quality related systems, procedures, and record retention?   □ ■ □ □ □
    • Are results and corrective actions reported to and reviewed by management?
    • Is self-audit performed at least quarterly?

6. Is there a system for organization and retention for all quality-related records?   ■ □ □ □ □
    • Are quality system records retained five years?
    • Are quality performance records retained two years?

Receiving

7. Are written inspection instructions utilized for incoming material?   □ ■ □ □ □
    • Is incoming material inspected and tested with results documented or does supplier
      receive certificate of analysis from subsuppliers?
    • Is verification of subsupplier certifications performed annually?
    • Is acceptance criteria zero defects?

8. Is incoming material identified to prevent mixing and misuse of defective stock?   □ ■ □ □ □
    • Is lot control utilized?

9. Are subsuppliers encouraged to use SPC?   □ ■ □ □ □
    • Is evidence of statistical control and capability required from subsuppliers?

10. Does supplier utilize a system to periodically audit subsuppliers?   □ ■ □ □ □
    • Is supplier survey performed annually?

Revision: D   Date: 06-15-92
\F\WF\SUPQLTYS.FRP

\\V⊭   Supplier Quality System Survey   Page: 3 of 6

In-process and Outgoing

1 2 3 4 5

11. Are written inspection instructions utilized for each in-process operation and for   ☐ ■ ☐ ☐ ☐
    outgoing material?
    • Are they displayed or on file at each inspection location?
    • Are in-process parameters tested with results documented?
    • Is acceptance criteria zero defects?

12. Do production operators have any responsibility for product quality or inspection?   ■ ☐ ☐ ☐ ☐
    • Do operators have the authority to shut an operation down when nonconformance
      is detected?

13. Is there an effective system for the control of all material, including segregation of   ☐ ■ ☐ ☐ ☐
    nonconforming material?
    • Is material identification, quarantine area, etc., utilized?

14. Is a certificate of analysis prepared on each lot of products supplied to WF?   ■ ☐ ☐ ☐ ☐
    Are containers identified with a shipping label?
    • Does the documentation contain the necessary information?
    • What information is provided to other customers?

15. Are the handling, storage, and packaging adequate to preserve product quality?   ☐ ■ ☐ ☐ ☐
    • Are plant cleanliness, housekeeping, environmental, and working conditions adequate?

Nonconformance Control

16. Is there an established plan for corrective action in the event discrepant material   ☐ ■ ☐ ☐ ☐
    is detected?
    • Are material(s) identified and segregated?
    • Is responsible management personnel alerted to quality concerns?
    • Is Western Foundry notified of suspect material that may have been shipped?

17. If discrepant material is reworked/sorted, is it reinspected and approved through the   ■ ☐ ☐ ☐ ☐
    normal inspection process prior to release?

18. Is there a system for documenting corrective actions to prevent recurrence?   ☐ ■ ☐ ☐ ☐
    • Statistical information where applicable?
    • Does it include the WF DPM Response Worksheet—8D?

Gage/test Equipment

19. Is there a documented program for control of calibration and maintenance of   ☐ ■ ☐ ☐ ☐
    test/inspection equipment?
    • Do records identify gage number, calibration procedure, specification, date calibrated,
      results, signed, date due, etc.?

20. Is gage accuracy verified at established frequency against masters?   ☐ ■ ☐ ☐ ☐
    • Is there traceability to NIST or international equivalent?

21. Are gage/test equipment repeatability and reproducibility studies performed?   ☐ ☐ ■ ☐ ☐
    • Is corrective action taken when the measurement system variation is determined
      to be excessive?

Continuous Improvement

	1 2 3 4 5

22. Are control charts utilized for process parameters and/or product characteristics?   □ ■ □ □ □
    - Are control charts properly constructed for the characteristic being controlled?
    - Are out-of-control conditions including nonrandom patterns being noted on charts and corrective action taken to bring the process back into control?
    - Are written plans for improvement generated to reduce sources of variation?

23. Are process capability studies conducted on process parameters and/or product characteristics?   □ ■ □ □ □
    - Can supplier exceed minimum Western Foundry C_{pk} requirements?
    - Are written plans for improvement generated when control and/or capability (product and process) are not indicated?
    - What capability is provided to other customers?

24. Does the supplier provide to WF a process capability quarterly summary ongoing? This summary to include the following: ■ □ □ □ □
    - Cover letter
    - Organizational chart, control plans, and flowcharts that are revised
    - Control charts
    - Long-term process capability form
    - WF DPM response worksheet—8D with timing, as required
    - Supplier verification document, as required
    - Continuous improvement plan, provided annually

25. Has a continuous improvement plan been developed to promote a total organizational commitment to continuously improve quality and productivity through reduction of variation and waste, with the aim to improve internal/external customer satisfaction?   □ ■ □ □ □
    - Does it plan for the education and training of all employees, including management and staff, to improve their understanding of theory and job-related skills relative to team building, problem solving, statistics, leadership, products, systems, etc.?
    - Does it describe future activities for improvement pertaining to this survey and full business assessment?
    - Is the plan endorsed by senior management and supported by the allocation of resources?
    - Is the plan updated quarterly and developed annually by all disciplines within the organization?

Supplier Quality System Survey   Page: 5 of 6

Guideline Values Established for All Questions

Rating	Points	
1	4	Excellent: Demonstrates high capability. Continuous improvement process in place. Performance history indicates past improvement.
2	3	Satisfactory: Effective planning and implementation demonstrated. System, operation, and commitment meets Western Foundry expectations.
3	2	Minor deficiency: Improvement in the system or its implementation are necessary to result in demonstrated performance improvements.
4	1	Major deficiency: Major improvement in the system or its implementation are necessary to meet Western Foundry expectations.
5	0	Unacceptable: System doesn't exist for the expectation under review. Commitment to improve not demonstrated with a documented plan.

Computation of System Survey Results

Quality system score:

Rating	Frequency	Factor	Total
1	8	4	32
2	15	3	45
3	2	2	4
4	___	1	___
5	___	0	___

Overall point score $\boxed{81}$ A

N/A   0   4 $\boxed{0}$ B

C $\boxed{25}$ Frequency total (should be 25)

Total possible points = 100 − B = $\boxed{100}$ D

Overall score = A/D X 100 = $\boxed{81\%}$ ⟶

Quality system category:

100 - 85	Excellent	☐
84 - 70	Satisfactory	☑
69 - 50	Minor deficiencies	☐
49 - 25	Major deficiencies	☐
24 - 0	Unacceptable	☐

Conformance to WF Supplier Quality System Survey

Requires a 70 percent minimum quality system score (category: satisfactory or higher). Regardless of the quality system category assigned, the supplier to forward the system survey improvement plan with timing for each question rated below satisfactory.

Revision: D   Date: 06-15-92
\F\WF\SUPQLTYS.FRP

\\V≶ Supplier Quality System Survey

Supplier Name_____ Auto Supply Ltd._____   Date __03_ / _19_ / _93_
                                                                       M   D   Y
                                                                          Previous

Item	Supplemental Remarks and Supplier Comments

WF survey rep._____

Western Foundry
Company Limited
Box 460, Wingham, Ontario, Canada N0G 2W0
519-357-3450　Fax: 519-357-2486

Supplier Quarterly Assessment
Quality and Delivery

Supplier Name	Auto Supply Ltd.	Year
Contact	Ed R. Haines	1992
Commodity	OEM automotive parts for passenger cars and light trucks	

			Quarter				Full business assessment
			1st	2nd	3rd	4th	
Quality	1	Quality system score	69%/76% 9/13	10/13	10/13	10/13	10/13
	2	Demonstrated product capability					
		• Average C_{pk} exceeds 2.00	9	9	9	9	9
		• Average C_{pk} exceeds 1.67	6	6	6	6	6
		• Average C_{pk} exceeds 1.33	3	3	3	3	3
		• Average C_{pk} less than 1.33	0	0	0	0	0
	3	Quality products, zero defects. Customer rejections—QR, PR/R, etc.					
		• Zero rejections 12 months	6	6	6	6	6
		• Zero rejections 3 months	4	4	4	4	4
		• One rejection issued	2	2	2	2	2
		• Multiple rejections issued	0	0	0	0	0
		Quality products, zero defects. Machine scrap—internal					
		• Less than 0.5%	3	3	3	3	3
		• Less than 1.0%	2	2	2	2	2
		• Less than 2.0%	1	1	1	1	1
		• Exceeds 2.0%	0	0	0	0	0
Delivery	1	Product delivered on time					
		• On time 12 months	6	6	6	6	6
		• On time 3 months	4	4	4	4	4
		• Late, customer not shutdown	2	2	2	2	2
		• Shutdown at customer plant	0	0	0	0	0
	2	Delivered product quantity					
		• Correct 12 months	6	6	6	6	6
		• Correct 3 months	4	4	4	4	4
		• Shortage, customer not shutdown	2	2	2	2	2
		• Shutdown at customer plant	0	0	0	0	0
	3	Packaging, labels, and documents					
		• Correct 12 months	6	6	6	6	6
		• Correct 3 months	4	4	4	4	4
		• One rejection issued	2	2	2	2	2
		• Multiple rejections issued	0	0	0	0	0
		Total points = 49	29	31	35	38	
		Overall score	59%	63%	71%	78%	

Signatures

WF lead assessor _____ Date 12/31/92
　　　　　　　　　　　　　　　　　　　　　　　　M　D　Y

Supplier acknowledgment _____ Date 01/05/93
　　　　　　　　　　　　　　　　　　　　　　　　M　D　Y

Legend

9	6	3	Excellent
6	4	2	Satisfactory
3	2	1	Deficiency
0	0	0	Unacceptable

Distribute copies to

☐ Supplier
☐ WF director sales
☐ WF materials mgr
☐ WF mgr corp qlty
☐ WF supplier—file

Revision: D　Date: 06-15-92
\F\WF\SUPQLTYS.FRP

Route original for WF acknowledgment

Director sales　Materials mgr　Mgr corp qlty　President & COO

Note: Supplier to return original copy to WF manager corporate quality

This chapter has examined some logic on the development of supplier ratings. These ratings must be established with a certain amount of care because there is a certain amount of concern that the supplier experiences when a rating is first proposed. The two examples show some different ways to approach supplier rating. It is important to look at what is necessary for your business to perform its day-to-day activities. What do you expect from your suppliers and what are things that are not required, but if done would enhance your partnership. There is an old adage which says, "What gets measured gets done," so measure what is important to you.

Basic Issues: Communications
Chapter 8

Key words: corrective action, disposition, nonconforming material costs, rejection reports.

Summary
- Types of communication
- Frequency of communication
- Nonconforming materials
- Problem identification and resolution

Whenever two parties get together, there is a potential for communication problems. Both parties have different ideas about what they want to get out of each meeting. What the customer and the supplier want is to create an atmosphere of openness and interest so that the business at hand is accomplished as quickly and as graciously as possible.

When developing a partnership with suppliers, the customer wants to establish a schedule of communication on routine issues. It also is a good idea to reinforce the issue of contacting the customer as quickly as possible when a problem arises. So, the two basic forms of communicating with suppliers are routine issues and nonroutine issues. Nonroutine issues can include problems, new people on board, new management, and so on.

Routine communications should initially take place once a month for both teams. If the teams are in the same area, this can be done face to face; if not, a conference call is a good way to address this. This communication allows teams to become familiar with each other. Until a level of confidence can be built up, openness with each other will be slow. In fact, during the initial meetings, most of the communication will be one-sided. The customer will do most of the talking. If the customer can quickly develop a trusting relationship, the process to a meaningful partnership will be expedited.

The first meeting of the teams should take place at the supplier's facility. This serves two purposes: (1) the customer's team can see the facility, and (2) it sends a positive message to the supplier. The message is that the customer is interested in the supplier and wants to help the supplier in any way. The customer is meeting the supplier on the supplier's turf. The supplier will be more comfortable in familiar surroundings, and this lends itself to open communications.

It is necessary for the customer's team to meet before the initial visit to discuss the purpose of the visit and the team's long-term goal. An agenda should be prepared jointly and sent to all team members. Generally, the initial meeting is one where the customer talks about the relationship that is beginning and where the customer hopes it will end. The customer also has the opportunity to show where and how the product being supplied will be used. This creates an opportunity for the supplier to make alternative suggestions about other materials that may be more suitable for the intended purpose. This can lead to the acceptance of a better-suited product if it can pass the accreditation testing.

At the end of the initial meeting, a schedule should be established for future meetings. If the supplier is located nearby, the monthly meetings could alternate from the supplier's facilities to the customer's facilities. If the supplier is not in the local area, then quarterly meetings should be set up at alternating facilities and, in between, meetings can be accomplished by conference call. This enables the customer and supplier teams to talk routinely and keep costs down.

Before every meeting, an agenda should be sent to both teams so that everyone is prepared. Routine monthly meetings can last as long as necessary, but experience has shown that after a year, these can be cut back unless there are problems or special circumstances. Some examples of special circumstances include new people brought onto the team due to retirements or personnel changes, new ownership, or a new location. A rule of thumb is to have each team visit the other facility at least once a year after the first year. This helps maintain good relations.

In some instances, the customer furnishes the raw material, parts, or assemblies for subsequent supplier operations or processes. It is important that the purchasing agreements establish the supplier's responsibilities to (1) receive, inspect, account for, and store such material, (2) contact the customer regarding disposition of any furnished nonconforming material prior to using it, and (3) determine the total cost of such material that may be unacceptable after the supplier has performed work on it.

Nonconforming material should be identified promptly and separated from other material pending material review. The purpose of reviewing nonconforming material is to determine causes of nonconformity and to obtain corrective action on serious or repetitive nonconformances. Quality assurance, design, engineering, marketing, or a materials review board may determine the disposition of nonconforming material.

Disposition may be to use-as-is, screen, repair, scrap, or rework nonconforming material in the customer's plant or to return material to the supplier for screening, rework, credit, or replacement. In the event the decision is to accept the nonconforming material, concurrence of production, engineering, and quality assurance may be obtained as required by company policy and customer specifications.

Feedback of information and samples of nonconformances are important to eliminate any misunderstanding on the part of the supplier and to obtain corrective action by the customer.

Costs incurred by receiving inspection will vary depending on lot size, the number of lots, the product mix, product complexity, special laboratory test requirements, specialized gaging, test equipment, inspection methods, and skills. Continuing pressures to reduce costs tend to optimize these factors for increased efficiency. Other costs also are there, but generally are hidden in most companies; accounts receivable labor, repackaging costs, downtime costs, and so forth.

Receiving inspection costs have traditionally been accumulated and apportioned among all products as a part of general overhead. However, the charging of receiving inspection costs directly to specific products is advantageous in determining true costs of each product, particularly when there are relatively large differences between the sales volumes, profits, and costs of the various products. The costs of collecting direct charges must be weighed against the anticipated advantages in controlling these charges.

The costs for shipping rejected material back to the supplier for screening, rework, or credit usually are billed to the supplier.

Costs of screening or reworking by the customer, in order to meet production schedules, usually can be recovered from the supplier provided these are negotiated for in advance between the supplier and customer. Certifications should be in the form of labeling or written statements and may be useful in reducing receiving inspection.

The labels attached to the product or lot package are intended to be informative and can include a description of the product, various product data, instructions for its use and maintenance, and safety precautions. These may be so worded as to imply that the supplier guarantees that the product conforms to the label. Another step of labeling is certification labeling that, in addition to describing the product, bears statements attesting that the product is free from specified hazards. Usually, certification labeling is based on testing done by the supplier or an independent testing laboratory. For example, Underwriter's Laboratories develops and publishes standards for materials that comply to protection from fire, burglary, hazardous chemicals, and so forth.

As stated earlier, when problems arise with respect to nonconformances, it is important that the customer notify the supplier as soon as possible. The customer should clearly identify the problem. Be as specific as possible. If a problem is stated in terms such as "will not assemble," or "will not mate," the supplier will have a difficult time identifying the source of the problem. For example, if the problem is the result of the distance between holes that are not to drawing or specification, the supplier can go back and rectify the problem.

If the holes are to specification, there may be a problem in the customer's process. It is the responsibility of both teams to identify the problem sources at their respective facilities, correct the nonconformances, and improve the process so that the nonconformances do not occur again.

All corrective action must be documented so that if a similar problem occurs, there is some traceable starting point. This is accomplished in many companies through the use of rejection or nonconformance reports. It lists the cause for rejection and has room for the supplier to identify what corrective action has been taken. A visit to the supplier may be necessary to demonstrate the problem and determine the appropriate corrective action.

Another tool for problem identification is a failure mode and effect analysis (FMEA). This tool is used widely in the automotive industry and has proven to be successful in the identification of potential problems and the actions necessary to fix the problem.

In summary, a good procurement program depends on good communication. Both teams must establish trust and confidence with each other so that an open exchange of information occurs. The frequency must be established at the first meeting. When problems arise, the cohesiveness of the team, along with the established protocols, will enable a swift resolution. The key thing to remember is that suppliers welcome feedback, so do not be afraid to give it.

Basic Issues: From Ship-to-Stock to Just-in-Time
Chapter 9

Key words: annual system audit, characteristic accountability, just-in-time (JIT), ship-to-stock (STS), source inspection, supplier certification.

Summary
- Evolution of ship-to-stock
- Supplier and product qualification
- Auditing the ship-to-stock system
- Advantages of a ship-to-stock program
- Relationship of ship-to-stock to just-in-time

Shipping suppliers products directly to stock is an alternative to the traditional method of assessing supplier quality by means of the incoming inspection process. The ship-to-stock (STS) program is a way to more efficiently and economically handle incoming material from high-quality suppliers. It requires purchaser and supplier personnel to talk (as partners rather than adversaries) about quality systems and product requirements. The principles were developed in a military environment and have since been implemented successfully in the commercial business world.

Traditionally, the purchasing company selected an approved supplier of material by evaluating its quality systems, assessing its financial position, and determining its design and manufacturing capabilities. From that point on, they monitored the supplier's product quality through incoming and source inspection.

Often, the unintended results of this approach were delays in the supplier-to-user time cycle, duplication of effort and equipment, discovery of problems at the wrong time and place, untimely corrective action, and inefficient use of human resources. These serious drawbacks are strong incentives to consider an STS program.

The STS program can be divided into three phases: (1) the candidacy phase, (2) the qualification phase, and (3) the maintenance phase. In the candidacy phase, past quality history indicates if a supplier's system is producing quality products, therefore making the supplier a potential candidate for the STS program. The supplier and the purchaser's STS representatives establish the STS agreement criteria that will form the requirements for the supplier's qualification. The STS agreement also outlines the quality rating, audit, and inspection requirements necessary to maintain the program.

After the background data has been collected and the STS agreement defined, the information is evaluated by the STS coordinating committee, which decides whether to consider the supplier as a candidate. The committee is comprised of a cross-section of major departmental functions and representatives from each manufacturing plant.

The qualification phase entails both supplier qualification and product qualification. The candidate supplier must undergo in-depth quality system and process surveys, which are performed with special attention to the supplier's adherence to process controls. These surveys, along with the quality history, form the basis for the decision to qualify the supplier for the program.

Because the STS program is based on supplier/product combinations, product qualification also is necessary for the program's success. The product qualification process requires

- A first article inspection and/or evaluation test
- A characteristic accountability, which is the process of reviewing each characteristic on the engineering drawing/specification for the supplier's method of manufacture and frequency of inspection (This review documents the quality plan for the specific product.)
- Successful completion of a minimum number of lot-by-lot inspections with a predetermined minimum quality rating
- Product manufacture using a mature production process
- Approval of the supplier QC engineer, who is responsible for monitoring the STS program with the supplier

After a product is qualified, that product may only be released and shipped by a designated supplier STS representative. The supplier STS representative audits each STS lot (after all processing and final inspection) to verify completion of all operations, verify critical and major characteristics, and ensure the completion of all paperwork. The representative's stamp and signature on the packing slip attest that the lot meets the requirements of the STS program.

The maintenance phase involves system audits, process audits, product audits, and inspections.

Annual *system auditing* verifies the effectiveness of the supplier's control of the quality system and process. It includes, but is not limited to

- Drawing and specification control
- Purchased material control
- Measuring and testing equipment control
- Process and product acceptance
- Material review and corrective action
- Finished material storage
- Packaging and shipping
- Record retention
- Quality management and reporting

System audits are much more strict than system surveys because they must ensure that the supplier's system is still capable of producing an acceptable product.

The second type of audit is the *process audit,* which is periodically performed to ensure that the quality parameters are adhered to during each process.

The third audit type is the *product audit,* which encompasses the following:

- One hundred percent dimensional inspection
- Nondestructive testing (NDT), if applicable
- Review of inspection, heat treat, plating, NDT, and material certification records
- Corrective action on any deficiencies

Product audits should be performed periodically (for example, each quarter, or every 1000 products), or a frequency considered necessary by the purchaser and the supplier.

Periodic incoming or *source inspection* of the key product parameters is the fourth element of the maintenance phase of the STS program.

Few commercial companies can afford the luxury of a staff of source inspectors or regional quality engineers located in various parts of the country, and they often have less expertise in supplier auditing than is found in military environments.

Consequently, the focus of incoming quality engineering should make each engineer responsible for all products produced by assigned suppliers. This should be done to make the engineers supplier-oriented and force them to concentrate on the supplier's total program and quality yield. Otherwise, they tend to be narrow in focus as long as their products are trouble-free. They will be unconcerned about other products assigned to other engineers, which breeds a disjointed effort in supplier quality management.

With the particular focus in place, the engineer has total responsibility for assigned suppliers, and the emphasis will shift from product/process to a total systems emphasis conducive to shipping products to stock.

The STS program may appear demanding on a supplier, but a close examination shows that all of the supplier requirements already are present in any good quality system. It is important that the supplier have an established quality system that contains the proper controls to continuously produce an acceptable product. With an established quality system, the purchaser need only audit the supplier to ensure continued conformance, and ship the product to stock.

The STS program described here has the following advantages.

- Establishes close interface between purchaser and supplier
- Establishes mutual trust between purchaser and supplier
- Places total responsibility on the supplier, leading to enhanced pride
- Encourages other companies to do business with the supplier
- Reduces inventory levels
- Reduces dock-to-line time
- Replaces incoming/source inspection activity with scheduled audits
- Reduces need for specialized test equipment
- Reduces rejections by placing emphasis on quality early in the process

If a supplier has effective and proven control systems producing good-quality products, it is redundant and perhaps foolish to perform incoming inspections on a lot-by-lot basis. Quality management's responsibility is to seek out alternative cost-saving methods, and a viable STS program is an excellent example.

Just-in-time (JIT) is a concept that can be broken up into two segments: JIT procurement and JIT inventory. JIT procurement involves scheduling and receiving purchased goods in such a manner that the customer carries almost no purchased goods inventory.

JIT inventory relates to work-in-process inventory at a near zero level and does not relate to STS.

STS is a program that focuses on the reduction of material acquisition costs related to the quality function.

STS operates under the premise that an effective total quality control system yields products that fit the customer's needs.

STS qualifies a product by verifying the design and the process which makes the product and then emphasizes auditing and periodic inspections to verify that the process does not change.

STS further emphasizes that the cost of qualification and preventative audits is less costly than the traditional methods of after-the-fact appraisal inspection.

JIT procurement focuses on the above, but also includes such additional elements of rigid forecasting and scheduling, inventory carrying costs, traffic and transportation costs, and so on.

In conclusion, one can see STS as a forerunner to JIT procurement. With STS in place, the company can then focus on the many additional issues involving JIT.[1] Appendix B includes some sample STS forms that have been used in industry.

Note

1. R. J. Laford, *Ship-to-Stock.* Milwaukee, Wis: ASQC Quality Press, 1986, p. 29.

Basic Issues: Data Evaluation
Chapter 10

Key words: average, Bossert charts, control charts, histograms, PCI, standard deviation, TCI.

Summary
- Some descriptive statistics
- Plot the data
- Keep it simple (KIS)

Every day, data is received from various suppliers. Depending on the company, this data can go directly into a file in the purchasing department, can be sent to the using area, or can be plotted. As more purchasing agents learn about quality and statistics, the data is going to be examined more closely. This chapter focuses on some basic statistical tools that will enable the customer to make decisions based on what the data is saying.

Today, data comes in many forms—certificates of analysis, raw numbers, histograms, and control charts, to name a few. Suppliers are deluged with requests for data in a variety of forms. For some it is not a difficult task, for others it is a tremendous obstacle. The question each supplier should ask is: "What are you going to do with the data?" The answer received can determine what the long-term plans are for that supplier. For example, the author had to develop a program for implementing SPC in the plant where he worked. There were five different supplier programs that had to be satisfied. Some supplier programs wanted control charts, some wanted histograms, and some just wanted raw data. The author ended up developing a program which satisfied the most stringent requirements. The data was collected in the same manner throughout the plant. This data was put into control chart form for in-plant purposes. The suppliers who wanted control charts received them, as did everyone else. All customers who came in and requested data were shown the program and told what they would receive. Everyone was happy; we had an SPC program that met our needs, and customers received good information on our process. The point is that if suppliers have a good documented plan for collecting and analyzing data, most customers will accommodate in terms of data requirements. They also tend to send more business to those suppliers.

The basic descriptive statistics that can be used on virtually any data are mean and standard deviation. Basically, the mean is a measure of location, and the standard deviation is a measure of the spread. There are times when the median may be preferred over the mean. This happens when there are some extreme points that will influence the mean. Sometimes these extreme values are called *outliers* or *fliers.* An easy way to identify possible outliers is by collecting data in groups of odd numbers (3, 5, 7, 9). Most of the data will be around the true average, the outliers will be in a distinct group apart from the main body (see Figure 10.1).

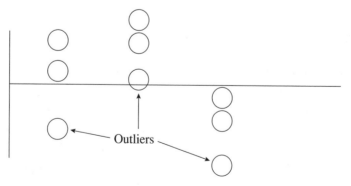

Figure 10.1.   Outlier identification.

Table 10.1.   Calculating standard deviation.

X = Readings taken

X	X^2
85	7,225
70	4,900
60	3,600
90	8,100
81	6,561
Sum of X = 386	Sum of X^2 = 30,386

The mean is the sum of all values divided by the number of values going into it. The median is the center point of all values in a group. So, if there were seven values in a group of data, the median would be the fourth point when ranked from low to high. The mean would be the sum of all the points divided by seven. The numbers may not be the same.

The standard deviation is a measure of the spread of the data. If you have a calculator that does not calculate the standard deviation, the simplest way to do so is by using Table 10.1.

$$S^2 = \frac{\text{Sum of } X^2 - (\text{Sum of } X)^2/n}{n-1}$$

$$= \frac{30,386 - (386)^2/5}{4} = \frac{30,386 - 29,799.2}{4}$$

$$= \frac{586.8}{4} = 146.7$$

S = the square root of S^2

$S = \sqrt{146.7} = 12.1$ – the standard deviation

Another measure of the spread is the range. This is simply the difference between the highest and lowest values in a group of data. From Table 10.1, the range is $90 - 60 = 30$.

So now, any set of data can be considered in terms of location (average or median) and the spread (standard deviation or range). Now percent conformance to a specification based on the sample can be estimated. If, for the data in Table 10.1, we have a specification of 80 ± 15, then the upper specification limit is 95 and the lower specification limit is 65.

$$Z_H = \frac{USL - X}{S} = \frac{95 - 77.2}{12.1} = \frac{17.8}{12.1} = 1.47$$

$$Z_L = \frac{LSL - X}{S} = \frac{65 - 77.2}{12.1} = \frac{-12.2}{12.1} = -1.01$$

Using a normal probability table, we can estimate the area under the normal curve:

$$
\begin{aligned}
Z_H &= .9292 \\
Z_L &= .1562 \\
\hline
.7730 &= 77.3 \text{ percent within } 80 \pm 15 \text{ specifications or} \\
&\quad\ 22.7 \text{ percent outside of specification} \\
&\quad\ (\text{See Table 10.2.})
\end{aligned}
$$

$Z_{1.47} = .9292$ To get the shaded area, subtract Z_L from Z_H.

$Z_{-1.01} = .1562$ Anything outside the shaded area is outside of the specification.

So, given the sample of five parts, one can estimate that these will be almost 23 percent nonconformance. This nonconformance is much greater than most companies could tolerate.

Proportion of total area under the curve that is under the portion of the curve from $-\infty$ to $\frac{Xi-\mu}{\sigma}$ (Xi represents any desired value of the variable X)

$\frac{Xi-\mu}{\sigma}$	0.09	0.08	0.07	0.06	0.05	0.04	0.03	0.02	0.01	0.00
-3.5	0.00017	0.00017	0.00018	0.00019	0.00019	0.00020	0.00021	0.00022	0.00022	0.00023
-3.4	0.00024	0.00025	0.00026	0.00027	0.00028	0.00029	0.00030	0.00031	0.00033	0.00034
-3.3	0.00035	0.00036	0.00038	0.00039	0.00040	0.00042	0.00043	0.00045	0.00047	0.00048
-3.2	0.00050	0.00052	0.00054	0.00056	0.00058	0.00060	0.00062	0.00064	0.00066	0.00069
-3.1	0.00071	0.00074	0.00076	0.00079	0.00082	0.00085	0.00087	0.00090	0.00094	0.00097
-3.0	0.00100	0.00104	0.00107	0.00111	0.00114	0.00118	0.00122	0.00126	0.00131	0.00135
-2.9	0.0014	0.0014	0.0015	0.0015	0.0016	0.0016	0.0017	0.0017	0.0018	0.0019
-2.8	0.0019	0.0020	0.0021	0.0021	0.0022	0.0023	0.0023	0.0024	0.0025	0.0026
-2.7	0.0026	0.0027	0.0028	0.0029	0.0030	0.0031	0.0032	0.0033	0.0034	0.0035
-2.6	0.0036	0.0037	0.0038	0.0039	0.0040	0.0041	0.0043	0.0044	0.0045	0.0047
-2.5	0.0048	0.0049	0.0051	0.0052	0.0054	0.0055	0.0057	0.0059	0.0060	0.0062
-2.4	0.0064	0.0066	0.0068	0.0069	0.0071	0.0073	0.0075	0.0078	0.0080	0.0082
-2.3	0.0084	0.0087	0.0089	0.0091	0.0094	0.0096	0.0099	0.0102	0.0104	0.0107
-2.2	0.0110	0.0113	0.0116	0.0119	0.0122	0.0125	0.0129	0.0132	0.0136	0.0139
-2.1	0.0143	0.0146	0.0150	0.0154	0.0158	0.0162	0.0166	0.0170	0.0174	0.0179
-2.0	0.0183	0.0188	0.0192	0.0197	0.0202	0.0207	0.0212	0.0217	0.0222	0.0228
-1.9	0.0233	0.0239	0.0244	0.0250	0.0256	0.0262	0.0268	0.0274	0.0281	0.0287
-1.8	0.0294	0.0301	0.0307	0.0314	0.0322	0.0329	0.0336	0.0344	0.0351	0.0359
-1.7	0.0367	0.0375	0.0384	0.0392	0.0401	0.0409	0.0418	0.0427	0.0436	0.0446
-1.6	0.0455	0.0465	0.0475	0.0485	0.0495	0.0505	0.0516	0.0526	0.0537	0.0548
-1.5	0.0559	0.0571	0.0582	0.0594	0.0606	0.0618	0.0630	0.0643	0.0652	0.0668
-1.4	0.0681	0.0694	0.0708	0.0721	0.0735	0.0749	0.0764	0.0778	0.0793	0.0808
-1.3	0.0823	0.0838	0.0853	0.0869	0.0885	0.0901	0.0918	0.0934	0.0951	0.0968
-1.2	0.0985	0.1003	0.1020	0.1038	0.1057	0.1075	0.1093	0.1112	0.1131	0.1151
-1.1	0.1170	0.1190	0.1210	0.1230	0.1251	0.1271	0.1292	0.1314	0.1335	0.1357
-1.0	0.1379	0.1401	0.1423	0.1446	0.1469	0.1492	0.1515	0.1539	0.1562	0.1587
-0.9	0.1611	0.1635	0.1660	0.1685	0.1711	0.1736	0.1762	0.1788	0.1814	0.1814
-0.8	0.1867	0.1894	0.1922	0.1949	0.1977	0.2005	0.2033	0.2061	0.2090	0.2119
-0.7	0.2148	0.2177	0.2207	0.2236	0.2266	0.2297	0.2327	0.2358	0.2389	0.2420
-0.6	0.2451	0.2483	0.2514	0.2546	0.2578	0.2611	0.2643	0.2676	0.2709	0.2743
-0.5	0.2776	0.2810	0.2843	0.2877	0.2912	0.2946	0.2981	0.3015	0.3050	0.3085
-0.4	0.3121	0.3156	0.3192	0.3228	0.3264	0.3300	0.3336	0.3372	0.3409	0.3446
-0.3	0.3483	0.3520	0.3557	0.3594	0.3632	0.3669	0.3707	0.3745	0.3783	0.3821
-0.2	0.3859	0.3897	0.3936	0.3974	0.4013	0.4052	0.4090	0.4129	0.4168	0.4207
-0.1	0.4247	0.4286	0.4325	0.4364	0.4404	0.4443	0.4483	0.4522	0.4562	0.4602
-0.0	0.4641	0.4681	0.4721	0.4761	0.4801	0.4840	0.4880	0.4920	0.4960	0.5000

Table 10.2.   Areas under normal curve.

$\dfrac{X-\mu}{\sigma}$	0.00	0.01	0.02	0.03	0.04	0.05	0.06	0.07	0.08	0.09
+0.0	0.5000	0.5040	0.5080	0.5120	0.5160	0.5199	0.5239	0.5279	0.5319	0.5359
+0.1	0.5398	0.5438	0.5478	0.5517	0.5557	0.5596	0.5636	0.5675	0.5714	0.5753
+0.2	0.5793	0.5832	0.5871	0.5910	0.5948	0.5987	0.6026	0.6064	0.6103	0.6141
+0.3	0.6179	0.6217	0.6255	0.6293	0.6331	0.6368	0.6406	0.6443	0.6480	0.6517
+0.4	0.6554	0.6591	0.6628	0.6664	0.6700	0.6736	0.6772	0.6808	0.6844	0.6879
+0.5	0.6915	0.6950	0.6985	0.7019	0.7054	0.7088	0.7123	0.7157	0.7190	0.7224
+0.6	0.7257	0.7291	0.7324	0.7357	0.7389	0.7422	0.7454	0.7486	0.7517	0.7549
+0.7	0.7580	0.7611	0.7642	0.7673	0.7704	0.7734	0.7764	0.7794	0.7823	0.7852
+0.8	0.7881	0.7910	0.7939	0.7967	0.7995	0.8023	0.8051	0.8079	0.8106	0.8133
+0.9	0.8159	0.8186	0.8212	0.8238	0.8264	0.8289	0.8315	0.8340	0.8365	0.8389
+1.0	0.8413	0.8438	0.8461	0.8485	0.8508	0.8531	0.8554	0.8577	0.8599	0.8621
+1.1	0.8643	0.8665	0.8686	0.8708	0.8729	0.8749	0.8770	0.8790	0.8810	0.8830
+1.2	0.8849	0.8869	0.8888	0.8907	0.8925	0.8944	0.8962	0.8980	0.8997	0.9015
+1.3	0.9032	0.9049	0.9066	0.9082	0.9099	0.9115	0.9131	0.9147	0.9162	0.9177
+1.4	0.9192	0.9207	0.9222	0.9236	0.9251	0.9265	0.9279	0.9292	0.9306	0.9319
+1.5	0.9332	0.9345	0.9357	0.9370	0.9382	0.9394	0.9406	0.9418	0.9429	0.9441
+1.6	0.9452	0.9463	0.9474	0.9484	0.9495	0.9505	0.9515	0.9525	0.9535	0.9545
+1.7	0.9554	0.9564	0.9573	0.9582	0.9591	0.9599	0.9608	0.9616	0.9625	0.9633
+1.8	0.9641	0.9649	0.9656	0.9664	0.9671	0.9678	0.9686	0.9693	0.9699	0.9706
+1.9	0.9713	0.9719	0.9726	0.9732	0.9738	0.9744	0.9750	0.9756	0.9761	0.9767
+2.0	0.9773	0.9778	0.9783	0.9788	0.9798	0.9798	0.9803	0.9808	0.9812	0.9817
+2.1	0.9821	0.9826	0.9830	0.9834	0.9838	0.9842	0.9846	0.9850	0.9854	0.9857
+2.2	0.9861	0.9864	0.9868	0.9871	0.9875	0.9878	0.9881	0.9884	0.9887	0.9890
+2.3	0.9893	0.9896	0.9898	0.9901	0.9904	0.9906	0.9909	0.9911	0.9913	0.9916
+2.4	0.9918	0.9920	0.9922	0.9925	0.9927	0.9929	0.9931	0.9932	0.9934	0.9936
+2.5	0.9938	0.9940	0.9941	0.9943	0.9945	0.9946	0.9948	0.9949	0.9951	0.9952
+2.6	0.9953	0.9955	0.9956	0.9957	0.9959	0.9960	0.9961	0.9962	0.9963	0.9964
+2.7	0.9965	0.9966	0.9967	0.9968	0.9969	0.9970	0.9971	0.9972	0.9973	0.9974
+2.8	0.9974	0.9975	0.9976	0.9977	0.9977	0.9978	0.9979	0.9979	0.9980	0.9981
+2.9	0.9981	0.9982	0.9983	0.9983	0.9984	0.9984	0.9985	0.9985	0.9986	0.9986
+3.0	0.99865	0.99869	0.99874	0.99878	0.99882	0.99886	0.99889	0.99893	0.99896	0.99900
+3.1	0.99903	0.99906	0.99910	0.99913	0.99915	0.99918	0.99921	0.99924	0.99926	0.99929
+3.2	0.99931	0.99934	0.99936	0.99938	0.99940	0.99942	0.99944	0.99946	0.99948	0.99950
+3.3	0.99952	0.99953	0.99955	0.99957	0.99958	0.99960	0.99951	0.99962	0.99964	0.99965
+3.4	0.99966	0.99967	0.99969	0.99970	0.99971	0.99972	0.99973	0.99974	0.99975	0.99976
+3.5	0.99977	0.99978	0.99978	0.99979	0.99980	0.99981	0.99981	0.99982	0.99983	0.99983

(Source: Grant, E. L. and Leavenworth, R. S., *Statistical Control*, 4th Ed., McGraw Hill, 1972.)

Table 10.2 (cont.)   Areas under normal curve.

Another way to use the data is to plot it. Plotting data enables the customer to see a picture, which can be very revealing. With supplier data, the three types of plots that work well are histograms, control charts, and Bossert charts. A *histogram* is "a plot of a frequency distribution in the form of rectangles whose bases are equal to the cell interval and whose areas are proportional to the frequencies."[1]

The shape of any histogram can best be determined when there are between 30 and 50 data points. When there are less than 30 data points, it may not be obvious whether or not the data is normally distributed. How many cells always is a question. A popular rule of thumb is to take the square root of the number of data points, as long as it is no less than five. There are many ways to calculate the cell intervals; the important thing is that it be consistently done. Histograms can have three basic shapes: skewed left, normal, and skewed right (see Figure 10.2).

If the data is skewed, there is reason to suspect that the underlying distribution is not normal. A nonnormal distribution can cause problems when determining specifications, and the type of control charts to use. For example, defects normally are not distributed so that a *c* chart is the most appropriate control chart to use.

A control chart is simply a chart of data graphed in a time sequence. This enables the receiver to see what is taking place over time. The most common charts are $\overline{X}$ and range/standard deviation charts; a chart of individuals with a moving range for variables (measured) data; and *p, np, c,* and *u* charts for attribute (counting) data.

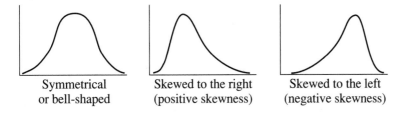

| Symmetrical or bell-shaped | Skewed to the right (positive skewness) | Skewed to the left (negative skewness) |

Figure 10.2. Three basic shapes of histograms.

There are other charts that are utilized for special cases, such as cumulative sum, exponentially weighted moving average charts, acceptance control charts, adaptive control charts, and multivariate control charts. There also are various rules for determining whether a process is in a state of control. The most common rules are the 1-, 2-, 4-, 8-point rules in which the control chart is divided into zones. The theory behind these rules is based on the probability of a particular number of points occurring in a normal population.

Another chart that can be used is called a Bossert chart. This chart plots the range or standard deviation of a grouping of data. If the customer is purchasing the same material from three suppliers, the characteristics of interest of all three suppliers can be plotted to determine each supplier's consistency.

These charts are simple to make and show a lot of information. For example, if one were looking at four suppliers of a chemical that had an iron specification of 0.0–8.0, the customer could gather all the data from the past year on each supplier. The customer then could obtain the range of iron for each and plot the range with a vertical bar for each supplier. The means are connected (see Figure 10.3). This plot illustrates how consistent the suppliers are to each other and compared to the specification. When there are more than nine data points, a standard deviation can be used (see Figure 10.4).

The bottom line on any plots is to keep it simple (KIS). An effective plot is one that tells a story with little or no explanation. A busy person cannot afford a busy plot. A clean chart enables a decision to be made quickly. A busy chart requires time and explanation.

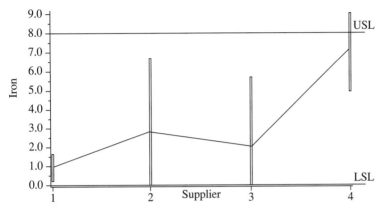

Figure 10.3.   Bossert chart example: supplier analysis by standard deviations.

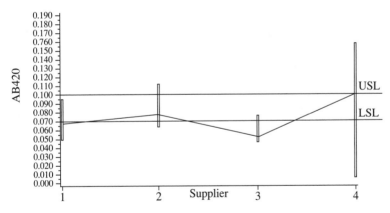

Figure 10.4.   Bossert chart example: supplier comparison by ranges.

Supplier Certification
Chapter 11

Key words: approved suppliers, certification, maintenance, partnerships, preferred suppliers, process documentation, quality system validation, recognition, service certification, supplier selection.

Summary
- The definition of certified supplier
- What are the certification steps?
- How to do service certification
- Two certification approaches

Suppliers to your facilities are the lifeblood of your business these days. As your business has grown more complex, you have made a series of strategic business decisions that set up this situation. You changed the level of both your own design controls and the percentage of your vertical integration in your finished products.

Because of this change in method of doing business you must find ways to get reengaged in understanding how to receive full assurances that the products and services you are buying from your suppliers are what you need and will be so tomorrow.

Many supplier certification processes focus on the gathering of data from history to try to predict the future of said product. That is like trying to say you have had three rain-filled days this week, so the entire week will be rain filled. You need to make a transition beyond looking backward to try to understand the method of what makes rain. Only when you understand all the variables in how to make rain or how to not make rain can you predict quality assurance or certification of future events.

One accepted definition of what a certified supplier is

A certified supplier is one that, after an extensive investigation is found to provide quality products or service of such a level that routine inspections are no longer needed.

Does this definition go far enough? There is a lot of room to define what actually is covered in the term *extensive investigation*. Some companies and government agencies take it at face value and only consider samples or short-term histories over three or six months. Others want to see a quality system that matches ANSI/ASQC Q-91. Still others want to tell the supplier how to set up its process of SPC. A few are even telling suppliers how to run the process and set in place the process parameters for them. The definition needs to cover the predictive nature of how to ensure tomorrow's production is going to be better or at least equal to yesterday's (if yesterday was a good day).

The following is a slight modification to the definition for the future.

A certified supplier is one that has shown a complete and thorough understanding of our needs. In doing so the supplier has set in place a process that has been investigated and has been found to yield products or services that meet or exceed our requirements.

You can see the subtle change in bringing in the fact that the supplier is setting up a consistent process. Now you must define how you will get the process documented and captured along with the history that many of us had relied on for certification in the past.

The steps of the certification process are

1. Documentation of the process
2. Selection of suppliers for the process
3. Establish partnership for improvement
4. Perform initial quality systems validation
5. Establish *approved* suppliers
6. Establish *preferred* suppliers
7. Review for certification
8. Certify suppliers
9. Recognize suppliers
10. Maintain certification

There must be a structured discussion for purposes of flow.

The elements needed can be organized into a booklet or flow-chart so you can educate management and suppliers to the process. Consider this as a key action because if you are to certify, both management and the supplier must understand what it is going to require to complete this task. It is not a short-term or grandfathering system of recognition.

The first step in any process includes the following:

1. Documentation of the process
   a. Define roles and responsibilities
   b. Develop goals and standards
   c. Develop methods of gathering evidence
   d. Orient management on process

Before you start any process you must decide who is going to be carrying out each role. The key players on your team must be identified and their tasks documented. For example, does engineering have the final say in supplier selection, or is it purchasing or quality assurance? Are the operations people asked to routinely visit the suppliers or only when there are problems? A role and departmental matrix is helpful here.

Next, establish the measures. Do you expect parts per billion from an industry that is measuring in percentages? Alignment of your internal expectations are required so when you start telling suppliers the standards, you speak with one voice.

Then, as you decide how you are going to measure, document the acceptable methods. As you study the process, document the results so that you will have evidence of why you are doing what you are doing.

This sounds simple, but try to obtain common forms from any technical group or groups that are to look at this evidence in support of a decision of certification. This may require months to reach agreement. The forms may include SPC forms, systems audit forms, process control details forms, or sample forms. If you are in a multi-plant system, this compounds the effort required.

Now that you have a package, you can start an orientation process for your own management. This is a key step so they will not expect perfection and will recognize the efforts made to date.

Next you must make some key decisions.

2. Selection of suppliers for process
   a. Existing suppliers
   b. New suppliers
   c. Perform orientation on suppliers

Which of your existing suppliers do you want or need to certify? If you have problem suppliers, do you start with them? Take a bit of advice—do *not* start with problem suppliers. You must gain confidence in your system, so start with a few good suppliers and then expand the system to gather the ones needing improvements after you are done with your own confidence building.

Set in place a decision point after which no new suppliers will be added to your supplier lists without entry into the system. This provides purchasing (or whomever is recommending or bringing in new suppliers) time to start telling prospective suppliers that you are doing business with suppliers that are willing to share process and performance information, as opposed to buying on price alone.

Your suppliers will need to get the same overview as your management of the new way of doing business. This can be done in a supplier conference, either in groups or one by one with their management. One caution should be mentioned. If you do a massive rollout of a program, you create expectations in the supply base that you may not be able to support. Support simply means having the resources to visit all of the suppliers. Inadvertently you can set up the process for failure. By doing some preselection of whom you want to orient, this pitfall can be avoided. Decide with which suppliers you are going to actively work.

Now, gain commitment and get the process started.

3. Establish partnership for improvement
   a. Commitment agreement for mutual discovery and improvement
   b. Commence documenting the process

In order for this process of mutual understanding and sharing to happen in an atmosphere of trust, you must get both parties to make certain commitments. Assure the supplier that disclosures to you will be used for mutual benefits, not against the supplier to put it at a competitive disadvantage. This commitment agreement is to disclose the work that is to be done. Include a listing of the methods, such as audits, SPC, process details, and so on. In addition, the commitment agreement can have a timeline for this process, but be careful about making time commitments you cannot keep.

Many of the certification processes put too much faith in this step of your process. A spot-check of a system for quality does not go far enough, but it provides necessary information.

4. Perform initial quality systems validation
   a. On-site or preregistered systems
   b. Establish corrective action

You can perform your own quality systems survey or you can find out if the supplier has been certified or registered by someone else. If you choose to accept another organization's work in the area, you must understand the details of the survey and the frequency, plus any potential open issues.

If you choose to perform your own systems verification, the tools are simple. Choose or develop a standard for a system and get a qualified individual(s) to measure the system against that standard.

Now that you have some suppliers committed and surveyed, you can move into your measurement phase. In the initial setup of your system, you should have set criteria about what it was going to take to have suppliers continue to do business with you. Or stated more bluntly, how bad would they have to become before you dropped them?

5. Establish approved suppliers
   a. Set requirements
   b. Measure performance

The typical approved supplier could be one that is performing to an acceptable level on cost, quality, and delivery that does not upset your process during normal times. Each of you has to set this threshold at a level you can live with in your production environment. At a minimum you should have basic agreement on the specifications and samples measured to determine if they comply to the standards. Using simple trend analysis with your receiving inspection history, you can show that you could expect to receive the same product tomorrow as today.

Next, measure and feed back the performance against the standard to the supplier. What good is it to measure a child in school and not issue a report card. The same goes for supplier performance reports. This is one of the commitments you should have made in the previously described commitment agreement.

Now you can start advancing your improvement cause.

6. Establish preferred suppliers
   a. Set requirements
   b. Measure performance
   c. Verify supplier is following documented process

As in the establishment of the approved level of suppliers, you now set a series of higher goals for those suppliers you wish to call preferred. This level of suppliers may turn out to be the top 25 percent of your supply base by performance.

When you started step three you found that you asked the supplier to document the process steps that it was to use to meet your specifications and standards. Now start to review this series of documents, called *process control details*. The information in these documents and forms show where each critical characteristic is made and how it is controlled to deliver the desired result. This is the key transition from the old historical certification to a preventive or proactive certification process. You are sharing the *how* rather than just the result. You can see the details of how the supplier is managing the process for mutual benefit to both parties. You must review these forms and approve them as part of the feedback you give the supplier.

You now have a view of both the supplier's system and the processes. You can start to decide if the performance and preventive actions taken by the supplier are of a level that should be recognized.

7. Review for certification
   a. Set final requirements
   b. Measure performance

The suppliers that reach this level will have a level of performance that make them stand out in all areas of the relationship. The performance at the top of your supply base should be measured across cost, quality, delivery, technical support, and management linkage or attitude. It follows the model of a full partnership. Typically these suppliers are in the top 5 percent to 10 percent in performance with nothing that has upset your process in either product or non-product areas for an extended period of time.

Suppliers reaching this level of certification should have the company value system that is an extension of your plant and production process.

You can now start the certification process.

8. Certify suppliers

In order to certify a supplier you must get your team together and gather all the objective evidence that has shown the supplier is at or above the performance level you had set at the beginning of this process.

At this point in your evidence gathering you should have created a listing of the products coming from this certified supplier that are to be given ship-to-use status. This prevents delaying certification for the new product or the experiment upon which engineering is still making design changes. Capture all of the information supporting the product in a certification agreement. Try to obtain all the supporting parties of both companies to sign off the agreement.

Now it is time to give recognition.

9. Recognize suppliers
a. Gather cost benefits

The act of certification should be special and unique to the supplier. Make a special effort to take your management to the supplier and help celebrate the status that has been attained. If you return to the school analogy, you now have a Ph.D. in supplied products; they are few and far between.

If you have a good cost of quality or nonconformance system, you can capture the cost/benefit aspect of certification. Those who have done this find they get a return on investment ranging from one to one, to one to 10. For each dollar spent you would like to be able to show management that the program is self-funding and returns money. However, there is a catch to this. It is an investment that must be made up front and the return may be one, two, or three years down the road.

All processes must be maintained for that period of time. Certification is not a short-term process. There are two processes here. The first is the certification of each supplier. The second is the process of your certification process itself.

   10. Maintain certification
        a. Process itself (annual review)
        b. Levels of certification

Build an annual review of the process details into your process. If you have an ongoing benchmarking system, you may have to benchmark your supplier certification process to determine if you are getting the returns expected, or to determine if new techniques are available that you can use to further improve the process. The status quo will not suffice in this dynamic world.

As you conduct the reviews, ensure that the supplier is maintaining the levels of performance you expected. If the supplier is not performing properly, take corrective action. If the response is not as expected, you may have to use a system of probation and supplier decertification. This process must be built in from the beginning. The manner in which this is handled is as critical as the building of the partnership. In many companies, this factor is not considered until the need arises. It is then too late to develop because some emotion is involved. Probation and decertification are difficult steps to go through, so a well-thought-out unemotional set of steps will ensure that all consideration is given fairly to all parties.

Business Sector Applicability

Most of the early work in supplier certification was in the high-volume hardware industries. These provide the most well-developed models to follow, but the process of certification has been expanded to all potential exchanges of goods or services. There are successes in businesses ranging from food processing to logging to the pure services, such as transportation and data entry. The traditional issues of capability and process flows have become issues of consistency, timeliness, and accuracy. Definitions of specifications through drawings have become discussions of expected performance factors. One model developed by the contract administration department of a company that was buying services such as security, cafeterias, and grounds maintenance flowed as follows:

The Model in Steps

1. Internal management orientation and buy-in
2. Role development
3. Supplier selection for the process
4. Definition of expectations and needs
5. Agreement on the definition of the needs by both parties
6. Agreement of controllable and uncontrollable factors
7. Commence process detail mapping
8. Joint setting of performance measurable
9. Set up feedback system
10. Performance measurement and feedback
11. Review process for weaknesses and commence improvement of same
12. Codify the improvements in revised process map
13. If required, pilot proposed improvements
14. Document quality agreement and sign
15. Review performance jointly
16. Recognize the select few top performers
17. Improve the improvement process itself
18. Annual review of agreements made and performance

Note that the themes of discussion, reviews, and agreements are identical to the hardware model discussed previously.

This text has discussed many issues around the philosophy and strategy of buying high-quality products. It is appropriate to show two examples of systems that work. The first example is a complex, but well-thought-out system that is used at Cummins Engine. The second example is what one company did to develop a model that conformed to the Deming philosophy in a simple format.

The Cummins supplier quality improvement process is a 20-step process that begins with a preliminary site inspection at a supplier and ends with the certification recognition. The flow diagram (Figure 11.1) shows the evolution of the partnership. Steps 1 to 4 are the dating phase, steps 5 to 15 are the engagement phase, step 16 is the marriage, step 17 is the honeymoon, and steps 18 to 20 comprise the blossoming of the long-term partnership.

The second example is one that is much simpler in format because the company was smaller. The work force totaled 120 people. It took four years to develop this program. They did not achieve instant success, but worked to establish a process that fit their culture. Understanding the culture, and making the process fit took time.

When raw material is received at the facility, the receiving personnel have a checklist that is followed for all incoming product. If any characteristic is not in conformance on the checklist, the material is returned immediately to the supplier. This condition is in all contracts. As the truck is pulling away, purchasing is calling the supplier to inform them why the material is being returned.

If the material passes the receiving inspection, a copy of the checklist is attached to the material. This checklist remains with the material until it is shipped out as product. All employees who handle the material will stamp the checklist as it passes through the transformation from raw material to product.

Each step of the operation has control charts in place. Even with control charts, there are critical steps in the process where audits are made to ensure conformance. At each process step, the specifications are displayed where all personnel can see them. No deviations are allowed. The equipment and personnel are routinely recertified to ensure performance expectations.

As the product leaves the plant, a control chart of the final process step accompanies it. This company maintains routine communication

The Ideal System

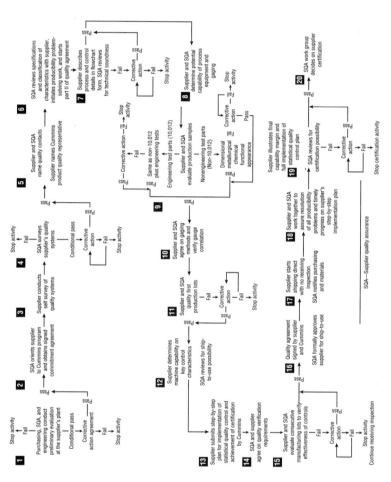

Figure 11.1.   Cummins supplier quality improvement process.

with all customers and has not had any product returned in over six years. It also has all the original equipment still working and in a state of control. The plant is over 45 years old.

Supplier certification can be a long and winding path, but there are rewards. From a classic management perspective, there is a return on the investment of working with suppliers. The ranges that have been quantified range from one to one, to one to 10. One electronics company measured it as percentage of units received that required inspection as 100 percent dropping to less than 30 percent in 18 months. From a human factor perspective, when you hand a token of recognition to a plant manager or a line worker at a key supplier and see its effect, you realize there are nonmonetary rewards that cannot be measured.

How to Conduct a Supplier Survey

Chapter 12

Key words: corrective action, documentation, evaluation, follow-up, preparation, team, visit.

Summary

- Goals
- Team organization
- Visit
- Evaluation of a period system
- Final report
- Follow-up

In conducting a supplier survey, you, as a quality professional, will be performing one of the most critical jobs you can do for your company.

To the supplier, you will represent your company. Up to this time, perhaps only a single salesperson from the supplier may have called on your organization. Now, virtually everyone in the supplier's plant will be watching you and judging your company by your acts and omissions. In fact, the quality surveyor may be the only person from your firm they ever see face-to-face.

This guide has one purpose—to help a professional in the field of quality do the best possible survey of a supplier. Some 20 of your fellow professionals have contributed toward this end. The guide begins from the point where your manager or supervisor assigns a survey task to you. It then follows through the preparation, the visit and tour, evaluation and judgment, report documentation, corrective action, and follow-up, ending when you sit back and review your activities, trying to decide whether you really conducted yourself as a quality professional.

Rather than presenting what to evaluate, we will stress the how-to aspect of surveying. We would like to make you aware of the philosophies, techniques, and realities of performing successful surveys. The methods described are applicable in virtually every industry or service, in all kinds of companies, large and small, with new suppliers or old, and within your own organization.

The guidelines presented are not intended to stand alone. ANSI/ASQC Standard C1-1985, *General Requirements for a Quality Program*, forms the basis of these survey guidelines and should be used in conjunction with any survey performed. In specialized cases, other standards also may apply, and should be used. However, all the guidelines and standards are of little use without the alert, inquiring mind that should characterize the quality professional, along with experience, training, and knowledge. Basic to everything is the guidance and support of the quality professional's manager or supervisor.

Goals of a Survey

We pluralize *goals* to stress that the survey will almost always have more than one goal. Most basic to understanding how to conduct a supplier survey is the recognition that a survey involves interaction between two or more people.

Unlike writing reports, which may be a solitary activity, surveying always involves more than one person. At the very minimum, it would involve you for your company and someone representing the supplier. Most surveys will involve many more people from at least two organizations.

While you may be trying to learn what quality standards an organization has, or is capable of, always remember that the supplier you are evaluating also has at least one aim: to present its organization in the best light (sometimes by hiding one or more defects). In conducting a survey, remember your company's goal(s), which often may depend on the type of supplier you are evaluating.

Circumstance–Typical question to be answered by survey.

New supplier–Can this operation provide the product quality we need?

Old supplier–Can this operation continue giving the product quality we need?

Problem supplier–What must be done so that this operation can give us the product quality we need?

Reformed supplier–Has this supplier really made the improvements necessary to give us the product quality we need?

System evaluation–Is this operation following all the procedures needed to give us the product quality we need?

Such listings could be extended greatly. Every new survey conducted can have its own matrix of goals. Although it may appear difficult to identify the proper goals of your company, this is much easier than trying to identify the goals of the organization you are surveying.

Not only may the supplier have a variety of goals, but the emotional interplay of the individuals must be considered. Imagine being told that your company will be surveyed by your customers— whether they are customers, government, wholesalers, and so forth. Further, try to imagine that how well you do on such a survey may determine if your company receives a large contract, or if your company will get further orders, or how your management may view your personal performance. Confidence, pride, anxiety, caution, worry, secretiveness, apprehension—just what kinds of emotions would the prospect of such a survey rouse in you?

If your counterparts in the company to be surveyed are good actors, you may never learn the supplier's real goals. Conversely, the supplier may never learn yours. If you are unsmiling by nature, you may give the impression that you are predisposed against the supplier. Then the supplier may rush through the survey considering each moment spent as wasted. If you are too friendly and easygoing, the supplier may believe you are a pushover, inclined to approve, and thus may not go into great depth about the quality system.

Such influences must be anticipated and allowed for whenever suspected. Otherwise, your company may pass by a capable source for needed materials, or unwittingly downgrade a supplier that might be able to offer a better product.

Preparation for the Survey

When you are preparing for a supplier survey, you will want to gather as many facts and figures about the supplier as possible. In doing this it is important to remember your company's goals and any existing history of relationships between the supplier and your company.

If a current supplier is to be surveyed, available documentation in your company files should be reviewed. These could include receiving inspection reports, purchasing agent's periodic reports, records of corrective action, delivery records, outstanding contract quantities, product specifications, and so forth.

If your company has been experiencing problems with the supplier, you may want to contact the designers, purchasers, inspectors, and production people in your plant for their opinions. However, you must be careful and realize that some of these people may themselves be associated with the causes of the problems.

For new or potential suppliers, your purchasing agent's visit report (if the supplier has been visited) is essential. Do not ignore information you might get from the supplier's annual reports, from Dun and Bradstreet, or from your professional colleagues in other companies. If you know the names of the supplier's quality control personnel, glance at the author index of various quality and other technical journals. Any articles published over their names may give you an insight into the supplier's quality philosophy. Similar information on other companies in the same business also is helpful, particularly if data on the company to be surveyed are difficult to locate.

It must always be kept in mind, however, that preliminary information should never be used to prejudge a supplier. The preliminary information is only a guide to what to look for in the survey.

When approaching an industry segment or supplier with whom you have never done business, be careful of the sophistication level you expect. Always keep in mind your company's needs and the supplier's ability to meet particular needs. Someone in the drug industry evaluating a plastics company for its capability to produce trays might be horrified at not finding a quality control manager, department, or inspector. However, the company may be fully capable of producing the right goods at the right price.

In such situations, the true quality professional will be armed with the knowledge of what is current practice in the strange industry, and will always keep in mind just what the company needs from that kind of supplier.

One final note on preparation. Whenever possible, try to document both positive and negative information. Receiving inspection may claim that a supplier is unacceptable. Yet, a fuller examination of the records may show that internal problems are the real culprit.

On the other hand, an A-OK report may really mean that the supplier's shipments came in so late that incoming inspection was dropped in favor of on-line culling to keep production going. These are supplier problems induced by the customer and capable of internal correction by the latter.

Team Organization

More often than not, the quality professional conducting the survey will have little to do with the makeup, selection, and organization of the team. The survey team may consist of only the quality professional who will visit the supplier for a few hours, or several professionals from varied disciplines who may stay a week. Whatever the scope of the survey, whether one person or several, remember that you are part of a team and you represent the company.

Even one-person surveys by a quality professional may bear information on labor negotiations, procurement policy, new design concepts, process capabilities, or security. The survey would be circulated to concerned departments, such as personnel, purchasing, development, engineering, or shipping. When favorable, such information usually is pointed out pridefully by the supplier, and the supplier would be surprised if your report did not mention them.

The effect on concerned departments in your company is reasonably predictable. Your personnel department is gratified that labor negotiations are progressing; development may want to follow up new design concepts; engineering may feel safer if it believes that production people are in charge of the process; and your shipping department may draw comfort from the impression that the safety of the product in transit is assured.

The moral is "Do not stick blindly to checklists. Keep your ears (and mind) open to receive useful information of any kind." This is easier with a team approach because rarely are two people on a team specialists in the same field. A forewarned quality professional will approach the survey with a receptive attitude.

On multimember teams, purchasing often will participate. Sometimes, with purchasing present, the impression may arise that purchasing should head the team in the belief that it must control intimate supplier contracts. Heading the survey team by someone from purchasing is not essential, unless a considered company policy so dictates. Whoever heads the team must take into account findings of others who usually are more expert in areas other than the team leader's specialty.

After the survey team is selected, an organization meeting must be held to set strategy and outline responsibilities. Such decisions should be made well in advance of the team's visit to the supplier. Do not schedule this important meeting for the airport waiting room, or en route, or at the hotel the night before the meeting. Someone may miss the plane, you may not be seated together, and you may be able to meet at the supplier's only a few minutes before you begin. Meetings to organize the survey team should take place well in advance of the actual survey. Your company goals should be clearly recognized and openly discussed. Team members should be assigned their areas of responsibility and their particular objectives. Information about the supplier of potential interest should be made available.

If the team includes more than one member with a given specialty, specific responsibilities should be clearly assigned so the team does not stumble over its own feet. It also is important at this time to agree on who will be the team leader responsible for the coordination and administration of the survey.

If necessary preliminary meetings are held early enough, it usually is possible to identify the need and supply extra personnel, information, or support by request to your management.

It may be decided that you need a facilities engineer, more product information, or a better analysis of the field complaints on the supplier's merchandise. If the upcoming survey is particularly important and the team roster is supposed to include an inexperienced person (remember everyone has to make a start sometime), it may be possible to place the learner in another team for training-by-doing or to otherwise give preliminary instruction.

Although it may seem perfectly obvious, many surveys run into problems for the lack of checking the following:

- Current address and phone number of the customer
- Name of the host individual you will contact
- Correct date for the survey
- Supplier's readiness for the survey

The Use of Quantification in the Evaluation Format

The end result of all surveys should be a decision. Ideally, the decision should be a clean-cut acceptance or rejection. With complex undertakings such as a manufacturing process, this may not always be feasible. An area of indecision, large or small, may remain and must be taken into account in any final recommendation of the survey team.

To minimize such a gray area, a survey team must clarify and formalize its approach to information collection and quantification. Many different tactics can be adopted as long as the major requirements for an adequate system are evaluated equally in each facility you review.

Valid and acceptable measurements are any that are reproducible within limits that do not compromise the usefulness of the initial quantity evaluated. A supplier survey is one form of measurement. Thus, all methodology that ensures accuracy, impartiality, and repeatability of physical measurements applies to supplier surveys of performance measurements. Numerical, alphabetical, or other regularly sequenced scores must be used to make valid judgments. The most direct way of checking repeatability of a survey is to quantify the measurements.

Mathematical tools are available to show interrelationships between cause and effect in a random system of events. The fundamental model for any production process is just that, a process whose variability is determined by a system of events that occur at random. Some manufacturing processes do not conform exactly to this model, but the mathematics can still be adapted to draw useful conclusions.

The prime reason for a survey is to estimate (or preferably measure) the extent to which the supplier being surveyed operates under a planned quality system. Never forget that the reason you are there is that your company needs the kind of products the supplier can produce. If the supplier has carefully quantified its product mechanics, provided a quality measuring system, and provided an adequate control and correct network, the survey will be significantly more accurate. If the survey team has to provide or extemporize means of such quantification, the results may not be as accurate or predictable, especially when they are reviewed by another individual remote from the survey's site.

Gather all the information you can to make decisions. Ask your supplier's staff to fill in a presurvey evaluation form before the visit. This evaluation form will tell the supplier what you want to know. Also, you will be able to judge how well your supplier reacts to communication from outside the company. The physical survey should follow soon after receiving the filled-in evaluation form from your supplier.

Your survey will be used by people who have not visited the plant under review, or who may not know you personally. Be careful to describe all quantification methods and the rating scales used. Make sure the report is comprehensive without personal explanation or amplification of the results.

Your survey will be used to compare competing sources of services or materials essential to your company's production. The award of contracts likely will depend on information contained in it. The survey must be straightforward and intelligible, and capable of supplying figures for cost and other computations that may have to be made during the selection process.

Finally, everyone has a personal error level, although not everyone is aware of it. This is a product of previous activity, experiences, and lifestyle. The format of any survey must seek to minimize variability from this cause.

Opening Conference

The first order of business when you arrive at the supplier's plant is the opening conference—it is get acquainted time! Explain exactly why you are there, what you are going to try to do, and, in a general way, the type of results you expect.

If your purchasing agent is a member of your team and has met the people from the supplier, allow him or her to introduce you. Have a purchasing agent emphasize the importance of your evaluation and its effect on future business with the supplier.

Ideally, for the supplier, the meeting should be attended by the representative's quality manager, sales manager, engineering department head, other operating managers, the executives(s) over all these groups, and the representative's boss. It is essential that all levels of supplier management understand the scope and purpose of the evaluation survey.

The explanation of your purpose should help calm the supplier's managers, especially if they have not been surveyed often or if (unhappily) they have been visited recently by an inept surveyor. It is unbelievable what some people imagine is going to happen, despite what they were told when you first arranged your visit. Reactions may range from, "They're just here to get out of their offices!", "This will be a military-type, white-glove inspection!", "Heck, it's just another Mickey Mouse program!", to a defiant, "We can teach them a few things." Since the truth lies somewhere in between, it is important that a correct perspective be established.

The opening conference also is the time to establish your credentials. False modesty is as out of place as a snow job. Stick to the facts. It is not wrong to impress the supplier's management with what you know.

Avoid bragging or exaggeration, because you will surely come out looking like a fool. Explain firmly that you are a professional in the field of quality, and that you have had training and experience in evaluation (if such is the case). If you are entitled to some special distinction or designation (such as ASQC certified quality engineer), tell them—this is not name dropping. The surveyor should briefly discuss his or her role in the company, any expertise in the supplier's field (but no lame excuses if he or she lacks such expertise), and his or her understanding of a component(s), material(s), or service(s) for which the supplier is being considered.

Handle the establishment of credentials in a calm, confident way. If you have any fears about this part of your visit, try a bit of role-playing with your peer group before the trip; rehearse your act. Above all, be honest and friendly.

Everything said up to now about the opening conference is to ensure that the supplier is comfortable with you. If the supplier is at ease and knows you are knowledgeable enough to give a fair and sound evaluation—it is likely to be open, cooperative, and nondefensive. However, if the supplier does not know where you stand, the meaning of every question will be pondered.

Of course, if the supplier has shaky quality, explanation of your credentials may tend to make them apprehensive. If you sense this, remind the supplier that your team has come only to see the present situation in the plant. Tell the supplier you are eager to try to indicate what kind of changes may put it in the ranks of a potential supplier. Your sincere reassurance may convince the supplier that it stands to benefit from your survey, and you may gain cooperation.

The next step is to ask one of the executives present for a general description of the company (for example, when founded, how many plants, people,and so forth) more or less to update/verify previous research on the company. Ask the quality manager to describe the quality system and the reporting level of the personnel with whom he or she works. The quality manager should briefly discuss the handling of design information, the manufacturing and test equipment, the nature of the inspections and tests, and the documentation that supports the entire program.

At this point, the survey team is trying to get a general feel for the quality program—how it works, how it fits together, the checkpoints. In brief, they try to understand what they will be viewing shortly on the plant tour. This is not the time to ask for detailed explanations, and certainly not the place to try to make a judgment of the workability on any facet of the quality program.

The opening conference, however, is a good time to make at least a preliminary judgment on management attitude toward quality. If the supplier's personnel are serious, yet excited, about their efforts to achieve high quality, you can do a lot with that supplier, even if they have not got it all together at the moment. If the company executives appear to look on their quality system as a necessary evil, a required but unwelcome overhead, then tread carefully and alertly.

A mention of the most significant features or critical characteristics of the component, material, or service to be provided should have a part in the opening conference. This will give the supplier's quality manager a chance to explain in fuller detail and depth how the system seeks to control such particular facets of requirements.

What if the company president quietly admits at the opening conference that he or she lacks a formal quality control organization? This requires careful thought and handling. The evaluator must ferret out who controls the quality of the product—despite actual titles. The evaluator must unravel the quality responsibilities granted to each part of the manufacturing and engineering functions. The surveyor must see the operation in action. Then, and only then, can it be determimed if the lack of a formal quality organization so weakens the assurance of quality as to disqualify the company. It is a fact that some (although few) companies that have no quality control group have as good a quality system as could be expected in their particular industry. Sometimes, especially in smaller companies, the top boss is very quality conscious and exacts a high-quality product.

What else can you do at an opening conference? At some time during the opening conference, the survey team should ask about significant problems the supplier has identified and is in the process of correcting. The opening conference also is a good time for the survey team to brief the supplier on the intended use of the product and to discuss design adequacy, limitation, and so forth. The good evaluator takes numerous notes. It is better to put down more than you need than miss important tidbits. Most of the time, there will be so many facts fired at you that it will be impossible to evaluate their significance at the moment. Often, such evaluation must wait until you are writing your report. If the supplier's group is not inhibited, a tape recorder may be helpful. However, there is a fringe benefit from trying to take written notes. The obvious effort of trying to keep up in writing with the spoken words tends to keep the pace more manageable. Both sides have more time to formulate questions and reflect a bit on their responses.

After you have taken enough notes, it is time for the next step in the survey—the plant tour.

Handle the opening conference carefully. It can spoil the entire evaluation if it is mismanaged. Carried off skillfully, it can make a valid and accurate survey much easier.

What to Look for in the Quality Program

A major concern of your survey team is how to look at the quality program. This is important because few quality programs are exactly alike. Programs differ and each must be considered in the context of its environment, top management policies, and employee personalities.

The objective of your survey is to determine if the combination of quality system and plant facility can consistently ensure that the purchased product meets specification requirements. Your prime task in the survey is to conduct an evaluation of the quality program, not to dictate specific system changes.

To be effective, a quality program must be supported by top management, even though it is carried out on lower levels. There must be a top management quality policy statement for guidance and as authority to initiate and operate the quality plan. The quality statement reflects a company's dedication to supply a product or service as stated. Because of its implications to quality, you must become familiar with the policy.

It is important that the quality function be separated from the manufacturing function, and reported to either top management, or to a level that has direct access to top management.

The combination of the quality system and plant facility may be viewed from the aspect of the system or the process. One or the other, or both, may be evaluated on the same visit, but not necessarily by the same member of the survey team.

Several basic considerations should be noted as the survey team considers the quality system. The plan should concentrate on defect prevention. The plan should try to provide best control where personnel capabilities are weakest or lacking. The plan must define responsibility for each of its elements. The plan should provide for planning and documentation of information feedback to measure the plan's effectiveness adequately. This should include a breakdown of quality costs in the broad sense.

When you evaluate process controls, become aware whether control elements are included in the operator's written process instructions. Are the supplier's minimum requirements for specification conformance a part of process control? Assuming you observe a satisfactory control that identifies, evaluates, and segregates nonconforming products, does the plan provide for action to prevent recurrence of the defects? You should end your process evaluation by assuring yourself that sufficient documentation is kept to verify the program's effectiveness.

How to Gain the Most from a Plant Tour

The decision to visit a plant usually results from the realization that required information or assurance of compliance with contractual agreements can only be obtained that way. As suggested previously, you will have outlined an agenda or plan long before your visit to make a plant tour as helpful as possible.

As your tour progresses, examine the corners of various rooms and areas to see if the floor has been recently swept or washed. If cleaning or washing of such areas look like a sometime thing, beware! The supplier may consider your visit very special, and may be taking extraordinary steps to try to impress you.

Check all instrumentation and/or testing equipment for noticeable patterns of dust marks, particularly in areas where there should be minimal dust if the instruments/equipment are used regularly. If any of the instruments/equipment have covers, check to see if they are dirty. This may indicate that the instruments/equipment are rarely used.

Try to look at some or all of the quality control procedure manuals, such as would be used by plant inspectors/monitors/auditors. Fingerprints, smudges, stains, frayed edges, and turned pages might mean that the procedures were in use at the plant. Conversely, it may mean that the procedures were not frequently updated. Look for dates of revision, particularly if given in open figures. You might casually inquire from plant personnel who should be using procedures if they have ever seen or heard of the quality control manual.

Try to determine how samples are chosen for inspection, where they are taken, and at what intervals. What you observe in this respect will tell you if quality inspection is well-planned and executed, or whether it is haphazard afterthought. With many plants and products, look for retained samples and how they are managed. Systematic operation of a retained sample library will tell you that top management is really quality conscious or that, having had a bad quality experience in the past, they are hoping to learn from problems and want to try to avoid them.

If you are going to discuss proprietary information, or visit areas where proprietary products or processes are open to view, your team should obtain competent legal instruction *before* your visit. Determine with the supplier which specific areas are considered proprietary, trying to distinguish between those that truly are proprietary and those that represent novel company practices that cannot be legally protected.

Do not sign secrecy agreements until your attorney has scrutinized their contents, has discussed the extent of your obligations under them, and has approved them. Hold to the essential few the members of your team who may involve themselves with access to proprietary data.

Naturally, under no conditions disclose proprietary data in violation of a signed agreement. Your team should interest itself only in those areas or processes that can affect your product of interest.

Evaluation of a Record System

Before you can evaluate a record system, you must define management and contractual requirements. In most procurements, the latter demand requires not only documentary evidence of the product's quality status, but also must include all facets that contribute to quality, such as inspection records, test data sheets, raw material certification, heat-treating records, calibration data, plating records, X rays, and so forth.

Perhaps the most effective way to evaluate a record system at the inspection level is to select a lot/part/assembly and trace it back to the raw material state. Select a specimen that is not too old, so the vendor cannot duck behind, "This is before my time," or so new that, "It isn't completed." Choose a sample within the oldest time frame acceptable to the supplier, in which time frame excuses for nonconformance cannot be supported. This also will check the accuracy of the data retrieval system. In the event of a failure, ability to retrieve relevant information is important when traceability, assignment of cause, and identification of similar potential time bombs already in the possession of customers may become vital. The degree to which you check your supplier's records should only be enough to make you feel confident of its record keeping.

Let us clarify this. If you select a complex assembly, ask for records of only one leg of the assembly. If (in your opinion) there are too many anomalies, reject the system. If there are no anomalies, accept the system. If you are not convinced one way or another, choose another leg to trace.

Do not try to trace every step. You are trying to evaluate the working effectiveness of the data-keeping system, not the acceptability of a single piece of hardware.

To sum up this phase: Choose a significant number of observations so that you may make a judgment as to the acceptability of the supplier's record system. If you need to take too many samples before you can decide, this indicates a weak or indifferent record system.

Avoid the type of surveys in which you, as the potential customer, examine in minute detail all records in order to identify each and every discrepancy that has existed. The supplier may correct everything you identify, but assume no responsibility for the correction of defects that may have been missed by your evaluation. Remember that you are trying to identify actual and potential problem areas. It is up to the supplier to correct these and all similar areas in which there may be similar conditions.

Up to this point, this text has been philosophizing about the conduct of a survey of a record system. Now, consider the specifics of actually looking at the records and how to evaluate after the examination of the records.

Are the records neat? Scribbled records, if legible, are not cause for rejection; illegible records are cause for rejection.

Are changes to records made properly? If a single line crosses out original data, but does not obliterate it, and the change is initialed by a responsible person, such changes may be acceptable. Other ways suggest sloppy practices and hint of cooking the books.

Are all blocks filled in on printed forms? Dashes or n/a (not applicable) are acceptable. Ignoring the blanks consistently may indicate failure to comply with requirements. Dashes or n/a suggest that the inspector has considered the requirements and acted accordingly.

Is the retrieval system timely and adequate? Unavailability or lost records may point to an inadequate system. Speedy retrieval indicates an accurate filing system run by competent personnel.

Are variable data being recorded? Lack of variable data is not cause for rejection unless it is in violation of the specific contractual requirements. However, its presence usually is a sign of a professional quality system, and should be noted favorably by the auditor.

What is the quality of the data? If the exact value is being recorded conspicuously, often for a given parameter (particularly if it just within an agreed limit), the data should be questioned. Perhaps it is the case of inspectors flinching; perhaps the measuring equipment is calibrated too coarsely. Normally you would expect most data to show some kind of unbiased distribution curve. Often, you can picture the distribution mentally as you are reviewing the data.

Refer back to original data. Reproduction can hide many sins.

Are the files current? A large backlog of unfiled data may include a lack of personnel, concern, or genuine quality activity. Collecting data is not quality control.

The most important question is whether the data are used to influence product quality? Most contracts with suppliers from prime contractors will not call for detailed variables data, quality cost trend analysis, control charts, and so forth. However, much of this will appear in plants that have an underlying commitment to quality. Maintenance of data to verify inspection status is required to protect hardware integrity. The use of data to adjust the quality plan to achieve the most economical cost balance identifies a true professional system. Serious consideration should be given to the effective use of quality data in a supplier's record system.

Closing Conference

The closing conference is your final contact with the supplier's management group before you leave the plant after the survey. Take time to prepare your presentation before the conference. Be specific on discrepancies you found during your survey. Write them down in descending order of importance. Be prepared to explain each one in terms of deficiencies and discrepancies. Be quick to point out good points of your potential supplier's quality system so that you keep its confidence. If there is anything particularly laudable, begin your presentation with it.

If the supplier's representatives cannot be made to understand a discrepancy, be fully prepared to accompany them to the area in question to show them. If the supplier fails to understand what is wrong, there may be a futile attempt at correction, perhaps resulting in another discrepancy, which might trigger another, perhaps unwarranted survey.

Do not try to lay the blame for discrepancies you find on the supplier group with which you are meeting. The intent is not to establish blame, but to establish corrective action to permanently fix the discrepancies. It is most probable that the group will have to secure higher management approval to make changes in its quality system.

After discussion, each discrepancy should be noted in writing at the closing conference. Your supplier should give an estimated date for completion of corrective action for each discrepancy. The discrepancy list should be signed by a representative from the supplier and from the survey group to indicate that there is full understanding.

Final Report

The end product of your survey or quality program evaluation should be an understandable final report. A good report effectively communicates the findings using the original observations to support the conclusions. The report must be an honest, objective summation of your efforts. Even when conveying results that are not always favorable, a properly written professional report should be of potential benefit to its recipients. The report should portray the situation dispassionately and give directions for suggested corrective action. When things are better than you had expected, do not forget to give full credit. However, take some care as unwarranted accolades, as well as improper criticism, destroy the credibility of any report.

An improper report destroys relationships, breeds dissension, and creates mistrust. Such a report may deal with personalities, avoid understanding, and overlook facts.

Know your audience. The report must always be in a format and language to suit those for whom it is written. Do not forget that even a formal report can be in narrative style. Unless you are certain that most of those who may read your report will understand them, use an absolute minimum of charts, tables, and ratings. If you do use these devices, keep them as simple as possible, stressing only the important points. Another way of handling such graphic or tabular material is to refer to them in the body of the report, but transmit them as attachments or appendices to the report itself. Remember the KIS principle in report writing.

List all individuals on both teams—don't overlook anyone. Make sure the names and positions are spelled correctly. A seeming lack of concern here might annoy someone needlessly and make the corrective task more difficult.

Unlike older, more formal reports, the best modern reports open with a capsule summary of the work carried out and salient recommendations. This allows the busy executive to gain an immediate overview of the basic facts. After this, the observations, supporting discussions, and, where necessary, detailed recommendations are added. Recommendations also should be given when a specification, procedure, or process is violated. An opinion for a better way to do something may be given as a suggestion or comment.

Your report should be sent to the management team with whom you met. Copies also should be sent to the quality control manager and the sales department, if they were not represented. In your own company, copies should be distributed through the quality control manager.

The supplier survey usually will indicate an acceptable supplier, a limited supplier, a potentially acceptable supplier, or an unacceptable supplier. Naturally, a report about an acceptable supplier is more pleasant to write. However, a report about an unacceptable supplier need not be marred by unpleasantness. Unless you should not have been there, most of the negative surveys will suggest how to rise into at least the potential or limited supplier category. In such cases, handling the report with finesse makes all the difference. It can lead the potential supplier to want to take suitable corrective action. Grace makes it easier for the limited supplier to accept its limitations, and may even bring the unacceptable supplier to understand the problems and work toward future acceptability.

Don't forget to close your report with expressions of appreciation for the supplier's time, assistance, and cooperation.

Follow-Up to Supplier Qualification Surveys

Survey follow-up is carried out to ensure that satisfactory corrective action has been taken by a supplier that did not qualify at the time of your previous survey visit. You may have to judge if a follow-up visit is warranted, balancing the nature of the findings against the costs to travel and work force involved. Accompanied by suitable documentation, a report from the supplier of corrective action may be enough.

Keep a genuinely helpful and constructive attitude at all times, and show it by timely support when you deal with all levels of the supplier's personnel. Doing this consistently may be difficult, but as a quality professional, you must do it.

The supplier and your company, should have reached agreement during the closing conference on the timetable for corrective action. Documentation of the corrective action schedule should be included in the survey report and the formal supplier response. You must thoroughly review the survey report and the formal supplier response before a follow-up visit.

Contact the supplier and arrange a mutually agreeable date for the follow-up visit. Schedule a date for the follow-up visit as soon as possible after the execution and reported completion of required corrective action. Make sure that all required corrective action has been completed. If corrective action has not been effected within the required time, your management's policy should provide directions for suitable alternative action.

Show a positive attitude during the follow-up visit. Your supplier has told you that the corrective actions you agreed on have been carried out. You are there to verify that the corrective actions have been taken satisfactorily. If all corrective actions are acceptable and no additional problems become known, the supplier should qualify as an approved supplier.

If you cannot verify adequate corrective actions, consider the following:

1. If the supplier has made an effort to comply, but has not met your requirements, you may have a communications problem. Review the survey report and reported corrective action with the responsible supplier personnel.

2. If requirements have not been satisfactorily fulfilled, the supplier should be advised that it has failed an approved supplier status. Mutually agreeable alternatives should be arranged before a visit and the supplier advised accordingly.

You may encounter a situation where the supplier has unique capabilities important to your company, but does not have the resources to invest to provide the quality assurance specified. If possible, the follow-up report should include suggestions for alternative controls, or for direct assistance to the supplier to overcome certain conditions. Competent, understanding assistance in critical situations can be a rewarding investment in securing a satisfactory supplier base.

Post-Survey Team Critique

So you have finished another survey. Congratulations are in order . . . . or are they? More than one team has faced that question after a survey. How can you answer it? One of the best ways is to conduct a team critique.

You carry out a critique to increase the professional competence of the surveyors. It may be tough to face, but the recognition of individual or team shortcomings is the first necessary step in correcting them. Hopefully, individual or team improvement may get noticed by management and by the individuals and groups your surveyors contact in your company.

Remind yourself that suppliers about to be surveyed by customers are never happy with what is about to happen. A survey takes time and time means money. A survey improperly handled opens the supplier to criticism by the customer. In a supplier's plant, each department is expected either to put on a good show or mislead the evaluators. Such efforts make good surveys difficult. A critique undertaken on the same basis is absolutely worthless.

A proper critique must be realistic. It should consider all the items normally encountered in a supplier or corporate quality survey. The headings of this chapter are an excellent list of subjects to consider in your team critique.

- Goals of a survey
- Preparation for the survey
- Team organization
- Use of quantification in the evaluation format
- Opening conference
- What to look for in the quality program
- How to gain the most from a plant tour
- Evaluation of a record system
- Closing conference
- Final report
- Follow-up to vendor qualification surveys
- Post-survey team critique
- International suppliers
- Supplier information and reassurance

A critique by an individual or a team can be a highly emotional activity, so conduct it in a professional manner to reduce emotion and increase effectiveness. Just as in all quality control operations, you must identify nonconformities and weaknesses rather than blame individuals for weaknesses and inadequacies. Timing of the critique can help set the proper frame of mind. A critique cannot be effective as a crash program or after some disaster. One good time for a critique is shortly after completing a survey when details are still fresh and before the next survey may be scheduled.

It probably is true that there is no perfect product, drawing, or specification. Likewise, there is no perfect survey, supplier, nor customer, and there can be no perfect evaluators. The critique is a search for self-improvement. Any individual or team who believes operations cannot be improved probably is very poor rather than very good.

Therefore, as individuals we must expect that a critique is going to point out areas for improvement and change. Such is the purpose of a critique. What was good yesterday may not be good enough tomorrow. All surveys look for improvements and ways to make them.

In a critique it is important that unsatisfactory results be identified, but it is equally important that areas where improvement can be achieved are identified. The one often means the other. Identification of areas that can be improved is the purpose of the critique. The areas are not the causes. It is necessary that the methods for improvement also be identified so that individuals can improve their performance and increase their efficiency and effectiveness. As an example, the critique may disclose that in a recent survey the reliability tests and results were not properly evaluated. Why did this happen? Were the individuals or perhaps the entire team inattentive? Did they have insufficient training in reliability methods, procedures, and statistics? Another question might be, "Why were the records not completely and properly evaluated?" Were they available to the members of the team or the individual conducting the survey (the same people now doing a critique)? Was it carelessness or failure to realize the importance of this area? Was this poor planning?

In conducting a critique, it is essential that the problem, not the people, be evaluated. This is a self-searching process to find a way to improve the operation.

To be worthwhile, a critique requires honesty and integrity. As with other data analysis situations, it is not a procedure aimed at finding excuses, but rather at finding areas of the program where major improvements can be effected. This may point to a study course in some particular area. Perhaps just a review with someone at the plant as to what is needed can provide insight that can be developed by home study material. An evaluator cannot be an expert in every field, nor necessarily as expert as someone who is conducting a particular kind of operation. However, the evaluator must have sufficient insight to recognize when things are patently wrong, or when things appear to be done properly.

At the end of the critique, a list of areas needing improvement should emerge. The next step is deciding how to obtain improvement in each named area. In some areas, provision of training and a program of study, counseling, or management consultation may be in order. In other instances, it may become obvious that the next survey team should include a specialist if specific areas are likely to arise. In any event, plans must be formalized and a commitment made to carry them through and improve the quality of performance of surveys.

As an alternative to the team critique, a peer review similar to those used for design reviews should be considered. In a supplier survey, communication is of prime importance; therefore, the form of the critique should be a confrontation situation in which the survey team defends its report and survey action to a peer group in the team's own company. The peer group should be drawn from the purchasing and production staff who would deal with the new supplier. They should have access to the history of the survey and copies of the proposed final report prior to the meeting.

The survey team must present its report and support its conclusions to this group plus a review chairperson supported by two observers. The plant team is then free to question the survey team or each member on specific recommendations or conclusions from the report. The in-house staff will have to finally accept or reject the report as a useful addition to its working information.

The chairperson and observers record significant points by both teams and produce an analysis of the proceedings after review. This method of in-house evaluation and improvement has proved most useful in many design fields, in value engineering, and in other situations where communication and action resulting from communication are vital.

The in-plant team gains from its exposure to the group who actually visited and measured the capabilities of the potential supplier. The review makes contact easier and the people in the supply source more three-dimensional.

Finally, the survey team witnesses the impact of its report on the other half of its own operation. The survey team members have to reason out why things were done and why conclusions were drawn. It is a satisfactory method of learning provided the chairperson and observers ensure that the confrontation is properly conducted and does not degenerate to personalities.

International Suppliers

What has been discussed to this point has been how to deal with the survey of a potential supplier in your own country. The situation may arise where you have to consider a supplier abroad. Here are a few tips on how to proceed.

Quality assurance has developed rapidly in Europe and Japan, where it is recognized as a very important part of export or international sales. When your company has commitments involving evaluation of international sources of production, be careful to check what information may be available to you from official or quasi-official bodies.

Most developed countries have state-sponsored organizations responsible for interfacing with foreign business interests; in this case, you are the foreign interest. These organizations usually can supply product and manufacturing quality references and approval to expedite sales and maintain their national image.

When the prospective supplier is located in Europe or a western-oriented country, contacts should be established with trade ministries, standards institutions, or professional organizations in quality work to obtain information on local quality practices (which are sometimes surprisingly good). Most countries have both certification and accreditation procedures that are applied to local quality assurance or testing organizations, usually backed by a national surveillance program to make valid evaluation data available to you. Use such sources whenever possible. In most cases, your professional affiliations will be able to give you information on how to contact indigenous groups in whichever country your company plans to do business at a given time.

Quality assurance is much more formalized outside of continental North America. Be sure to benefit from any bona fide source of evaluation data available to your organization from such nation bodies. Although it may be a costly mistake to assume that some given quality information from abroad is fully equivalent to one with which you are familiar, it is not unusual to discover that in certain fields of quality accreditation, suppliers abroad may have to regularly meet standards that would strain some of your domestic suppliers to their limits. Treat quality accreditation information abroad with the same open attitude as a quality survey of a domestic supplier. It may save you from accepting as qualified a supplier that is not, and it also may save you from rejecting a supplier that is more qualified than any you might find at home.

Supplier Information and Reassurance

So, you are going to take part in a supplier survey, but it is your plant that is being surveyed. You may wonder how to get ready for the survey. First of all, relax and remember that tens of thousands of supplier surveys take place every year. You are not alone.

You may be surveyed by competent quality professionals, perhaps someone who has read this book. Because you are reading it too, you have an idea of how to get ready. It also would be useful for you to review any specific standards that might apply. In short, start by arming yourself with knowledge. Determine what the surveyors may be looking for.

The next step is to make a realistic appraisal of your plant's quality situation. Do you have a good quality system?

If the answer is "no," it is practically certain that it is too late to build one before the survey date. Your best bet is to inform your management of existing deficiencies. Try to sell management on support of a quality control program. Then when a survey team shows up, learn as much as you can and take your lumps. Point out that your management has (hopefully) given the support for necessary corrective action. It is foolish to try to hide true facts from competent evaluators. They almost surely will find out, and you will look even worse.

If you have a good system, stand firmly. It may not be perfect—nothing ever is. Doubtless the evaluators will find deficiencies somewhere, and you may end up debating necessary corrective action. However, do not make the mistake of trying to dress up the operation with a lot of spit and polish. Such effort will make your operation appear artificial. Competent evaluators know what a working facility looks like. They rarely are impressed by a snow job, but may become suspicious and wonder what and how much you are trying to cover up.

Make sure that the key people have been thoroughly briefed and that their schedules will permit them to be available at the time of the survey for introductions and to answer questions pertaining to their functions. Have an organization chart available (most quality control manuals have charts you can use for models) that can be presented to the survey team and indicate who carries out what function in your plant. Also make sure the documentation that should be available is accessible.

Recognize that no two systems are alike. Know your own system and how it works. Do not be afraid to defend your system if it does work. Competent evaluators are interested in new techniques and new ideas, but do not be so defensive that you are unwilling to learn from them if they suggest a better idea.

It is not out of place to extend a modest show of professional courtesy to the survey team. The team represents a potential purchaser, which means sales and income for your firm.

The survey team almost surely will appreciate the availability of office space. Some hospitality (for example, lunch) is not out of line.

Your evaluators may need overnight accommodations. Because you are at the site, you are in the best position to arrange this. The same goes for transportation to visit your facility. You do not have to be pushy, but your offer of help may be appreciated. Eventually, when you are an approved supplier and the same evaluators return on regular checkup visits, you may develop a warm personal relationship. However, do not rely on charm to hide deficiencies—it can only delay the ugly discovery of shortcomings.

If it is the evaluators' first trip to your plant, they probably will expect you to take them on a tour. Plan such a tour in advance and estimate the timing. Make sure that the plant personnel has been informed of who the evaluators are, what their purpose is, and how your personnel can help by giving straight replies to the evaluators' questions. After the evaluators have seen your plant as a whole, they may ask to revisit specific stations for in-depth study. Do not be alarmed: Perhaps they have found something unusually good. If it is not, they may be in a position to suggest how those sections of your plant could be improved. Usually you will win if you deal fairly with the survey team.

This chapter has briefly discussed the key points concerning what is necessary to conduct a supplier survey. The hints and suggestions will aid the novice in preparation and execution of the survey. The experienced auditor will have some thoughts and ideas reinforced. The essential point to remember is that in most cases, the supplier knows your company through you. How you conduct yourself is the impression that the supplier has of your company. The professionalism that you show will be reflected on your company's image. So, by following the steps, you will ensure some consistency of format. The rest is up to you.

How to Evaluate a Supplier's Product

Chapter 13

Key words: certification program, design control, drawings, process audit, product qualification, purchase orders, tolerances.

Summary
- Preaward conference
- Initial production
- Source inspection
- Utilizing supplier data
- Nonconforming product
- Performance evaluation

Evaluating a supplier's product is an important element of a company quality control program. This chapter describes some of the more commonly used methods of evaluating purchased products. Obviously, a cookbook approach to evaluation is not practical as each product requires specific decisions; however, the methods discussed here have proven effective. Using these concepts, the customer can develop operating procedures that will maintain an ongoing program for evaluating supplier products.

Each aspect of the program is important, but higher priorities must be assigned those areas that offer the customer the greatest payback. Considerations also must be given to the types of products and processes, especially when new procedures are being established.

Product evaluation procedures can range from simple to complex, and the degree of formality in any program depends on product and customer requirements. Individual ingenuity and integrity on the part of both customer and supplier quality control personnel are essential to optimize operating procedures and to provide maximum effectiveness to the program.

This chapter describes successful methods of supplier product evaluation. These are not the only ways to evaluate a supplier's product, but they are the most important for developing a purchased material quality control program.

Preaward Conference

Prior to evaluation of a supplier's product, contractual requirements applying to that specific product must be established. Both the supplier and the customer must have a clear understanding of the basic product requirements, as well as any special quality requirements. A most effective way to accomplish this understanding is to schedule a preaward conference.

Need for a preaward conference usually is determined by discussion between the supplier's purchasing and quality assurance department. A conference should be called where high cost or special circumstances are involved in the contract. Often a preaward conference is considered when the job is new to the supplier. The conference provides an opportunity to finalize product or process requirements.

The preaward conference brings together technical and management personnel representing both the supplier and customer. The departments generally involved are product design/development, manufacturing, testing, purchasing/sales, and quality assurance. Depending on the type of product, representatives from service, financial, legal, marketing, and other functions also may be involved. Attendance could be governed by the requirements of the contract.

After the need for a conference is established, it is the responsibility of the supplier quality assurance department to develop an agenda that ensures all applicable product quality requirements will be covered. Normally, the customer's purchasing department schedules and chairs the initial meeting. The customer's quality representative serves as secretary and coordinator to ensure that product requirements are understood and accepted, responsibilities are assigned, and agreements made at the meeting are documented.

The agenda is used by both supplier and customer staffs to prepare for the meeting as a guide in conducting the meeting. A typical agenda could include the following items.

- Design acceptance
- Production facilities
- First-article inspection
- Process requirements
- Production quality control
- Packaging
- Records
- Quality audits and past performance
- Warranty provisions
- Communications
- Schedules

The preaward conference should be as extensive as necessary to cover all subjects pertinent to satisfactory completion of the contract. A successful meeting virtually eliminates the "I didn't know we had to do that," or "That's going to cost more" response when the product goes into production. The importance of the preaward conference becomes clear as the various agenda items are discussed.

Perhaps the most critical factor is design acceptance because it is difficult to evaluate a product that is not clearly defined. Questions that must be answered include

- Who is responsible for design control?
- Are tolerances and specifications realistic and within the capability of the supplier?
- Are test requirements adequate to ensure fit and function?

These important questions must be discussed at the preaward conference and it is essential that clear agreements be reached prior to release of the contract.

After product requirements and specifications are agreed to, consideration must be given to the facilities and equipment necessary to produce and check the product. In many cases, the customer may furnish tools or equipment. Yet, without mutual agreement as to the design and use of this equipment, the supplier may be unable or unwilling to use it. Possibly the supplier may have a better or more economical method of production. The point is that production and test methods must be clearly agreed on prior to release of the contract or purchase order.

First-article complete inspection is the first real product evaluation. Product requirements must be defined in detail to allow the supplier to understand what is expected. The first article may be a sample, a dozen items, or any specified quantity or volume. The conditions of first-article inspection must be understood, accepted, and documented. Requirements for inspections, tests, reports, and so on, must be defined and responsibilities established for future implementation.

Many jobs, particularly in the chemical field, are controlled through specific process requirements. Therefore, an understanding should be reached as to responsibility for authorizing process control changes. Communication channels must be defined. Both the supplier and customer must understand and agree on specific areas of responsibility for approving product or process deviation.

Production quality controls planned by the supplier are another major topic of the preaward conference. For instance, some jobs require special operator skills or qualifications; therefore, details of these requirements must be discussed. All significant elements of the supplier's quality plan should be reviewed and agreement reached regarding methods of inspection, sampling plans, acceptance standards, and so forth.

Manufacture of a product in conformance with customer specifications is not the only important subject discussed at the preaward conference. Special attention also should be given to packing, protection, and shipping. If the product is damaged or deteriorates during shipment and storage, all the efforts to ensure conformance are wasted. For many products, the loading, handling, and packaging requirements are as tightly controlled as the product itself. Again, the requirements of the specific product must be clearly defined and a mutual understanding achieved between the supplier and customer.

Some products require special records so that traceability may be maintained in reference to applicable inspection and test reports. All aspects of this identification, inspection, and reporting must be discussed and agreements documented so that they become an integral portion of the purchase contract.

Information gained while reviewing the supplier's quality proposal often can be used to plan subsequent audits of the supplier's production operation. After agreements are reached, it is easy to plan objective audits to determine if the conference agreements are being fulfilled.

The preaward conference also provides an opportunity to review prior problems and plan for prevention. When the potential supplier is to furnish an existing product with which the customer has had extensive experience, the customer can provide information that will help reduce future problems and defect costs. The conference's discussion of warranty should cover a multitude of activities ranging from customer complaints to responsibility for returned product. In many instances, special warranty coverage may have to be negotiated. A factor that should not be overlooked is handling and evaluating returned goods to ensure that the supplier can plan and implement corrective action. Guidelines for cost recovery on warranty returns, as well as an agreement on product improvement costs, should be established at this time.

Finally, a preaward conference should include an open session where all parties may submit relevant subjects for discussion. In this manner, anything of importance not previously discussed may be covered. Everyone involved with the conference has an opportunity to contribute and all viewpoints are considered.

After a preaward conference has been completed, it is customary to include all agreements as a part of the purchase contract. This is done by amendment of the purchase order to require conformance to the agreements of the conference. A copy of the conference report accompanies the purchase documents.

Some conferences recommend the proposed contract be revised or cancelled. It is best to prevent an unsatisfactory project from starting if agreements cannot be reached. One of the prime reasons for a contract being revised or cancelled is the supplier's inability to comply with the customer requirements.

The preaward conference is one of the most productive prevention-oriented quality functions performed as an element of purchased material control. Often it is the initial step in evaluation of the supplier's product. Each company must develop its own preaward conference program. The information presented here simply highlights some significant factors of such a program. The preaward conference alone cannot ensure freedom from problems, but combined with sound planning and implementation of the product evaluation techniques discussed in this chapter, it can significantly minimize the potential for problems involved with purchased products.

Initial Production

The first evaluation of a product or a process is the most critical stage in establishing a good working relationship with a supplier and in ensuring that the product to be received on a production basis conforms to the desired characteristics. Assurance that the received product is correct begins on the initial purchase order with appropriate performance requirements. First-article or process evaluation not only ensures that drawing and specification requirements are met, but that the product is consistent with contractual requirements.

Product Qualification

Prior to receiving the initial product, a checklist of evaluation characteristics should be established. The list should consider all significant elements of the product and its performance. Inputs from each design/development group that will be involved with the product should be obtained and added to the checklist.

Upon receipt, the product should be checked for problems incurred in shipping. Once this is done, the evaluation procedure already developed should begin. At each step, both acceptable and unacceptable test results should be documented. For uncomplicated products, a standard form for documenting results is helpful. It ensures that all steps are adequately and consistently evaluated. The results of each step should be considered while the product is being processed so that any additional evaluation parameter may be included in the tests. The documented test results should then be reviewed with engineering, manufacturing, and other concerned groups, and compared with the supplier's results to identify problems. After the evaluation, the package should be sent to the supplier either to request corrective action in areas where discrepancies exist, or to provide documented acceptance of the product. If the product is complex, a joint review of the results may be necessary to ensure measurement correlations between supplier and customer.

Methods for accomplishing this correlation are negotiable. The negotiations should be handled by the purchasing department and, once the methods of corrective action are finalized, they should be transmitted by purchasing to the supplier.

Prior to receipt of the corrected product, a new checklist should reidentify the characteristics to be evaluated. Close scrutiny should ensure that the corrections do not affect original product characteristics. The supplier should be requested to provide a written description of the process or procedural changes necessary to correct the product. This description provides verification or correction. The procedures should be included in future evaluation requirements.

Upon receipt, the corrected product should be checked again for packing and handling discrepancies and then evaluated according to the new checklist. If the product still does not meet required performance characteristics, the same review and negotiations for correction may be required as when the product was first received. If the product is acceptable, recognition by design/development, manufacturing, and quality control should be transmitted to the supplier through the purchasing department.

Process Identification

Prior to a process evaluation, a checklist should identify characteristics to be evaluated. As part of the checklist, a flowchart should point out the step-by-step characteristics and controlling parameters of the process. The checklist also should identify manufacturing system control parameters. These parameters include material routing procedures, change control, defect identification, isolation, evaluation and disposition, production capabilities, calibration capabilities, process documentation, system audit, and tool control procedures.

A description of the production facility, its management, and quality policy is helpful before any evaluation. These can and should be obtained through the customer purchasing department.

Process Audit

After the checklist is developed, arrangements for process audit can be made through the purchasing department. If possible, the timing of the audit should coincide with the movement of preproduction or actual production parts through the process. This allows the evaluation team to review the product characteristics as described in the original design parameters under working conditions.

After visit arrangements are made, the supplier should have a chance to review the scope of the evaluation plan to ensure that none of the processing activities are proprietary and to determine if any special activity will be required.

Auditors should arrive promptly to conduct the audit. They must evaluate the details of the process and system control as part of the supplier's manufacturing cycle. Records on process parameters must be checked for out-of-control conditions and evidence of corrective action. Where practical, process parameters should be compared with daily records. Each operation must be checked to ensure that enough safeguards are in place to maintain the process in control or to identify an impending out-of-control condition. Weakness or deviations from the expected results should be recorded. Most processes are likely to maintain the desired output if normal controls will prevent deviation; however, special controls established specifically for the product should be emphasized as they are likely to be overlooked in routine operation.

When the audit is complete, a summary of findings should be reviewed with the supplier. If needed, a plan for corrective action with implementation dates should be developed. Methods for demonstrating corrective action also should be developed and accepted. A complete, documented report, including the agreed upon corrective action, should be sent to the supplier by the purchasing department. A follow-up by telephone should confirm that the supplier has received and understood the report. Additional telephone contacts can follow the progress of the corrective action, although additional visits to the supplier's facility may be required to evaluate implementation of corrective action.

Qualification by Suppliers

Product, process, and article requirements developed for first-article inspection and process evaluation should again be reviewed before establishing characteristics of supplier qualifications. After these requirements are determined, the records can be developed to achieve the desired evaluation results.

These requirements should be documented and transmitted through the purchasing department to the supplier. The supplier should be contacted to ensure that the requirements are understood and to establish timing for completion of the evaluation. An on-site inspector can help ensure that the evaluation is carried out accurately and completely.

The evaluated product and the results of this evaluation (both provided by the supplier) must be audited for accuracy and completeness. This audit can include evaluation of critical characteristics and parameters. If the audit procedures show results different than those shown in the supplier evaluation tests, additional parameters should be measured or additional information requested from the supplier. The review and audit results should be documented and transmitted by the purchasing department to the supplier. Discrepancies should be followed up and corrective action obtained.

Qualification by Independent Laboratory

Qualification of an article or process by an independent laboratory is essentially the same as qualification by the supplier. *However, the capability of the independent laboratory must be determined prior to any tests.*

The scope of the desired task, cost, expected reports, and outputs should be established and agreed on by the contracting parties. When the results are received they should be reviewed, audited, and transmitted to the supplier for its information. Any questionable areas should be clarified with the laboratory or the supplier with appropriate corrective action and follow-up evaluations performed until an acceptable correlation or product can be demonstrated. Several independent laboratories' analyses may be needed, depending on the complexity and diversity of the evaluation.

Certification Program

An alternative to the quality control methods described herein is a ship-to-stock or certified product program. As the name implies, the product essentially is treated as a free lot in skip lot inspection and is released without being subjected to the conventional receiving inspection.

This alternate method depends on a strong supplier–customer relationship that emphasizes preventive planning, detailed product and process audits by the customer, and a high degree of integrity on the part of the supplier. Extensive planning liaison is required and agreements are reached prior to release of the purchase contract.

As with all sound quality planning, the job requirements must be defined and documented. Specific audit guidelines must be developed and a schedule established for periodic evaluation during the production schedule. The supplier's plan for control of the process and product must be documented carefully and included as an integral part of the purchase agreement. This plan becomes the benchmark for planning and auditing throughout the life of the contract.

The certification program normally is not used with a new supplier because a history of demonstrated ability by the supplier to control operations is essential. New products may be considered for this plan when a good supplier–customer relationship exists, but again extensive planning must be done and detailed agreements reached prior to production. When the supplier has a strong operational quality program and the customer maintains timely and effective audits of the specific job, this program can be an alternate to receiving inspection.

Incoming Inspection

Incoming inspection is one of the most important functions in the overall quality assurance program. In simple terms, incoming inspection reveals whether the supplier can produce and deliver what it said it could in the manner it claimed it would! The following is a sequence of events that can be used as a guide in formulating specific flowcharts and procedures for use in the incoming inspection area of any specific plant or operation.

Purchase Orders and Drawings

Access to copies of every purchase order and drawings/specifications is necessary. The receiving copy of the purchase order can save duplicate files, and other paperwork.

Upon receipt of the parts from the supplier, the receiving department normally will pull the purchase order, count the parts, and check for damage. If the cartons and/or parts show physical damage, the receiving department should immediately process a shipping damage claim to the carrier and/or the insurance company with whose procedures they should be familiar. If everything is in order, the receiving department will put the purchase order with the items and forward the order to incoming inspection for the required inspection and test.

In a small company, it may be advantageous to have the supplier of metal work, printed wiring boards, or similar items return with the shipment the original drawings/specifications used to produce the part or finished item. In many cases, receipt of all the drawings/specifications will prevent future supplier problems related to design changes. This method provides some confidence that the supplier cannot build more parts without new or updated drawings/specifications. Receiving the drawings/specifications with the parts also saves the cost of maintaining a drawing file in receiving inspection.

The incoming inspector with the purchase order, the drawings/specifications, and parts, now can begin to ensure the following:

1.   The purchase order is accurate and calls for the specific item(s), part number and revision, test data (if required), and so forth.

2.   Parts are not damaged due to defective packing and packaging.

3. Parts are as called for on the purchase order with draw-ing/specification by part number, color code, and so forth.

Inspection, Test Records

Under normal circumstances, the quality system or program will require the incoming inspector to select a sample per an approved sampling plan if quantities will allow. If not, all parts should be inspected and/or tested to ensure conformance to the drawings/speci-fications or inspection instructions.

The inspector must have the necessary tools, gages, and equip-ment to inspect and/or test the items properly. All inspection tools, gages, and equipment must be calibrated to ensure accuracy. Either the sample or the total quantity should conform in order to be accepted and released to stock. The incoming inspector should complete the incoming inspection record in detail and process the items to stock if they are accepted.

Rejected Material and Records

If for any reason the items do not conform to the drawings, specifica-tions, standards, or inspection instructions, the items should be rejected. A rejection report should be completed and placed with the items for review and disposition by quality management. Under nor-mal circumstances, the defective item(s) would be processed through purchasing for return to the supplier for corrective action or replace-ment. Under special conditions (if they were required because of time and if they could be corrected/or used within the facilities) the items might be presented for material review board action. Material review procedures would control these activities.

The intent of incoming inspection is to ensure that the item(s) received are as stated on the purchase order and that the item(s) con-form to specifications and drawings. The intent of incoming inspec-tion records is to document the facts with regard to the performance of suppliers and to provide purchasing and quality management with data from which decisions can be made.

Source Inspection

Source inspection is inspection by the buyer's designated representative to confirm a product's compliance to contractual obligations prior to shipment of the material. Source inspection does not necessarily eliminate receiving inspection. Source inspection does have some benefits. The customer saves money on equipment that does not have to be purchased because the supplier does the testing; the customer utilizes the expertise of the supplier in the product the supplier is providing; and if a nonconforming product is formed, the supplier can correct the problem prior to shipment.

Source inspection can take place for three types of materials or assemblies.

1. *Complete assembly/material*–A product that will be used without further processing or modification. The need for source inspection should be predicated on the ability of the customer to determine, at the customer's point of receipt, the supplier's compliance to the purchase documents, specifications, and agreements as economically and completely as necessary to establish the acceptability of the delivered material.

In some instances, it is impossible to perform a meaningful evaluation without destroying the product, or at a minimum, making it unfit for use. This must be included in the cost. Some items may be of such a delicate nature that both the supplier and customer agree that handling must be kept to a minimum and, by mutual agreement, decide that inspection at source is indicated. Some items may be of such a complex nature requiring adjustment, calibrations, tests, or combinations of subassemblies, that it would be impossible to check them without upsetting or destroying all of the supplier's settings or impossible to check them in any manner. Here it is apparent that source inspection would be of considerable value to the customer because of the participation by the inspector in the supplier's procedures. Some items may be of such a nature that the failure of the assembly to meet specification could result in the loss of life, the loss of equipment life, (and the loss of governmental projects or missions military/scientific), as well as endangering public health and safety.

No economy can justify inspection cost saving programs against the possible danger factor.

2. *Subassemblies/materials*–A product that will be used in conjunction with one or more other subassemblies, components, or processes to make a deliverable product. Subassemblies would have all the same considerations applied in determining the *why* of source inspections, as do complete assemblies, plus the added requirement of compatibility and assembly feasibility with other subassemblies, components, or processes that they may be subjected to by the customer.

- Would the subsequent assembly procedures affect a delicate or complex subassembly or, more importantly, the completed assembly? This could be monitored closely on the source inspector's own assembly lines by virtue of the inspector's knowledge of the subassembly acquired during source inspection.
- A safety-sensitive subassembly, in addition to the above, also could be monitored on the customer's assembly line to ensure that nothing is done in the subsequent assembly or processing that might result in an unsafe product.

3. *Components*–A part to be used in conjunction with other parts and/or subassemblies to produce other subassemblies, complete assemblies, or deliverable products. For source inspection on components, the customer must consider all aspects as discussed under prior sections, as well as the relative importance of the individual components to the subassembly and/or completed deliverable product. For instance, how would an individual component affect a delicate, complex, or safety-type subassembly and complete assembly in the customer's deliverable unit? Other things to consider for component source inspection are

- Is the item proprietary to the supplier or customer? Who controls the design?
- Is the customer requesting modifications to an existing product to fit a specific need?
- Is the supplier new? Is the market new?
- Is the component a developmental or state-of-the-art item?

Successful source inspection begins with the first supplier contact, whether it occurs during a preaward conference or during evaluation of the supplier's facilities. It is important that source inspection effort be regarded, by the supplier and the customer, as a desirable method of proving the supplier's production to the purchaser's satisfaction.

For a good working relationship, the customer quality personnel must maintain direct contact with the supplier quality personnel. Their first such contact should be made through the purchasing department, whether at a preaward conference or by telephone. Subsequent contacts could be made directly between the quality personnel of the two companies. Of course, the purchasing department should be informed of any substantive conversations. This interchange of intercompany quality data is vital to a good working relationship.

Good source inspection depends on a thorough understanding of the product. Thus, careful review of the drawings, specifications, and purchase order is necessary for the quality professional who will conduct the inspection. Source inspection criteria, whether developed by design or quality, should be selected carefully and reviewed by design, purchasing, production control, manufacturing, and quality. All concerned parties should agree that the salient points have been covered. At this point, agreements also should be reached concerning assistance, by any of the aforementioned functions, for the quality professional assigned the source inspection.

With the customer quality team in agreement as to what will be done and who will do it, the quality professional is ready for his/her first survey trip to the supplier's plant. The trip should have three purposes: (1) establishment of good working relations, (2) evaluation of the supplier's quality system, and (3) discussion of the areas to be inspected during source inspection. If first-article inspection is planned, changes in the source inspection as a result of that inspection should be discussed and agreement reached on how and when such changes should be implemented. An estimated production schedule should be provided by the supplier during this plant visit. That schedule should be updated as necessary by the supplier's quality personnel to ensure timely response by the customer when the hold points for the source inspection are reached. The customer's quality professional, in turn, should notify those who are to assist if there are any schedule changes.

Actual source inspection could include detailed inspection of dimensions, visual examination of parts, functional testing, review of records, and any other aspect of the product. It is important that the customer representative create minimum disturbance in the supplier's manufacturing process. Proper communication ensures availability of the source inspector(s) when the product has reached inspection hold points. Thorough preparation will ensure familiarity with the product and reduce the time required for source inspection. Proper attitude will result in a good relationship with the supplier and prevent needless conflict. Source control should be implemented only after the supplier has validated product acceptability; this also may be done concurrently by joint agreement.

After source inspection is completed for the first item/lot, the results must be evaluated carefully. Most likely the initial quality plan will need changes, reducing some requirements and strengthening others. It is important that the source inspection requirement be flexible enough to allow the customer's quality professional to reduce inspection of subsequent lots if the initial ones prove satisfactory, or to increase control if production proves to be out of control. Whether or not a reduction takes place, the quality professional should monitor any defects found during the company's receiving inspection and/or the company's production cycle. Defects found are justification for increased or modified source inspection criteria during the supplier's production cycle.

After the supplier's production line is running and actual source inspection has been reduced, the customer's quality professional might consider surveying the product by random audits or visits to ensure that all continues to go well. Such surveillance would take up little time and could be conducted in conjunction with trips to other plants. Additionally, it would maintain the good working relationship between partners, which is necessary in a source inspection program.

During the production phase, the source inspector (in addition to the normal functions of determining the acceptability of the submitted material) performs other duties essential to the successful operation of the buyer's production line.

- Constant evaluation of the supplier's performance. Under this function, in addition to the quality evaluation, the source inspector becomes aware of any and all situations that may affect the production and delivery schedule, and keeps management informed.
- Coordination with the supplier of all changes to specifications or the purchase order and report on the effectivity of implementation.
- Coordination of any problems the supplier's company may have with items purchased. If the trouble is within the supplier's realm, the necessary steps should be taken to preclude their repetition.
- Release for shipment only those items the supplier finds acceptable for use as defined by the specifications, samples, or purchase order.

The choice of a source inspector is a delicate and critical decision. The effectiveness of the source inspector largely depends on the inspector's ability to obtain the fullest cooperation from the supplier, while at the same time insisting that the product meet the required specifications.

The character, personal, and professional habits of the inspector are equal in importance to the inspector's knowledge of the job. The ability to absorb information, observe operations, and make discreet investigations without being obvious is essential. The inspector also must be able to gain the confidence and cooperation of the supplier's inspectors and floor supervisors without becoming so personally involved that the inspector can no longer make an objective judgment. The ability to make firm, positive, decisions also is necessary. Therefore, the source inspector must combine the attributes of a technician, detective, politician, diplomat, baby-sitter, and disciplinarian.

The amount of technical knowledge that the source inspector would be expected to have depends on the type of inspection being performed.

One of the most critical functions performed during source inspection is record keeping. Accuracy is paramount. The minimum amount of information maintained is

- Supplier's name and address
- Drawing number, revision, and purchase order
- Quantity inspected
- Quantity accepted
- Reasons for rejection
- Contractor's personnel contacted with regard to rejects
- Corrective action to be taken

In addition, any shipping papers to all source-inspected items must reference the fact that the items comprising the shipment have been inspected, tested, and/or accepted at the source by an agent of the buyer's company. Usually, this is accomplished by the source inspector signing or stamping the shipping papers.

Too often the source inspector, particularly if a resident at the supplier's facility, is out-of-sight and out-of-mind, which means that the inspector has been forgotten by the home company. This is an unhappy situation. Therefore, it is imperative that the source inspector be regularly informed of events at the home company. If there is an opening for advancement, the source inspector should be considered, if eligible. When the source inspector returns to the company for any reasonable length of time, the inspector should not be treated as an alien, but made to feel welcome and an essential part of the quality assurance group. The source inspector must be made aware of all changes in the scope of work by the supplier as reflected in revisions to drawings and/or purchase orders. The source inspector should be invited to all supplier/customer meetings at the supplier plant that may impact the scope of work. If unable to attend, the inspector should be on distribution of the minutes of the meeting.

The source inspector has responsibilities to the home company that must not be overlooked. These include

1. Advising management of conditions at the supplier's plant.
2. Maintaining accurate records and ensuring their availability when required.
3. Working without interfering with the supplier's production.
4. Reporting to work at hours consistent with those of the supplier.
5. Remembering at all times that the inspector is the sole representative of the home company, who deals with line personnel at the supplier's plant. Nothing should be done that could bring discredit to the home company.

Utilizing Supplier Data

Supplier data includes product, process, or equipment information obtained from a supplier. This may be a description of the equipment and/or process, process/product yields, product input/output variable or attribute measurements, X ray films, laboratory analysis, or other related sampling or 100 percent measurement. Data should be required contractually by drawings and specifications described in the purchase order. Acquiring and processing data costs money, thus, the necessity for contractual understanding. Supplier data are used primarily to ascertain compliance to specification. Data also are used to evaluate process capabilities, equipment correlations, trend information, and product-related factors. Data from more than one supplier may be combined for performance comparisons in one of the many supplier rating schemes, but that is a separate subject.

This section is limited primarily to the use of supplier data to verify conformance for acceptance of purchased material. References here to the inspection include test activities, where applicable. Similarly, references to equipment and process encompass those required by manufacturing and quality.

Optimum benefits are derived when data are reviewed in a timely manner. Depending on the phase of development or production, review may take place at the supplier's or customer's facility. Many mathematical models exist for data analysis at various stages of production. During the preproduction or development phase, data may be used to review available process capabilities, including manufacturing and inspection measuring equipment. Assessments of product and equipment design, and the adequacy of quality assurance functions, often are made through data review in the early stages of production.

Experienced quality management will arrange for the analysis of specific supplier data from the first production units. Timely review of first-lot data is essential when the production situation dictates limited expenditures. This investment in supplier quality assurance often becomes critical in terms of quality and schedule assurance.

First production unit data review will highlight any corrections that may be necessary before full production. Depending on the type of material and its end use, supplier data may be used in lieu of customer inspection and tests.

One such alternative involves calculating the degree of correlation between supplier and customer testing. Normally, the customer must perform comprehensive testing on initial receipt to determine if the material conforms to contractual specifications. It should be understood that inspection costs are included in product prices so the customer already is paying for material in the supplier's inspection. Therefore, a purchase order requirement for the supplier to furnish specified inspection data should not be a significant additional cost.

With the supplier's data in hand, plus his or her own inspection information, the customer can perform a correlation analysis to determine the relation between in-house tests and the supplier's plant inspection. If the correlation is satisfactory, subsequent receipts may be accepted upon a verification-type review of the supplier's inspection data. This plan may be augmented by testing selected parameters on each receipt. Other modifications may require complete customer testing periodically to ensure a continuing correlation. The correlation study method can be readily applied to metals, raw material, and mechanical piecepart-type products.

Another alternative is to arrange for evaluation and approval of the supplier's inspection equipment and associated calibration controls. This method is particularly appropriate for control and acceptance of electronic/electrical components. Approval of the supplier's equipment is given on a specific basis defined in customer standards. As with all methods using supplier data, adequate measures must be applied contractually to control any changes or modifications affecting equipment, standards, or processes after they have been approved. Additionally, all or selected parameters may be verified on the initial receipt, usually as part of the customer's formal qualification approval. Selected parameters may be tested periodically by the customer to maintain a satisfactory confidence level of the continuing verification. Again, depending on the degree of the high-reliability requirements, correlation studies can be included in this alternative.

For purchased material not requiring critical high reliability, supplier data may be used without performing correlation studies, equipment approvals, or verification testing. The basis for this judgment may be the quality history of previous receipts, the quality of similar material, and the supplier's established reputation within the industry or a cost-type measure of next assembly failures.

The bottom line on controlled use of supplier data is to be cost effective, primarily by eliminating redundant inspection equipment and associated receiving inspection operations.

Nonconforming Product

After inspection, a supplier product may be reported as nonconforming to one or more of the established standards: form and appearance, material, fit and dimensional characteristics, or function. The inspection report must then be reviewed to determine if the product can be used and what corrective actions are required. Acceptance will depend on whether the product can be modified to perform its intended function without risk to user and whether the added cost of the modifications or corrections is acceptable. Other questions will need answers: Will the corrective actions be carried out at the supplier plant or possibly in the customer's operation? Does the variation appear to be repetitive or an isolated case?

Key aids in this analysis are inspection history sheets, the latest supplier survey, the histogram of the defect, the repeatability of the inspection or testing method, the type and completeness of the qualification test or proof sample, and knowledge of the specific process that created the discrepancy. An excellent vehicle for carrying out the analysis is a materials review board (MRB) with representatives from the functions responsible for the item. This review, however, is effective only if a complete history can be presented to the board by the inspection supervisor or the quality engineer.

If it is determined that the supplier is at fault, the purchasing department should arrange a meeting with the supplier, or relay the information via a cover letter plus a copy of the report and corrective action request. A decision on the most effective method of repair usually is made by the MRB. Visits to the supplier in connection with the MRB action may be made by purchasing, the quality engineer, and, if necessary, other engineering functions (such as product design, tool design, and manufacturing engineering). If the problem is recurrent and/or very serious, plant management or a higher representative also should be invited.

Before visiting the supplier's plant, the adequacy of in-house inspection procedures and the way they are being carried out should be checked and verified. When visiting the supplier's plant, the customer should take along all current data, prior history, and, if applicable, analysis of the most likely cause of the problem. Concluding the fixed tooling needs repair or that a design change is required will have different backup than a recommendation to increase or improve detectability.

Supplier Total Performance Evaluation

The purpose of performance evaluation is to permit both the supplier and customer to react quickly to unfavorable trends affecting product quality, product availability, and mutual profitability. A supplier's performance can be evaluated in many ways, but quality, delivery, and cost must all be considered if the measure of supplier performance is to be comprehensive. It is important to measure the conformance of a specific part or lot, but the supplier's past performance must also be measured so that special action may be taken if problems are repetitive.

With increased emphasis on quality cost, both the supplier and customer must be aware of the economic consequences of a nonconforming product. To maintain an effective quality program, even a small company must recognize its quality costs. The emphasis in today's quality program is prevention. Effective quality planning must be done to optimize quality costs. It has often been said that "Hindsight has 20/20 vision whereas foresight is very seldom good." Taking advantage of all available information can help identify potential problems.

Measuring the elements of quality, delivery, and cost constitute a form of supplier rating based on objective information. Because no single guideline can define a workable system for everyone, a rating program must be developed and implemented by each organization.

All companies, regardless of size, accumulate much of the information required to perform a complete supplier analysis. A major problem, however, is retrieval. Having records in a computer is an advantage if the information is accessible in a usable format. For discussion purposes, the quality factor will be considered as the percent defective. The most readily available information is based on the relation of rejections to receipts. If actual usage quantities are available for this factor, all the better.

The units of measure must be consistent with those received whether they are in pieces, pounds, gallons, meters, and so forth. No considerations are given for theoretical percent defective based on a sample, because a lot rejected is unavailable to production and generally would be returned to the supplier, reworked, repaired, or used as is. In another sense, this is comparing the quantity of product requiring special action to that which was accepted or processed through normal procedures.

In the quest for simplicity, no attempt is made to weigh or adjust the numbers based on formulas or computations as percent defective is more a measure of nuisance than anything else. As an example, a supplier may have a 40 percent reject rate, but if the total value of the product rejected is only $20, no one gets excited and little if any action can be economically justified.

The most universally understood unit of measure is the dollar and the cost factor of supplier performance evaluation is the most effective measure of supplier performance. When purchasing advises a supplier that $1500 worth of a product has been rejected, it has far greater impact than saying a lot is 7 percent defective.

All manufacturing operations work to a budget and quality costs such as scrap and rework generally are budget items closely monitored by management. Where purchased material is involved, the purchasing department usually is charged for the rejected material and it is that department's responsibility to ensure that nonconforming product is repaired or replaced, and that the defect costs are recovered.

Ideally, the customer should be able to collect and report all defect costs (such as rework and repair) and establish the cost of a product at the time of rejection. It is conceivable to also include costs of extra inspection, testing, engineering, and so forth. Many companies operate on a standard cost system and have values assigned for the various stages of product completion. Rework or repair costs usually are accumulated through a shop labor reporting system.

Using total defect cost data, the customer can evaluate the distribution and rank suppliers in terms of defect cost contribution. In this way, the reasons for the defect costs can be determined and the responsible suppliers directed toward corrective action. The information gained through this program also helps in quality planning so that preventive measures may be incorporated in future quality requirements.

Again, this means dealing with factual values—dollars charged to a rejection. This can be especially meaningful when dealing with a relatively inexpensive product that can create defect costs far in excess of its purchase price. It is not uncommon in some industries to find costs of several hundred dollars to remove and replace a part that may only cost a dollar or two. In this situation, a 5 percent reject rate of some $2 parts could cost the customer over $1000 in labor to remove and replace five pieces from a 100-piece lot. When only $10 is involved, few persons become interested, but increase the cost to the actual $1000 and management of both companies undoubtedly will seek immediate corrective action.

It doesn't take many such illustrations to point out problem areas where substantial savings can be made for both the customer and supplier. If neither the supplier nor the customer has an effective form of quality cost tracking, it is doubtful that the impact created by defective product will be realized until the year-end financial statement is reviewed. Then profits will be far less than anticipated.

When defect cost information is available, perhaps the most significant indicator of supplier performance is the relationship of defect cost to the purchase cost of the product. Depending on the complexity of the customer's defect cost reporting system, the evaluation may be summarized as comparison within commodity, by part number, total by supplier, and so forth. Again, it must be stressed that objective data are recommended without resort to formulas, weighting, or other mathematical manipulations.

When objective quality cost information is available to the customer's purchasing department, it can effectively use the information when analyzing jobs for potential resourcing and for placement of new jobs. A supplier with the lowest quoted price may not present lowest overall cost to customer when defect costs are considered. The customer's purchasing department can improve its source selection by combining the defect cost potential with the quoted price. Paying more than the lowest bid may be justified to achieve a lower total cost.

The last element of supplier performance evaluation is delivery, or a measure of the supplier's ability to react to schedules. This aids a purchasing department in reviewing past performance. Although expeditors may be aware of specific jobs, it is important to follow the overall trend of a supplier's delivery performance so that special action may be initiated for unsatisfactory performance.

In summary, supplier performance evaluation is essential to measure the effectiveness of the supplier's quality program. Analyzing data obtained from a review of the supplier's past performance identifies problem areas and permits planning action to prevent recurrence of the reported problems.

How to Establish Effective Quality Control for the Small Supplier

Chapter 14

Key words: independent laboratories, in-process inspection, interpreting product requirements, measurement assurance, planning, quality procedures, source inspection.

Summary
- Organization
- Planning
- Certification of personnel and equipment
- Testing, inspection, and measurement
- Handling nonconforming material

In today's world of consumer affairs, with product liability and an endless listing of government and industry regulations, the small business must develop a quality control system that satisfies customer requirements and remains cost effective. To this end, the small business manager must rely heavily on customer requirements. Initial contacts with potential customers should aim at understanding these requirements and regulations.

For the small business, the basic understanding of quality control has been less critical than in major industry. However, the division between commercial and military procurement that historically dictated separate control by product line has changed rapidly. Consumer actions in the private sector now require quality system control equal to, if not exceeding, military procurement.

The small business is therefore faced with required product controls that demand additional expenditures. To keep these expenditures in check, the small business manager must develop a quality program that meets customer requirements while controlling and maintaining product conformance. Certain assumptions have been made in this chapter. With due respect to the reader, it is assumed that the reader is primarily concerned with the technical and financial aspects of the business and has little knowledge of the quality control function. Thus, the quality professional's jargon has been reduced to a bare necessity. It also has been assumed that there is a business in place, producing a product that a quality organization can support. This chapter (authored by experienced quality professionals) is intended to serve as a useful guide in establishing an effective quality control system. However, it has not been designed as a do-it-yourself guide as it does not contain the scope or depth required to formulate a professional quality organization.

Organization

An owner of a small business stated, "I would like to establish a quality control organization, but where do I start?" That's a reasonable question, but extremely difficult to answer because there are no concise answers.

First, the owner must understand the primary objective of quality control. Many volumes have been written on this subject and to reduce it to a single statement may seem presumptuous, but an attempt follows:

Quality control is that effort applied to assure the end product/service meets its intended requirements and achieves consumer's satisfaction.

In a well-designed product, requirements and customer satisfaction should be synonymous. As products and requirements have many variations, so must quality control. Each organization must meet the requirements of the customer and the business. The objective is to apply only the required effort to economically control the end product or service. To illustrate this point let us take an authentic situation involving a Chicago plastic manufacturer. The manufacturer's primary business was producing containers for major pharmaceutical firms under the rigid requirements of the Food and Drug Administration. Taking advantage of his expertise, he also manufactured plastic flower pots. This was done on an automatic molding machine that ran 24 hours a day. The only attendance given the machine was to fill the hopper periodically with raw material. On the container line he employed a complement of trained quality personnel. Why?

In the first situation, rejection would impose severe dollar losses, invoke the customer's displeasure due to production line delays, and result in probable loss of future business. On the flower pot line, his quality control consisted of a visual check by the employee who filled the hopper to ensure that the pots were whole and free of cracks. Why? A malfunction of the machine could be easily detected visually and the parts not shipped. He did not have a customer dependent on the product. Furthermore, unacceptable material could be ground up and recycled. The manufacturer would be hard pressed to justify more than a few dollars a day devoted to quality control on the flower pot line. This may be a unique situation that covers the extreme ends of the spectrum, but it illustrates the need for examining the requirements and evaluating the penalties of failure. Most applications are not as simple as the preceding example and require knowledgeable management decisions.

Quality control has developed in a pattern because of the requirements imposed at the various stages of industrial growth of an individual organization. If quality control grew in this pattern, then perhaps quality organizations should grow in the same progression.

In the days of a single-person shop with apprentices, inspection was nonexistent, except for a cursory review by the master journeyman. Inspection came into being with the multiperson shop and was intensified with the high-volume production line when operators performed a single operation.

The first addition to inspection came during World War I. The U.S. Navy discovered that shells from one manufacturer would fit a gun breech and shells from another would not fit. Exhaustive investigation revealed that the equipment used by the gun manufacturer and both shell manufacturers did not give identical results. It was only by luck that one shell fit. The requirement for calibration came from this experience.

Between World War I and World War II, the significant change was the introduction of statistical sampling and statistical process controls. These were necessitated by high-volume production making 100 percent inspection costly, if not impossible. During World War II and into the 1960s the industrial/military complex came into existence. Many small businesses found themselves facing a myriad of complex requirements, some of which were unnecessary. They passed on these rigid requirements to suppliers' plants. Quality organization in prime contractors flourished. As in any expanding market, many nonprofessionals did a great deal to tarnish the quality control image. The saving grace was the recognition that quality control be structured to be a contributing member of the management team.

One measure of success or failure of a quality system is quality costs. In simple terms, it recognized inspection as the backbone of quality. The cost of scrap, rework, reinspection, and customer rejections are accumulated and analyzed as to the cause. By taking corrective action to determine cause and eliminate this cost, these dollars can be saved. Additionally, by careful preplanning as to the complete understanding of requirements, these rejections can be minimized and productivity will increase as cost decreases.

Today's high-technology products often make it impossible to detect failures until the final test. The cost at this stage of manufacture is prohibitive and the replacement cycle unacceptable. Quality again has adapted to the changing environment with a trend toward controlling the process. Process control (be it tooling, pressure, temperature, speed, feed, fixtures, process, or chemical solutions) must be maintained at optimum values to significantly improve the chances of final acceptance.

Inspection and calibration are essential elements of a system that generates information that is fed back and used to maintain a process that yields good products. This is quality control. From this point, the small business must make its own decisions. What is the extra cost of rejected material including rework, reinspection, scrap, and cost of customer complaints? Can the business come out ahead by saving more money than is spent on an effective quality control system?

Other considerations are customer satisfaction, degree of technology, company image, program delays, and their impact on future business. Only an astute manager can make this evaluation, as these considerations have nebulous values. It is incumbent for the manager to make a flowchart of the business, identify the strong and weak areas, place inspection in the most critical areas, assign responsibilities, and rearrange or hire personnel as required.

The small business must make a total commitment to quality. It must guard against the natural impulse to favor shipments and monthly billing at the expense of a quality product. Quality must be given management support to accomplish its objectives.

Above all, the small business should be aware that a properly managed quality control organization will contribute to the company's profits and project a favorable quality image to the customer.

Interpreting and Reviewing Product Requirements

Interpreting and reviewing product requirements when accepting a purchase order is primarily the responsibility of sales and marketing. Product requirements can be explicit, implicit, or both. Explicit requirements are readily apparent in customer drawings, specifications, inspection procedures, technically descriptive letters, and requests for quotations. Implicit requirements are in undefined areas and usually are difficult to ferret out.

Review of explicit requirements starts with information supplied with the quotation request, which generally supplies either a number or a description as a cornerstone for building details of the requirements. The most important blocks in constructing the total requirements picture are the customer's drawings and specifications for products to be supplied. Similarly, technical descriptions and/or specifications are keys to the services to be performed.

The supplier must review the drawing for tolerance limits, conflicts, and buildups that might affect assembly. The supplier should examine requirements and determine whether the dimensional reference surfaces or baselines are clearly defined and adaptable to the processes. Wherever necessary, the supplier should prepare recommendations for changing the dimensioning methods and tolerances, and improving clarity. The supplier must make sure that material requirements are fully defined, as well as physical conditions (such as hardness, finish, and conductivity). Information might be contained in references such as specifications, other drawings, and gages. The supplier must determine the type of verification or certification required for completed work.

The supplier should analyze the specifications to see whether the item is to be built to performance specifications with dimensions and materials as a reference, or to the dimensions and materials with performance as a reference. One possible combination is to supply the item within several material and dimensional constraints and a set of performance requirements.

In addition, the supplier has to determine what type of testing is required by the customer to prove conformance with the specification. Is the testing of both design qualification and production lot-by-lot? The supplier must know how to conduct the tests and have the appropriate equipment and people or the ability to use a qualified outside laboratory. If the customer is supplying test equipment or gages, the supplier should review the operating procedure as well as calibration methods and potential drifts or wear.

The customer's inspection procedure is a guide to the significant dimensions and performance requirements. For example, this may lead the supplier to assure that the method of manufacture and drawing dimensions are compatible. If not, the supplier must be sure that there won't be a conflict or recommend a change in inspection methods. The request for quotation should be read carefully for such items as marking, packaging, shipping instructions, special quality requirements, and delivery schedules. At this point the supplier should be able to determine if it is capable of handling the contract. If the supplier is supplying a service, the request should be reviewed for conflicting or incomplete requirements, and for the method of determining satisfactory fulfillment of the requirements. This is the supplier's opportunity to recommend standard procedures, materials, and packaging.

Quality Manual

A quality manual is a compilation of the company policies and procedures that implement the quality policy established by the senior company executive. It is the documented statement of the quality standards the company has established for its product and employees. The quality manual is a companion document to similar manuals published by engineering, manufacturing, or procurement and, as such, should be comparable in structure and depth. The manual must be a living document. It is the guide to day-to-day practices.

The quality manual should be prefaced with a written statement by the chief executive establishing the company's quality policy and philosophies. The statement should be explicit about how the company will guarantee and support the integrity of its product or services. This statement by the chief executive is essential and establishes the quality program and a system to monitor the achievement of the stated goals. The quality manual provides several important elements for the conduct of business.

- Makes both the customer and employee aware of the company's quality philosophy, standards, and goals
- Provides a documented baseline for measuring the effectiveness of the quality programs
- Serves as the basis from which audits are performed to assure compliance to the company's quality objectives and methods
- Provides written instructions and guidance to assure repeatability, uniformity, and consistency in application of work elements and process standards
- Establishes the responsibilities of each department

The size and complexity of the manual depends on the organization's operational needs. Several factors must be considered.

- Number of employees and their skill levels
- Complexity of the manufacturing processes required to produce the product or service
- End use of the product and extent of internal controls necessary to assure customer satisfaction
- Requirements of any regulatory agency involved with the particular industry

The quality manual should provide the policy statement, procedures, work instructions, and process specifications as applicable. In small, less complex operations, these elements may be contained in a single document. In larger, more complex organizations, it may be necessary to divide the elements into separate documents or manuals for effective use.

Quality policy–Here the company's quality policy and objectives are described narratively. It may be necessary to describe operating policy in several functional areas, such as warranty claims, correction action, design review, subcontracting, process control, and so forth. It also may describe how decisions are to be made regarding conformance and suitability of product or services.

Quality procedures–These documents define responsibility and authority for implementing the quality program. They outline the information and work flow and provide a generalized how to series of instructions.

Work instructions–In some cases, it is necessary to provide step-by-step instructions for specific activities such as plating, heat treating, wire bonding, and completing test reports. It is beneficial to separate this type of instruction from the more generalized procedures already described. In this case, a separate package of detailed work instructions can be made available to the work force.

Process specifications–These technical documents provide for control of operations where verification of the end result is not practical under ordinary inspection techniques. Some examples are heat treating, chemical formulation, aging/curing, plating, impregnation, and nondestructive examination.

The format of the quality procedures and work instructions can be shaped to the company's desires and needs. The documents, however, should identify the subject, purpose, scope, method or procedures and responsibilities. The quality manual should be divided into sections based either on functional or organizational areas. Dividing the manual according to function permits compiling all directives pertaining to a particular operation into a single section. Dividing the manual on an organizational basis permits compiling all directives pertaining to a specific department into a single section. In either method, all organizations responsible for achieving the objectives of the directive must be identified and their participation clearly outlined. The contents of the manual should be coordinated with all departments to ensure agreement and understanding.

The procedures, work instructions,and so forth, should be numbered to assure control and identification. In a typical industrial application, a quality manual's table of contents may include the following:

- Preface
- Introduction
- Company quality policy
  —Statement of quality objectives
  —Organizational chart
  —Description of manual or instructions for use
- Index or Table of Contents
- Section 1 Configuration Control
  —1.01 Product configuration control
  —1.02 Documentation control
  —1.03 Service bulletins
  —1.04 Government conformity inspection
- Section 2 Receiving Inspection
  —2.01 Receiving inspection—raw material
  —2.02 Receiving inspection—high-value material
  —2.03 Receiving inspection—hazardous/toxic material
  —2.04 Identification of incoming material
- Section 3 Material Storage and Release
- Section 4 Inspection Marking
- Section 5 (and so on)

Additional subjects to be considered include

- Purchase order review
- Control of suppliers and subcontractors
- In-process inspection
- Assembly inspection
- Final inspection and test
- Control of nonconforming material
- Tool and gage control
- Packaging and shipping
- Control of special processes
- Training and skill certification
- Sampling inspection
- Quality system audits

The quality manager should establish a cycle periodically reviewing the manual to ensure its applicability and to purge unnecessary or obsolete instructions. The table of contents should carry the date of the latest revision. Copies of the manual should be distributed to everyone who needs it to perform their duties and to those who should be aware of its contents. A distribution list should record the copy number of the manual provided to each person. This way changes, revisions, and new publications can be sent periodically to all appropriate individuals. The manual holder will be responsible for updating the manual. Unused manuals should be returned to the quality assurance organization.

Under some conditions, a customer or regulatory agency may request a copy of the manual. A determination must be made whether the issue is on a one-time, uncontrolled basis whereby no updating material will be furnished, or on a controlled basis that requires forwarding new releases and modifications. In the latter instance, the manual holder is responsible for keeping the manual up-to-date.

The quality manual serves as the baseline for the audit, both internally and by customers and regulatory agencies. It must reflect the methods actually being used. Either the methods conform to the manual or changes are made to make them conform.

Overall, a quality manual is an instruction to company personnel on how to perform in a uniform and consistent manner. This avoids confusion and mistakes. To achieve this objective, a quality manual should be as simple as possible.

Inspection

Major purchase orders may require a plan for quality control that begins with preproduction activities and extends through full production. A quality plan should include measures for defect prevention and provide controls for processes and product.

Inspection instructions must outline, in general sequences, the process to be followed and the minimum inspection requirements.

The instructions provide a uniform method for performing inspection and tests, and reporting results. Drawings, specifications, and related manufacturing instructions must be reviewed to prepare inspection inscriptions. Therefore, an ongoing evaluation for clarity, completeness, and accuracy should be made for all documentation. Potential manufacturing and inspection problems must be identified at the preproduction stage. This includes equipment, personnel capability, and any special requirements or controls.

The instructions must define, by part number, the characteristics to be inspected and the sampling plan, equipment, and method to be applied. The basic information can be found in drawings and specifications, manufacturing instructions, equipment operating instructions, and schedules. Considerations must include functional requirements, reliability, quality history of this or similar products, and quality costs.

The quality plan also must consider the supplier's requirements: test data, material analysis, certifications, and special process approvals. These requirements must be included in the purchase order so that necessary documentation of inspections and tests may be obtained contractually and used as objective evidence for acceptance. Inspection instructions require a review of the referenced drawings, specifications, and other documents to verify that the instructions are compatible with the authorized product definition.

Sampling plans provide for effective and economical inspection. Although economical, sampling does provide a degree of risk to both the producer and consumer.

A commonly used reference, complete with sampling tables, is MIL-STD-105E issued by the Department of Defense. MIL-STD-105E provides sampling plans for various levels of protection depending on the criticalness of the dimension.

In addition, many companies define critical, major, and minor defects on their drawings using symbols. Many impose quality requirements for critical defects such as 100 percent inspection for conformance to specification, adequate documentation, and part identification that is traceable to inspection reports. Often, the customer will dictate the sampling level or require approval of the plan selected by the supplier. Use of statistical or plotted sampling can reduce expenses. Inspection results can be tabulated or plotted in a manner that allows periodic reviews to identify trends and problem areas.

Consideration should be given to the use of inspection stamps to identify final acceptance, in-process acceptance, and defective material. Obviously, the issuance and use of inspection stamps must be formally controlled. In some cases, signatures, dates, and the use of specific inks are required on final inspection documents.

Receiving Inspection

For manufacturing operations, the inspection function normally is divided into receiving inspection, in-process inspection, and final inspection. Receiving inspection requirements are determined by functional considerations, operating costs, and applicable specifications. The requirements are interrelated and may be affected by inventory, flow time, and seller warranties.

Functional considerations include the need to verify selected measurements and tests prior to assembly operations; for example, to ensure that bar stock is a specified stainless steel prior to investing costly machining operations, to ensure that an inexpensive component is performing within specified limits before installing into a costly assembly, or to ensure that a costly purchased product conforms to specified requirements within warranty limitations. In short, ordinary good judgment should determine the amount of receiving inspection required for functional considerations. Good judgment, however, must be based on facts.

Operating costs determine whether to verify the conformance of purchased material by performing receiving inspection or by applying next assembly measurements. For example, when there is little or no flow time through an inventory, incoming material may be checked initially only for count, shipping damage, and identification. Controls then can be applied to measure the product for conformance in conjunction with next assembly inspection and/or test. The decision to perform receiving inspection at next assembly must be weighed against the potential cost of processing rejected materials at that stage as well as warranty time limitations. This alternative normally would be advisable when historical data indicate that the supplier can be relied on to provide acceptable material with a minimum of rejections

Customers may specify the degree of receiving inspection to be applied. This is common practice among large prime contractors in government procurement. These requirements should be analyzed for abnormal costs prior to submitting a price quotation. For example, requirements to test all raw and fabricated material and to verify raw material certifications periodically by independent testing laboratories can significantly affect flow times and operating expenses.

The receiving function should have a system for checking in materials on receipt. This should include examining the material for shipping damage, verifying the count, and checking for the presence of certification or test data, shipping document identification, and lot control information.

The writing and issuance of inspection instructions should be controlled sufficiently to define purchase order requirements including applicable specifications, inspection equipment, sampling plans (if applicable), and material control requirements.

Receiving inspection must be able to withhold acceptance of material until it verifies that required certifications, specifications, and specified parameters are conforming. Inspection results should be documented; made available to appropriate purchasing, engineering, and quality personnel; and maintained in a retrievable file. Source inspection may be substituted for receiving inspection by the customer when it is economical, auch as (1) where duplication of costly inspection or test fixtures or equipment can be eliminated, (2) where direct shipment to field site is advisable, or (3) where shipping costs would make the return of large and bulky items expensive.

Nonconforming material must be identified, segregated, and held for disposition. The buyer should advise the supplier of rejected material and be responsible for obtaining corrective actions. Follow-up measures should be applied by the quality assurance function.

In-process Inspection

In-process inspection can be used in certain operations to provide early detection of processes producing nonconforming products. Similiar to receiving inspection, the requirements for in-process inspection are determined by the interrelations of functional considerations, operating costs, and customer specifications. Functional considerations primarily involve parameters that must conform to specification before they are sealed or otherwise covered up by a subsequent operation. Failure costs (in-house and customer) must be weighed against the cost of in-process inspection. Reliability, consumer acceptance (reputation), truth in advertising, and the potential for liability suits resulting from latent defects must be included in the determinations.

In-process inspection frequently involves a first-article inspection before a production run is approved. This verifies that the operator, machine, and associated setup are capable of producing acceptable products. As with other specified inspection, documentation should be available for review when required.

Final Inspection

Final inspection is the last opportunity before shipment to assure that the product conforms to customer requirements. The extent of inspection should depend on the amount of receiving and in-process inspection already applied, complexity, shop defect levels, customer use information, and the potential for liability suits.

Some customers specify the level of inspection and test required, ranging from sampling to 100 percent. Test results and record maintenance also may be specified. Inspection records should include the quantity received, lot and/or serial number, number accepted, number defective, nature of defects, date, and inspector identification. Records should be maintained in such a manner that retrieval and review can be performed readily upon receipt of any authorized request. Such records, reflecting reasonable quality control practices, can be extremely important in cases of a product failure causing an accident, or otherwise involving large sums of money.

It is good practice to identify and segregate nonconforming material. Nonconforming material subjected to repair or rework must be resubmitted to inspection for acceptance. Authorizations for shipping nonconforming material must be well documented and controlled. When possible, units accepted at final inspection should bear an inspection stamp (or marking) denoting acceptance and identifying the inspector.

Management should provide procedures that describe receiving, in-process, and final inspection requirements, including the assignment of specific responsibilities. All functions should be audited periodically by a representative of quality management for conformance to policies and procedures. This can be performed in a constructive manner, and the results can be of mutual benefit to the company, customers, suppliers, and the profit margin.

A checklist of items to be considered for all inspection operations follows:

- Product definition (adequately specified and control assured for making changes)
- Inspection instructions
- Adequate (size and segregation) area for products in work, to be worked, accepted, rejected, and hold
- Adequate work benches [lighting, environmental controls, Occupational Safety and Health Administration (OSHA) requirements]
- Current calibration of acceptance equipment
- Adequate handling equipment
- Clean work area
- Adequate supervision (with identified authority and responsibilities)
- Trained inspection personnel
- Flow time controls through inspection
- Current product status (in work, to be worked, and hold)
- Record of inspection results
- Timely measurements
- Identification of accepted material

- Identification and segregation of nonconforming material
- Material certifications (as required)
- Identification of inspector (and qualification, as required)

Independent Laboratories for Testing and Evaluation

Many small business firms require, on an occasional or continuous basis, the services of a laboratory for testing purposes. The cost of a test laboratory, in terms of capital cost for facilities and equipment plus operating costs, may be prohibitive. Therefore, a business logically might choose to purchase testing services from an independent laboratory.

After a business has determined the type and frequency of the testing services it requires, it should find sources capable of fulfilling the requirements. As in any subcontract activity, a small business should attempt to locate two or more qualified sources. Adequate timely test or evaluation reports may be critical to a company meeting commitments to its own customers; consequently, reliance on only one source of testing services may be inadequate. An initial list of firms having the required capability may be obtained by

- Reviewing trade indexes or trade journals
- Discussing with colleagues in industry, government, or academia
- Contacting trade associations such as the American Council of Independent Laboratories, Inc., 1725 K Street NW, Washington, DC 20006; or Canadian Testing Association, Box 13033, Kanata Postal Station, Ottawa, Ontario, Canada K2K 1X3
- Reviewing telephone directories
- Contacting sources already approved by the customer

After the potential source list is prepared, some laboratories may be eliminated because of geographic location or other reasons. All remaining firms should then be contacted to determine if they are interested in providing the needed service. At this time the customer should make it clearly understood that the laboratory's facilities will be evaluated from a technical and managerial viewpoint.

The next step is to evaluate the selected laboratories. The following items aid in performing a meaningful evaluation.

- A checklist of equipment required to conduct the tests
- Copies of applicable standards and methods
- A list of additional requirements for review and/or observation
  —Sample identification and control/disposal
  —Test reports, format
  —Qualifications of testing personnel
  —Security of samples and/or test reports
  —Ownership of firm
  —Receiving and shipping
  —Laboratory capacity (where timeliness of tests is critical)
  —Laboratory quality control procedures
  —Test equipment calibration procedures and records
  —Traceability to national standards

(Evaluating a testing laboratory is similar to evaluating suppliers. See chapter 13.)

Upon completion of the evaluation, the contractor may wish to invite the firms to visit the business location. This will help laboratory personnel understand the requirements from both a technical and a business viewpoint.

Two of the standard methods of billing used by testing laboratories are flat rate for standard tests and hourly rate for equipment and personnel. Both methods normally are negotiable subject to volume, and so forth. Once a laboratory has conducted the required tests a number of times at an hourly rate, it may be willing to negotiate a standard cost per test.

Because critical decisions will be based on the laboratory test results, confidence in a laboratory's capability to provide accurate test results is imperative. This may be achieved by

- Periodic visits and/or reviews of test results with laboratory personnel and management
- Use of an audit sample. This is a sample where one portion is sent to another qualified test laboratory (referee) and one portion to the laboratory being audited. There will be some variation in test results from laboratory to laboratory or sample to sample; however, if the results from two laboratories are widely divergent the problem may be resolved by
  —Reviewing test methods with both firms
  —Discussing test results with both firms independently, or together
  —Where feasible, it is advisable to retain an archive sample that is fully representative of the sample submitted for tests.

Inspection, Measurement, and Test Equipment

Accurate inspections and tests depend on the calibration and control of all inspection and test equipment, and on the proper maintenance of all measuring instruments, tools, fixtures, gages, and measurement standards. A calibration and control program should provide for

- Selection of appropriate standards and measuring equipment
- Periodic documented calibration
- Identification of equipment
- Training and qualifications of personnel
- Documented calibration procedures
- Records of calibration and historical data
- Tool and gage control
- Maintenance, modification, storage, and handling of equipment

Equipment selected for inspection and measurement should have adequate accuracy, stability, and range for the intended use. When several different types of equipment can perform a specific measuring function adequately, selection should be based on availability, equipment history (including repair work), initial cost, maintenance costs, and the manufacturer's service.

Whenever practical, equipment should have a rated accuracy of about 10 percent of the tolerance being measured. Similarly, standards used to calibrate measuring equipment and instruments should have appropriate capability. As a general rule, and within state-of-the-art or economic limitations, the standards of measurement systems used should have a tolerance no greater than 10 percent of the allowable tolerance of the equipment being calibrated.

Through the proper selection of standards of appropriately higher accuracy levels, the equipment should be maintained in a state of calibration with the measurement of parameters traceable to the National Institute of Standards and Technology, or other acceptable levels of reference.

Equipment should be calibrated at regular intervals on the basis of stability, purpose, degree of usage, accuracy requirements, standard practices, and operating history. There can be no rigid formula for the frequency of calibration because so many factors come into play; however, the following partial list of basic inspection instruments and test equipment, initially, may have the calibration intervals shown.

Equipment	Calibration frequency
Digital indicators	Quarterly
Digital voltmeters	Monthly
Micrometer	Quarterly (plus each time before use)
Optical comparators	Annually
Pressure gages	Semiannually
Scales	Semiannually
Torque wrenches	Quarterly
Voltmeters	Quarterly

To ensure required accuracy, calibration intervals should be monitored continuously and lengthened or shortened according to the results of preceding calibrations recorded by the calibration agency. If a gage is not used for an extended period, the calibration cost could be avoided by placing it out of service in a controlled access area. The gage then needs to be calibrated only when it is returned to service.

Records on all equipment should denote location and calibration status. The records should contain identification information, calibration maintenance history, calibration status, calibration interval, and repair history. The records and historic information are useful in determining future recall requirements of the equipment.

All equipment should carry labels, seals, or tags, identifying serviceability and calibration status. When equipment use is meant to be limited, it should be identified accordingly. When necessary, seals should be used to ensure that instrument calibration will not be disturbed. When an instrument is too small to be tagged or labeled, its container or storage box should be appropriately identified.

Tools, gages, jigs, fixtures, and production tooling that control or measure dimensions, contours, or locations affecting quality characteristics should be checked for accuracy prior to use. Periodic check and recalibration should be made at predetermined intervals to ensure continued accuracy.

Periodic audits should assure compliance with, and effective implementation of, procedures established for calibration and control of equipment. The surveillance should verify that

- Applicable procedures are available and being used
- Calibration personnel are qualified
- Records and data are being maintained
- Proper equipment is being used
- Appropriate labels, seals, and tags, are attached to equipment
- Calibration dates are being adhered to in a timely manner

Additional information on calibration program implementation appears in military standard MIL-STD-45662, *Calibration System Requirements.*

Frequently Used Calibration Terms and Definitions

Accuracy–The degree of agreement of the measurement with the true value of that parameter. The difference between the measured and the true value is defined as error.

Calibration–The comparison of an instrument or equipment to a measurement standard of known accuracy, to detect, correlate, report, and adjust, as required, any deviation from the standard.

Precision–The ability of an instrument to repeat the same reading when making the same measurement in the same manner and under identical conditions.

Preventive maintenance–The service, cleaning, lubrication of parts, alignment, adjustment, functional test, repair, modification, and overhaul, as required, to ensure there is no deterioration of equipment performance.

Reliability–The susceptibility of a measurement device with a visual display to having its indications converted to a meaningful number, also expressed as the legibility of a visual display, normally expressed as the minimum measure and increment that can be discriminated in the terms of the display.

Resolution–The smallest change in input necessary to produce the smallest detectable change in output of the instrument under test.

Sensitivity–The ability of a measuring device to detect small differences in a quantity being measured.

Standard–An item designated as an authorized measurement reference and used to calibrate other standards or measuring and test equipment.

Documentation and Traceability

A manufacturer is accountable for the product quality of items delivered to its distributor and ultimately, to the end user. Consequently, it also is responsible for the quality of materials and components procured from suppliers and subcontractors, and incorporated into the product. Increasing emphasis on product liability and growing public pressure is forcing manufacturers to recall and correct defective products that could endanger consumers.

Customers are requiring assurance that the products they buy are safe to use and will perform to expectations. Various regulatory commissions are directing that critical components have documented certifications that are traceable from inception through all fabrication phases to ultimate distribution. Critical components are items (such as metals, chemicals, and finished assemblies) whose defect or failure would likely result in hazardous or unsafe conditions for individuals using, maintaining, or depending on the product, or whose defect is likely to prevent performance of a major end item (such as a ship, aircraft, safety equipment, or hospital unit). Products that require certifications cross over almost every industry: metals, chemicals, petroleums, food, drugs, textiles, lumber, and rubber compounds. The list is endless.

For quality assurance purposes, a certification of compliance is

A document signed by an authorized party affirming that the supplier of a product or service has met the requirements of the relevant specifications, contract, or regulation. (Comment: Compliance can pertain to a broad spectrum of requirements which may include procedural, conformance, timely deliver, reliability, or other elements.)[1]

For effective supplier control, the definition can be expanded to

A statement of fact pertaining to the quality of products or services, which is based on observations, measurements, or tests that can be fully verified. It is evidence that is expressed in terms of specific quality requirements or characteristics, which are identified in drawings, specifications, and other documents that describe the item process or procedure.

Certification or objective quality evidence (OQE) can be looked upon as protection. OQE is proof to the customer that the product has been manufactured and tested to specifications. In some instances, OQE is the basis on which regulatory agencies issue a license for the product's sale and use. In the event of product liability claims, OQE may be the basis for substantiating that the product met all the material and design criteria. Purchase orders for critical items usually specify objective data to be furnished with the product. In many instances, the documents and data are as essential as the hardware itself. Without the documentation, materials and hardware components cannot be incorporated into assemblies or placed into service. Many operating activities will not accept materials or authorize payment when documentation is missing, incomplete, or in error. Incoming materials usually are rejected or held until documentation problems are resolved.

In many instances, a simple part is the same as or similar to a component used in a critical application. Often, these similar or look-alike parts are fabricated in the same shop using identical product lines. The difference is the additional testing imposed to certify that the item meets the needs of a critical application. Adequate controls are required to prevent similar components from being mixed in the manufacturing process or at the supplier's location.

Certifications that are merely statements of compliance to specification or phrases (such as *equal to* or *is similar to*) usually are not reliable, and generally are worthless and unacceptable to user activities. Some companies will forward, along with their purchase orders, specific instructions for data format and preparation. Other companies are much less explicit and must be contacted for their requirements.

In order to satisfy the minimum requirements of most activities, certification data should contain

1. The original or exact copies of the quantitative test reports. It should indicate the specification to which the tests were performed, the methods used, and the actual test results obtained.

2. Identification of the activity or laboratory where the tests were performed, date, and laboratory control numbers. Test reports must be signed by an appropriate official of the testing organization.

3. Documentation traceable to purchase order numbers, lots, heat, batch, or traceability code numbers marked on the materials. Normally, original analysis and test reports furnished by material producers are accepted as verification of furnished materials; however, if any subsequent processes are performed (for example, heat treating, forging, cold working, and aging) that could change the characteristics of the materials, additional tests will be required that are representative of the finished state.

Traceability and Marking

The best certifications are of little value without traceability to the material. Anyone must be able to look at a part and (using the identifying code numbers) be able to find documentation verifying that the part has been tested and conforms with specifications/performance requirements. This must be accomplished using objective data. Traceability is best accomplished by permanent codes marked directly on the material. Some buying activities will issue specific instructions as to type, depth of marking, location, and so forth. Normally, component manufacturers are allowed to use their own code numbers provided they are traceable to the original heat, lot, batch, laboratory analysis, and performance test reports.

In practice, parts, containers, or tags should be marked permanently with unique code numbers and any other identification required by the purchase document/specification plan. Markings should be located so as not to affect form, fit, or function and preferably so they will be visible after assembly. Critical items installed internally in an assembly by a prime or subcontractor should carry a certified document listing each item in the assembly and its associated identity code numbers and data. Items too small to mark, should be packaged and labeled, or tagged, as required for permanent markings.

Traceability begins with a review of all incoming purchase orders to determine customer requirements. All outgoing orders also must be reviewed and quality requirements transmitted to suppliers or subcontractors.

Written instructions should go to receiving personnel to review all test reports and certifications, ensuring conformance to the drawing specifications. All certified materials must be marked and identified with the same unique, traceable numbers recorded on the certificate. Items such as chemicals and rubber products should be checked to determine that shelf life and cure dates have not been exceeded. A certification from the supplier does not always assure compliance with the purchase order requirements. As a safeguard against breakdowns in a supplier's quality system, the supplier's data should be checked routinely by having a sample of the material verified by inhouse or independent testing. Often this can be accomplished by testing only a few of the more critical elements.

Every business handling certified materials must keep incoming logs and material segregated. This requires a formal procedure for permanently marking materials and finished parts with heat, lot, batch, or code numbers that are traceable directly to the test reports and laboratory analyses covering them. These requirements should be demanded of the supplier (subcontractor). There also must be strictly enforced procedures requiring identity markings obliterated during manufacture to be reapplied immediately after the operation during which they were removed.

Permanently documented and maintained records must be kept on all contractually specified tests and special processes performed. This includes operational and/or reliability testing, nondestructive tests, chemical analysis, physical properties, pressure tests, welding, heat treating, plating, and so forth. In order for the tests and special processes to be valid, they must be performed by a certified employee and accomplished according to procedures for which the license was granted. Records must verify that personnel qualifications and process approvals were valid at the time the tests or special processes were performed. In most instances, documented data for the product itself must be retained for its operating life. The average record retention period is seven years, but may extend indefinitely for certain specialized industries. Many companies reduce these records to microfilm after several years.

The traceability story is an example of total quality assurance from planning, procuring, manufacturing, handling, inspecting, and more. It could fill a complete volume in itself. This brief discussion should provide a reference point for establishing document control.

Personal Skills and Equipment Certification

During development of a business plan to produce and market a product, company management determines the types of equipment and facilities needed. Management also determines what employee skills are necessary. These employee skills cover a spectrum from engineering to fabrication through inspection to packaging for shipment. Manufacturing skills can include special methods of joining or bonding machining of exotic materials, handling of hazardous materials, performing chemical processes, soldering, performing nondestructive testing/inspection, and so forth.

It is not unusual for management to find that the inventory of personal skills available is not adequate and must be acquired or developed. Depending on their size, companies conduct training programs ranging from simple on-the-job training to sophisticated classroom and bench-type programs that may extend for several months. Training also is available at educational institutions as short courses or extended programs leading to a degree. Some professional societies (such as the American Society for Quality Control, and the American Society for Nondestructive Testing) have developed training material and assist local groups and educational institutions in conducting training and certification programs.

Once acquired, some skills need no further on-the-job or classroom training, because expertise is added and maintained by continued use. Other skills require occasional upgrading due to advances in technology. Still other skills require periodic demonstration of operator proficiency due to the nature of the operation or product itself. In these cases, success depends on the aptitude of the operator because final determination of adherence to the process usually requires subjective evaluation or destructive testing of the product.

For some operations, fabrication or assembly tools are certified periodically (in addition to their regular calibration) to ensure repeatability of the process and to reduce the variables resulting from operator techniques. Certification of equipment and processes will be discussed later in this chapter.

In discussing personal skills, two terms should be defined: *qualification* and *certification.* Qualification is the skill, training, and/or work experience required for a person to properly perform assigned duties. Certification is a written document indicating that the holder has demonstrated, through written or oral questioning or examination of work samples, a knowledge and ability to perform specialized duties. The customer may determine which skills need certification. A Department of Defense contract may cite one or more of the following specifications, each of which requires periodic skill demonstration.

- MIL-STD-1537, Military Standard Electrical Conductivity Test for Measurement of Heat Treatment of Aluminum Alloys, Eddy Current Methods
- MIL-STD-410, Military Standard Nondestructive Testing Personnel Qualification and Certification (Eddy Current, Liquid Penetrant, Magnetic Particle, Radiographic and Ultrasonic)
- MIL-STD-5021, Military Specification Test; Aircraft and Missile Welding Operator's Qualification

Prime contractors or manufacturers may require additional certification and periodic validation of skills they believe are necessary to ensure quality and reliability. Beyond the mandatory certifications established in the contract, a manufacturer must examine its own requirements. Professional or trade associations can offer further assistance and guidance.

The differences between training and certification must be examined in light of the operation's complexity and the ability to verify the end result. A machinist may require only initial training to operate a numerical controlled machine. Similarly, because the dimensions of an end product are easily validated by standard measuring instruments, a machined parts inspector usually needs one-time training in basic mathematics and the functions of micrometers, calipers, parallel bars, and other standard measuring instruments. However, skill in interpreting X-ray film requires extended periods of training because the interpretation is subjective due to the medium iteself. Company management must carefully determine which skills require one-time training and which require certification.

Another factor to be considered is the cost of periodic certification. Continuation of certification requires a periodic evaluation of the individual by obtaining special work samples, requiring a written or oral examination, or by keeping a record of work results to establish error patterns. A combination of testing and an actual demonstration of skill is required by some military specifications. If the skill is not defined in a military specification or in a trade standard, a testing program should be developed and enforced. Test results should be kept for an appropriate length of time.

Training and skill certification programs are best administered by designated centers. If the certification is prescribed by a military specification or trade association, the requirements are documented and available. If the skill or process, or the need for such is unique to the manufacturer, the requirements should be documented and made part of the company's manufacturing or quality records.

Some skills, such as nondestructive testing, require that the person who certifies others must have special education and work experience. Program surveillance normally is assigned to the product assurance organization. A number of methods can help verify that currently certified employees are performing work predetermined to require a certified operator.

1. Issuing each operator a card indicating his/her name, employee number, the skill for which he/she is certified, and the period of certification. The card should be in his/her possession whenever he/she performs that operation so that his/her current qualification can be checked at any time.

2. Posting the names of certified operators at the work station, so management of inspection can match the operator to the name on the list.

3. Certifying all operators in the work area (cost center, and so forth) so that work assignments can be done without fear of using a noncertified operator.

4. Issuing an identification stamp to the employee so that the product and/or documentation can be traced to him/her. This also will indicate that the process has been accomplished by a certified person.

The product assurance manager must decide whether the inspectors require training similar to that of operators, so they can more objectively determine product acceptability. For example, should an inspector of welds be qualified to weld if the weld inspection is accomplished using nondestructive test methods? Whatever approach the product assurance manager finds appropriate, he or she must establish a program for monitoring the skills of the employees. The specification (drawing, work instruction, procedure, contact) must identify where a certified skill, process, or operation is required.

Manufacturing and the product assurance managers must determine whether the shop paper (assembly instructions) should identify operations requiring a certified skill. Verifying the performance of an operation by a certified operator is easier for management when the shop paper is annotated. Whatever method is used, manufactured and product assurance must agree on the identification of skills, the period that the certification is valid (when not controlled by military or customer specification), and the method of confirming use of skilled operators.

The product assurance manager further enforces the skill certification program when, through failure reports or observation, he/she determines that the quality of the work performed by a certified operator falls below an acceptable level. At this point, the product assurance manager should initiate action to suspend the certified status of the operator and require retraining, or other action as necessary to restore the skill level.

Some manufacturing operations require similar certification consideration due to the process itself. Some examples are bonding leads on micro devices, crimping or insulation stripping, or a spot welding operation where the inspection or test of each weld is not feasible due to cost or the destructive nature of validation. In these instances, it is customary to initiate a two step program.

Step 1–The machine, instrument, or process is tested to the appropriate specification or manufacturer's instruction. When the operation is performed within acceptable limits, all adjusting features (such as screws, slides, and power settings) are sealed to prevent unauthorized or inadvertent adjustment. These seals should remain undisturbed until maintenance or recalibration is required.

Step 2–A schedule is developed to produce an adequate number of test specimens at the beginning of each work shift, or other predetermined cycle. These specimens are verified through destructive or nondestructive means prior to production.

Verifying the repeatability of equipment or process is a certification action. A log maintained at the equipment or process area records the original proofing and certification. It may be necessary to repeat this step several times during the work shift if the process is time- or quantity-oriented, or at the beginning of each shift if the process is operator-oriented. In any case, work specimens should be retained long enough to permit examination during failure analysis or post audit.

Certification does not guarantee product quality. It is a program to reduce or eliminate process and operator variables.

Handling Nonconforming Material

Because most production processes inevitably yield some defective product, every production facility must establish a method to prevent further processing, completion, or delivery of defective products. The products must be segregated as soon as the nonconformance is recognized to ensure that appropriate action is taken to control or localize the defective items. The defective material must be marked clearly and removed from the normal work flow to a special holding area. Once nonconforming material is isolated, someone must decide what needs to be done before the material can either be returned to production or scrapped. Evaluating nonconforming material is an important quality control activity between the supplier and the customer. Excessive nonconforming material usually occurs because of a breakdown of the producer's operations.

Many things produce nonconformance. It may be caused by chance alone. The design may be so advanced that no means yet exists for eliminating the causes. The cost of elimination may not be economically possible; in other words, it may be cheaper to scrap items. The design criteria may be too severe. The process capability may be wider than the tolerance. In any case, the parties involved should be concerned because of its effect on the operation's efficiency and the potential of hidden costs in the production process or end product.

Prompt, effective corrective action is good business. Nonconforming items cost money, because scrap, repairs, or rework mean additional operations. The producer should find and correct the causes of nonconformance wherever economically feasible. The supplier should use both its own expertise and that of the customers through informal consultation or, if warranted, a formal review board appointed by top management.

Whether formal or informal, the decision-making group should review all aspects of the process and material used to produce the nonconforming item. The investigation should continue until proper disposition of the material can be made. The group must find the causes of nonconformance, individually or collectively, and ensure that appropriate corrective action is taken. A summary of the group's findings should include product identification, the stage in production under review, nature and extent of nonconformance, technical assessment and decision, disposition action to be taken by the producer, and advice of corrective action to all concerned.

Methods of disposing of nonconforming material include scrap, rework, or repair, and use as is under concession from the proper authority for return to the supplier. All material to be used in production either as is or after repair or rework must remain segregated until it is cleared up by inspection or test for production use. Records of nonconformance, corrective action, and disposition should be saved for comparison in future reviews.

When parts fail to meet the customer's requirements, the producer is obligated to notify the customer and make a decision as to acceptability or possible repair. It is not ethical to knowingly ship out-of-specification material.

Planning for Customer Quality Survey

The primary purpose of a customer quality survey is to determine whether the supplier has a quality system capable of measuring and controlling contract requirements. Obviously, the customer's procurement organization believes the supplier has something to offer or the survey would not be performed. The supplier must present itself honestly. If a supplier convinces a customer that it can do something and subsequently fails to perform as contracted, both customer and supplier lose, but the supplier also loses on future contracts.

A survey has three basic parts: opening conference, plant tour, and closing conference. The opening conference is a key part of the survey. At this time, the customer's survey personnel will present their credentials and explain their function. They will define the products, intended use, and design requirements. At this time, they also should briefly outline the quality controls that will be required. It is important for the supplier to have manufacturing and quality personnel who are thoroughly familiar with the operations at this conference. They should give the survey team a brief accurate overview of their quality system, however detailed or informal it may be. Overstatements at this time will be negated during the detail survey. This is the time to describe the quality controls as they exist. This allows the survey team to determine whether the controls are adequate for the product or process under consideration.

Evaluation of the supplier's quality system begins with a review of the quality manual. In a small company, it may only be a few typewritten pages, but it must accurately represent the quality controls being used. A major problem can occur if a manual promises more than actual procedures deliver. When this happens, the evaluator can only assume that the supplier is giving a false impression.

Basic survey categories include

- Drawing and specification control
- Purchased material control/receiving inspection
- Manufacturing control/in-process inspection/final inspection
- Gage, calibration, and test equipment control
- Storage, packaging, and shipment control
- Nonconforming material control
- Quality program management

During the plant tour, the supplier also should demonstrate the procedures in each of these areas. Because the survey is a classic show-and-tell situation, and all things will not be immediately visible to the surveyor, the supplier should provide information in any area that an evaluator surveys. If the evaluator does not witness the controls in action, no credit can be given for them. Conversely, the supplier should not babble endlessly about how good its control is. The supplier should understand what the evaluator is seeking and openly demonstrate the quality system.

When evaluating drawing and specification control, the surveyor wants to determine if the supplier has a method of ensuring that requirements (including changes) are transmitted to manufacturing and verified by quality.

Many surveyors like to start with the incoming rough product and follow it through to completion and shipping. So that important procedures are visible and operational, it is best that the presentation be made by individuals knowledgeable in the operation, rather than by an executive who may be more concerned with making an impression. Beginning in receiving inspection, the supplier must be able to document that requirements have been communicated to the suppliers, and that the incoming product has been inspected and appropriate records maintained. This is the first area where the importance of visibility becomes evident.

Being able to randomly check a lot of material that is properly identified and carries evidence of inspection helps demonstrate control of operations. Identification alone, however, is not going to satisfy the surveyor. It is important to show evidence of planning for the characteristics to be checked and to specify sampling frequency. Demonstrating the use of a recognized sampling plan (such as MIL-STD-105E) is far more meaningful than claiming that everything is checked *real heavy,* or 10 percent, or something else.

Many small companies depend on outside laboratories for testing or evaluation material. Here, again, it is important to have this information available, as well as examples of current reports for review. It is embarrassing to say, "We have stuff checked all the time," but not be able to remember the laboratory's name or find any reports for the last

18 months. If laboratory work is required for the product, it is essential to demonstrate a good working relationship with the laboratory.

In the area of in-process operations, several important items must be checked. These deal with the importance of written work instructions in the shop. Documentation of controls follows the fundamental steps to telling the worker and inspector what to do, and giving them the tools to measure their work and the means to record the results. In some small operations, an operation sheet can be combined with an inspection plan and inspection record. It is difficult to fault objective plans and data. A sound, handwritten instruction performed by qualified people who use calibrated equipment and record the results of their checks is far more meaningful than fancy printed forms that are incomplete or improperly used.

If the surveyor can stop at a work station and find that the operator has the applicable drawings, specifications, work instructions, inspection equipment, and record sheets, the supplier is on the right track. Having only one complete work station is not going to impress a surveyor because control should be evident throughout the shop. Furthermore, it is quite obvious when a supplier has made a quick tour through the shop, hanging tags on everything and getting all the proper forms on the job the day before a survey; it is best to be honest and demonstrate something that can be substantiated. After all, the objective is to evaluate the quality program. Surveyors generally expect to see documentation of inspection instructions and to find the use of sampling plans in receiving inspection. The response that "Charlie has checked them for years and knows all about it" will only draw the counter, "What do you do if Charlie isn't here?" There is no substitute for being able to show: "These are the characteristics that we check; this is our inspection frequency. These are our criteria for acceptance and here are our records of inspection."

Also regarding inspection or testing, surveyors will notice the presence of equipment required to check the parts being reviewed. It is not wise to make claims for doing things without having the equipment or capability to perform. Rusty JO blocks, damaged gages, and lack of standards will not establish confidence in the supplier's calibration and maintenance of inspection tools. If inspection tools or gages cannot be found, it is difficult to convince the surveyor that the items are calibrated and in use. Again, the supplier who can demonstrate well-maintained equipment, records of calibration, and traceability to known standards is on the right track to a satisfactory survey evaluation. The show-and-tell concept continues and the importance of the tour guide's knowledge of the quality program becomes more evident. The survey is nothing more than a review of operating methods to determine the capability to produce in conformance with specifications and requirements.

Inspection is not the final element because the survey is a comprehensive evaluation of operations. The supplier will have to demonstrate controls in warehousing, packing, and shipping. If a part of product is not packaged or identified properly, it may present more problems than if it were nonconforming to some other requirements. In numerous instances, product may be damaged during handling and shipment. Therefore, it is important to show that customer requirement information is available to shipping personnel.

Thus far, the survey has revolved around positive preplanned elements. However, control of nonconforming material must be evaluated too. It is essential to be able to show the surveyor positive identification and, in the case of some contracts, segregation from production. As with the other elements, this means the ability to control operations. Information feedback on the evaluation of rejected material and corrective action often is covered. Therefore, it is necessary to be prepared to explain what is done in response to customer complaints. A system should be operational for evaluating the returns and documenting the findings and action taken.

The survey category dealing with quality program management includes not only the quality manual mentioned previously, but also management's philosophy toward the growth and development of people responsible for quality. This is the time to demonstrate whether one person can take over if another is out. Are there automatic stand-ins for key quality persons? Are the inspectors taking or have they taken any courses in quality control? Are they members of a professional society such as the ASQC?

Other elements are covered in some surveys and a standard recipe cannot be provided for receiving an outstanding rating every time. The supplier will do best if it is honest with the surveyor and presents the system as it is operating and in effect. If the supplier follows sound, accepted principles and can demonstrate control of operations for the type of product or process being considered, an acceptable rating should follow. The key to a successful survey is planning and demonstrating control of operations.

At the closing conference, the survey team can summarize for the supplier which areas were good and which had discrepancies. It is important for the supplier to understand each discrepancy. Possibly the surveyor did not see a particular control or procedure and, at this time, the supplier can clarify a misunderstanding. On the other hand, if the discrepancy is valid, the supplier can find out what the customer is looking for so that appropriate corrective action can be taken. The supplier receives a written report detailing discrepant areas. Upon its receipt the supplier should respond in writing, designating any improvements made or planned and their estimated dates of completion. If the price of the order does not justify the changes required to upgrade the system, the supplier should indicate this at this time. (The supplier should provide an adequate meeting place to hold both the opening and closing conferences.) In conclusion, when the customer defines what is needed and the supplier successfully demonstrates what can be done, the result could be receipt of orders with the supplier's capabilities, benefitting both the customer and supplier. Generally, customers are willing to assist a supplier that is candid, open to suggestion, and honestly strives to maintain an effective quality program to produce products meeting contractual requirements.

Planning for Source Inspection

Source inspection is a process wherein the customer, or an agency representing the customer, inspects the supplier's product at the facility prior to shipment. Source inspection has the following advantages over normal incoming inspection.

1. It avoids duplication of costly specialized inspection or test equipment at the customer's plant.
2. It expedites the flow of needed items to the production line by eliminating or reducing the need for incoming inspection.
3. Material needing rework can be corrected while the product is in the supplier's plant, thus avoiding time lost in returning defective material.
4. When certain parameters cannot be fully tested after assembly, source inspection allows verification while the product is being manufactured.
5. Awareness of the supplier's processes, systems, and people allow for better control by the source inspector.
6. The presence of a source inspector allows the supplier to discuss and seek advice about customer specifications and requirements.
7. Source inspection allows closer relations between the customer and supplier.
8. It permits direct shipment to locations other than the customer's plant.

During contract negotiations and purchase order review, the supplier should inquire whether in-process and final source inspection requirements exist.

The supplier should notify the customer's purchasing agent at least three days prior to the date when source inspection is needed. (Every supplier cannot get source inspection coverage the last day of the month.) When notifying the customer, it is best to provide the name of the person whom the source inspector should contact and the specific plant location.

When the source inspector arrives, plant personnel should be courteous and brief. The source inspector has a busy schedule and does not have time for idle chatter. More importantly, inspection records and any certification of outside testing, such as nondestructive testing or laboratory analysis, should be ready and available for the source inspector.

As the product already has passed the supplier's final inspection, source inspection is basically an audit to verify that the supplier has completed the appropriate contractual requirement. Source inspection is not intended to replace the supplier's quality responsibility.

The product should be ready and in an appropriate area for the source inspector to work. Nothing is more upsetting to a source inspector than to wait for the supplier to locate the product, find the gages, and set them up. Someone should be assigned to escort and assist the source inspector. If the assignee is familiar with the inspection of the product, this person often can demonstrate a complicated inspection setup or test for the source inspector.

It is good practice for the supplier's management to arrange a brief closing interview during which the source inspector can explain his or her observations. Often the inspector can provide valuable information. Supplier management also should be available to make decisions if rework, repair, or correction is required. Follow-up activities should ensure that appropriate releases, acceptance paperwork certifications, and so forth, are included in the shipment.

Regarding hospitality, an occasional lunch may be in order, as this gives supplier management and the source inspector an opportunity to recap earlier events. Local use of the supplier's phone is normal, as most calls are related to the product.

Most source inspectors want to accept the supplier's product. If a discrepancy is found and corrected, the source inspector may have prevented the supplier's product from causing a failure in the customer's assembly, which could have become costly for the supplier and the customer.

When the product has been made to specifications and has been controlled and inspected properly, the supplier has nothing to fear from the source inspector. The supplier's openness and willingness to demonstrate compliance with the customer's requirements will help create positive relations with the source inspector and, thus, with the customer.

Finding and Hiring a Consultant

Industrial corporations hire lawyers and accountants as consultants on a regular basis. Few manage without these outside aides, yet many overlook the advantage of consultants. The professional engineering consultant can be an invaluable aid to profit. In the use of outside advisors, the key is proper identification of the problems and the correct combination of attitudes on the part of corporate management, engineering advisor, and staff. The manager who has not used consultants probably is not aware of where to find or how to choose a consultant.

The relationship's success depends both on the client and consultant. The client should select the consultant only after carefully considering what the client wishes to accomplish. The ethical consultant will have no qualms in refusing an assignment outside his/her field or one he/she considers impossible. The consultant is an extra hand who has skills and special competence. When these skills are combined with client needs, success can be achieved.

There must be a specific need for hiring a consultant. A consultant should not be employed to manage a department. A consultant is most effective solving specific problems, analyzing problem areas, suggesting methods of finding solutions, writing manuals and reports, training, advising, and assisting a staff to develop required skills and procedures. The consultant also may provide management with systems and procedures that improve product, processes, and operations.

The organization looking for special assistance can use one or more of the following methods.

- Advertise for a consultant (this method is least recommended)
- Ask the quality control or reliability engineer to search for one

- Consult the business card index (advertisements) of organizations that provide consulting services in journals such as *Quality Progress* (published by ASQC)
- Call the ASQC office and request the names of one or more quality control or reliability engineering consultants in the client's area
- Call friends or acquaintances for similar suggestions

If the firm's quality manager or others in its quality department are members of the ASQC, they may know of appropriate consultants. Because the quality manager will have a good deal of contact with the consultant and must develop a good working relationship with the consultant, having the quality manager help in the selection will be an advantage. Choosing a consultant in this manner is less likely to cause friction or create the false impression that the quality manager may lose his/her job to the consultant. Competent people can be trusted to hire competent help.

After the manager (executive) has found one or more consultants, he/she must decide whether the consultant is suitable, competent, and will be valuable to the organization. The manager should interview the consultant but, even before that, he/she will be interested in the consultant's background, training and experience, the cost of the services, and whether the consultant can devote sufficient time to the task. In the initial contact, the need for a quality control consultant is explained. Is the consultant able to help? When can the consultant meet to view operations and discuss problems? At that time the consultant can determine what he/she believes can be done and how he/she proposes to work in the particular situation.

The consulting engineer will indicate whether he/she can undertake the task on the basis of his/her experience, competence, availability, and familiarity with the field. The consultant will want to discuss any possible conflict of interest with present clients. Sometimes clients will not object to an arrangement where the consultant services two or more organizations in the same business.

Fees

Many consultants will make an initial visit without charge if the client is local and the potential assignment lengthy. Others may want to be reimbursed for transportation costs. Trips can sometimes run into substantial costs. If the interview precedes a task or contract of short duration, the travel expense and fee are more usual.

How much do consulting engineers charge? Most fees are quoted on a per diem basis. They may run from $500 to more than $1000 per day. To this is added travel expense, food, and lodging, if necessary. The usual work day is approximately eight hours. In some instances the eight hours are on-site; in others, time is based on portal-to-portal pay scale. The consultant is an expert available at a fraction of what it would cost to have a full-time employee. Extremely competent engineers are available on this basis. This can be a bargain to the small firm that does not need full-time services, provided the job is accomplished properly. Even for large firms it is a distinct advantage.

How much time should the professional engineering consultant devote to the task? This is part of the negotiation. To complete a quality manual will take days—anywhere from four to 40, or more, depending on the complexity of the problem and the extent of existing material.

To install an operation and train the company in the proper use of the manual and its procedures is even more time consuming. It can be done slowly or on a crash basis over a shorter period. The consultant and company will have to agree on a schedule, the amount of time to be devoted to the task, the fees, and when they become payable. Some contracts between company and consultant last for days, others for years, depending on what is needed. Most consultants bill on a monthly basis.

Time and Availability of Services

How can a consultant devote a great amount of time to one organization, particularly when it may need many weeks of continued effort? This depends on whether the consultant is

- A large consulting company—more than 50 people
- A medium-size consulting company—five to 50 people
- A small group—two to five people who operate cooperatively
- The individual consultant—a full-time professional or a moonlighter, such as a university professor

The size of the consulting group is no indication of its competence, although a small group obviously cannot provide as many people as a much larger group. Whether dealing with a large or small firm, a good rule is to be sure the responsible executive meets and knows the actual consultants assigned to the task.

There are two ways to use a consultant. Let the consultant do the work or have the consultant help train employees. The latter usually is cheaper. Furthermore, control is in the hands of management, where it belongs.

One item most consultants cannot estimate with precision is how much time it will take to accomplish a task in a given company. They can come in, survey the plant, and write a report within specific time limits, but to tell management that tasks will take specific periods of time when the organization's staff is involved, means that they, and not the staff, are doing the work. Although estimates are possible, few consultants will do more than estimate, because corporate management and the work force can work with or against a consultant's recommendation.

If the corporate staff and the consultant cannot work together effectively, the program should be halted. It will not work. For this reason alone, most arrangements with consultants are agreements and not line-time contracts. If it is not working, it is not worthwhile to either party. Both parties should exercise this responsibility. Furthermore, when the job is finished, it is time to call a halt.

One of the common concerns expressed by purchasing and quality professionals is how can a small supplier do some of this so-called quality stuff. It always has been a challenge to incorporate some of the tools that are so common in large industries, to the small shops which are resource constrained. In most of these businesses the employees traditionally wear multiple hats. This chapter has examined the issues facing the small supplier and has attempted to show some of the key points that all suppliers whether large or small have to address. How to do so is limited only by the creativity and patience of both the customer and the supplier. Quality improvement is a never-ending journey, where all efforts will yield some rewards.

Note

1. ANSI/ASQC Standard A3-1978. American National Standard Quality Systems Terminology. Milwaukee, Wis: American Society for Quality Control, p. 4.

Procurement Quality in the Food Industry

Chapter 15

Key words: best value, bulk material, destructive testing, food safety, government regulations, HACCP, homogeneity, identity check, organoleptic methods, qualitative methods, representative sample, shelf life.

Summary
- Best value
- Terminology
- Bulk materials
- Destructive testing
- Qualitative methods
- Shelf life
- Food safety

As you read through this book you should notice that the role of procurement is changing. Procurement departments are becoming the orchestrators of many activities aimed at buying the best value raw material. Focus is on the best value vs. the lowest purchase order price.

The term *best value* encompasses not only the cost of the raw material, but also the costs associated with the use of that product. Price negotiation includes the quality and service criteria necessary for production to operate without scrap, rework, and excess variation that causes production shutdown. To determine best value, a measurement system must be in place to monitor the purchase price plus the cost-of-use. This fact-based approach is useful for negotiating and monitoring improvement.

As the gatekeepers of incoming quality, procurement departments from any industry are responsible for

- Communicating all requirements
- Determining capability of a supplier to satisfy requirements
- Monitoring conformance to requirements
- Providing feedback to suppliers
- Working together with suppliers to plan corrective actions and improvements

In other words, procurement drives the selection, motivation, and evaluation of its suppliers.

Although this approach is generic enough for all industries, the food industry presents some unique opportunities to apply these approaches. Several things that set the food industry apart from most other manufacturing industries are

1. High percentage of bulk material suppliers.
2. Destructive testing is necessary to obtain analytical information.
3. Qualitative methods are frequently used, especially in organoleptic or sensory evaluation.
4. Food has a limited shelf life and continues to change, sometimes very rapidly, during the life of the product.
5. Food safety is paramount.

Terminology

Before we discuss each of these issues in more detail, it is appropriate to comment on some terminology of the food industry. Whereas most manufacturers utilize engineers to design the product, the food industry utilizes scientists to develop new products. Engineers are utilized to design the package and the equipment that produces the food product. When you see the term *design engineer* in other chapters of this book, substitute *product development scientist* to align terminology with the food industry. Design engineers develop the drawings; product development scientists develop the formula (or recipe) and define the processing (or cooking) steps.

Reliability and life testing, the measure of the product's ability to perform in the intended manner over the period of its expected useful life, relate to what the food industry commonly refers to as the shelf life of a product. The shelf life represents the useful storage life of the food product under appropriate storage conditions. At the end of its shelf life, the food is beginning to develop undesirable characteristics caused by microbiological, chemical, or physical changes.

On-line monitoring is accomplished with gages when manufacturing parts and assemblies. Gages are used to measure physical dimensions of product produced in terms of millimeters, inches, and so forth. Gaging is used to some extent in the food industry when size and shape of a product produced are critical. However, the majority of on-line control in the manufacture of food items is accomplished with laboratory equipment or instrumentation. Monitoring chemical parameters (such as moisture, solids, fat, and acidity) and physical parameters (such as color and viscosity) are accomplished by the use of instrumentation specific to each parameter being monitored.

Part number identification, or verification, is analogous to identity checks. This important aspect of the receiving inspection verifies that what you are receiving is what you purchased. Examples of identity checks are grading of food products according to established standards, such as many vegetables, cheeses, and meats have.

MRBs decide on the disposition of product that does not conform to the requirements and assure adequacy of corrective actions. This structured approach is not widely utilized in the food industry. They use a less formal process whereby the quality assurance department working with the production department reaches a consensus regarding the usability of the product in question.

Bulk Materials

Purchasing of bulk materials can present some unique problems. Bulk materials in the food industry many times are agricultural commodities, whose price and quality can drastically fluctuate, depending on growth conditions.

For many industries, bulk materials are assumed to be homogeneous or uniform. In the food industry, this is not always the rule. Sedimentation and stratification are common in bulk fluid products. During sedimentation, the solids portion of the fluid begins to settle to the bottom of the container (such as with fruit and vegetable juices and purees). During stratification, layers of the fluid or solid components begin to form based on the varying densities or sizes of the components (cream rising to the top of a tank of fluid milk is an example of stratification). In addition, microbial levels are rarely distributed homogeneously throughout a lot.

Nonhomogeneity in bulk lots of food products puts greater emphasis on sampling methods. When procuring food of this nature, it is important that both supplier and customer follow the same sampling methods. When different methods are used, samples may not be representative of the lot. The objective of sampling is to obtain a representative sample of the entire lot, so that upon analysis, a decision can be made regarding the lot's conformance to requirements or price to be paid (payment schedules based on components such as solids or fat are common in the food industry). A representative sample should exhibit the same composition of the lot from which it was obtained. If a sample is not representative of the lot, the producer could erroneously ship nonconforming product or not ship conforming product. Likewise, if the customer sample is not representative, decisions made to accept or reject the lot may be made in error. Therefore, sampling methods should be included on the specification to prevent the potential of sampling errors.

Several techniques can be employed to achieve a representative sample depending on the type of product being sampled. Agitation of the bulk lot to produce a homogeneous mixture can be used in many fluid products such as milk and juices. When this technique is utilized, two critical areas must be addressed. First, it is necessary to determine the amount of agitation time to produce a homogeneous mixture. The supplier may have this information, but if not, it needs to be determined experimentally. The goal is to achieve homogeneity with the minimum amount of agitation, to save time and to minimize the deleterious effects that agitation could impart to the product. Begin by agitating a minimum amount and increase the time until several sample locations within the lot yield the same result. A number of statistical tests can be employed to verify that the results are statistically the same and that no outliers are present.

Second, after an agitation time is determined, it is important to ensure that the agitation time remain consitent from shipment to shipment. A written sampling procedure documenting agitation time is a useful tool to clearly define the steps required to obtain a representative sample.

Solid and semisolid products cannot be agitated to achieve homogeneity. Subsamples from several areas of the lot should be taken and then one or several composite samples can be formed to ensure a representative sampling of the lot. To determine the number of samples to obtain, consider the criticalness of the parameter you are monitoring. The more critical the parameter, the more samples you are likely to obtain.

Some industries have conducted studies to determine the most representative sampling areas in a solid food product, thereby reducing the number of samples needed to make decisions about the food product. An example of this type of study was one supervised by the National Cheese Institute and the University of Wisconsin to determine the most representative sampling areas for moisture in barrels of cheese containing 225 to 250 kg. Over 9000 moisture analyses were made from representative geographical regions. The results were statistically analyzed to generate a moisture profile in barrel cheese. The resultant sampling procedure is very specific and indicates that a cheese trier with a blade length of 30.5 cm be inserted 7 cm from the edge of the cheese and toward the nearest outside edge of the barrel at 11 degrees from vertical. For a cheese plug between 25.5 and 30.5 cm, the top 11.4 cm is used for sealing the plug hole. The next 10.2 cm portion is the representative sample and placed into a sample container. The remaining bottom portion of the plug is discarded.

Consult reference manuals that publish approved methods or contact industry groups (such as the National Cheese Institute, American Meat Institute, or the American Institute of Baking) to determine if specific sampling protocols exist for food products. A comprehensive list of food industry associations is included in Appendix C.

Destructive Testing

As discussed, sampling plans for bulk items are important so that meaningful analytical results are obtained. For foods, however, product must be destroyed for a majority of analytical methods to obtain results.

Because of the destructive nature of conducting food analyses and the costs involved with sampling and testing, minimal sample sizes are desirable. It is important to remember, however, that the smaller the sample size the greater the probability of error, or risk that the sample(s) is not representative of the lot. A lot could be rejected when it actually does conform to the specification (known as the alpha- or producer's risk). Likewise, a lot could be accepted when it does not conform to the specification (known as the beta- or consumer's risk). Although sampling and analyzing larger sample sizes will add cost, rejecting good loads and accepting bad loads will add greater costs.

A sampling plan should be chosen to make the correct decisions regarding the incoming quality of food products. A sampling plan is the instruction that specifies the number of samples, or units, to be obtained for analysis and the criteria for accepting or rejecting the lot. The cost to sample and analyze must be weighed against the risks associated with the characteristic being analyzed. Several factors must be considered when choosing a sampling plan for incoming inspection to utilize available resources most effectively.

1. *Hazard to the customer*–The manufacturer's responsibility is to provide customers with safe and wholesome food. Typically, unsafe food occurs one of two ways. First, the food is grown or produced in a manner that makes it hazardous. Examples of these types of hazards include pesticides, antibiotics, mercury, lead, and radioactivity. Second, the food becomes contaminated during distribution, storage, or subsequent processing. Insect infestation or the growth of organisms that produce hazardous substances (such as mycotoxins) can render food unsafe during distribution and storage of agricultural products. Microbial contamination, improper use of food additives, and accidental incorporation of physical dangers (such as glass or metal) are potential hazards that can occur during processing. Hazards vary in degree of severity. As the severity of the hazard increases, the sampling plan selected should reduce the probability of accepting an unsafe lot.

2. *Legal requirements*–Legal requirements for foods are established by the federal, state, or municipal agencies and generally are mandatory. These standardized food items may require more samples to be analyzed to achieve a higher degree of confidence in the lot composition.

3. *Homogeneity*–Lots that are homogeneous can be sampled representatively with fewer sample units than lots that are not homogeneous. Nonhomogeneous lots will require a larger number of sample units to confidently assess their composition.

4. *Supplier's quality history*–A supplier demonstrates good process control and reliability by consistently meeting requirements. Confidence increases and reduced sampling may be justified over time.

5. *Ability of suppliers to provide accurate data*–Many customers request suppliers to provide analytical information with each incoming lot of food product. As we move toward total cost reduction and supplier certification strategies, more emphasis is placed on verifying compliance to specifications through supplier-generated data. Relying on your supplier's data can eliminate your need to sample product, except on an audit basis. However, the supplier's analytical information is meaningless unless you have confidence in its accuracy. The accuracy of the supplier's analytical information must be verified. This can be done several ways: conducting laboratory audits, verifying statistically that no difference exists between the results of split samples analyzed at both a supplier's lab and your own, and having your suppliers participate in proficiency testing programs. A proficiency testing program is a systematic program in which a sample is analyzed by a number of laboratories to assess continuing capability and relative performance of each participating laboratory.

The destructive nature of food analyses and the time involved to conduct analyses are factors that tend to keep sample sizes to a minimum. Although small sample sizes keep receiving costs down, it is important to note that the probability of decision error is greater the smaller the sample size. Sampling plans should be established at the start of a relationship with a supplier, and the supplier should be fully aware of your criteria for accepting and rejecting product. It is a good idea to include sampling plans as part of your specification.

Qualitative Methods

How a food product looks, tastes, and smells are as important as its actual composition. Composition will affect appearance, flavor, and odor, but a food product can meet your compositional requirements yet still possess an unpleasant flavor or odor. Methods used to evaluate food usually involve sense organs and are referred to as sensory or organoleptic methods. These methods are subjective, in that they are based on the opinions of the investigators. Quantitative methods allow us to conduct a test and get an exact number, such as 34.3 percent solids, to make a determination on whether the product meets our requirements. Qualitative methods are less exact and rely on a customer having a good understanding of the organoleptic requirements and communicating them as precisely as possible to the supplier.

Because sensory characteristics are critical to most foods, they should be included in the specification to the supplier. Flavor, odor, color, appearance, texture, and consistency should all be considered if they are critical to the performance of the product in the consumer's kitchen. Be as descriptive as possible in characterizing each of these attributes. Try to identify not only what it should taste or smell like, but also what it should not taste or smell like. Various industries have resources available where sensory attributes have been described and correspond to a grade. The United States Department of Agriculture has established Federal Grade Standards for over 100 foods, including dairy products, meat, poultry, fruits, vegetables, and seafood products. Whenever possible, work from an established uniform set of criteria.

In addition to the description of the sensory attribute, it is important to agree on a test method. Granted, this will not be as simple as referencing an approved method. Chances are that no approved method exists for checking flavor, odor, or appearance of the food item you are procuring. When discussing methods for organoleptic evaluations, elements to consider are temperature and age that the food will be when evaluated, and conditions under which the food item will be evaluated (such as lighting, or as an ingredient in a finished product).

Various equipment is available to evaluate characteristics such as color, texture, and viscosity. Utilizing equipment such as colorimeters, texturemeters, and viscometers, helps to quantify the characteristic being measured. If specific equipment is used, it still is important for the customer and the supplier to agree on how the test will be conducted. Ideally, any testing method that is not an approved and referenced method should be included as a part of the specification.

As a customer, the more specific you can be in identifying how you want the food item you are procuring to taste, smell, appear, feel, and perform, the more informed your supplier becomes. The more informed your supplier, the less guessing the supplier will have to do to meet your requirements. A clear understanding of your requirements greatly improves your chances of consistently receiving product that meets your requirements.

Limited Shelf Life

All food is perishable. Beginning when it is harvested, slaughtered, or manufactured, food progressively deteriorates to the point it is no longer fit for human consumption. The speed at which a food product deteriorates depends on how the food product is handled. This is an important concept in the procurement process. How food is handled in your supplier's facility, how it is transported to your facility, and how it is stored in your facility prior to its use can all affect the quality of the food product.

It should not be assumed that those involved in the transport and storage of food products are aware of how important certain conditions are to maintaining quality and safety of the products. To determine the best storage and handling conditions for the food product you are procuring, ask the supplier. The supplier should be able to recommend the optimum handling and storage conditions for the food product that is being sold to you. After you obtain this information, make sure that it is communicated to the shipper and the necessary departments within your own company, such as receiving, warehousing, and production. Temperature often is a critical condition to the keeping quality of food products.

To assure that temperature is maintained properly, include it in the specification. Many companies even include the temperature requirements on the purchase orders and the shipping instructions. It is a good practice to have the supplier take product temperatures when loading and record them on the shipping document. To verify that the product was maintained at the proper temperature during transport, temperatures are taken at various points in the lot when it is received. Receipt temperatures are compared to loading temperatures. If temperatures have changed or do not meet an established temperature requirement, the lot may be rejected. Temperature recording devices also are employed to monitor the temperature of the shipping container during its transportation. When visiting with the supplier, verify that the proper temperatures are maintained. Determine how temperatures are monitored, how often they are monitored, if and where this information is recorded, and what actions are taken when a problem temperature is recorded.

The proper handling of food products during transport and storage is an important component in the food procurement process. Do not wait until a disaster shows up at your receiving dock to address the shipping and storage requirements.

Food Safety

Food safety concerns are growing. Today's consumers are increasingly aware of the diverse health hazards associated with the production, processing, and marketing of foods. Although the United States has one of the safest food supplies in the world, our food still makes millions of people ill each year and causes numerous deaths. To help protect the consumers, there are numerous local, state, and national government agencies that monitor and regulate the origin, composition, quality, safety, weight, labeling, packaging, marketing, and distribution of food sold in the United States. Most food industries are aware of the need to provide their consumers safe and wholesome food products. Adverse publicity about product safety or a company's negligence in complying with government safety regulations can result in large monetary losses, not to mention product liability lawsuits.

In 1938, the new Federal Food, Drug, and Cosmetic (FD&C) Act was signed into law. This law gave the Food and Drug Administration (FDA) the responsibility for ensuring the safety of consumer products. Section 402(a)(3) of the FD&C Act defines a food as adulterated if, "it consists in whole or in part of any filthy, putrid, or decomposed substance or if it is otherwise unfit for food"; Section 402(a)(4) elaborates on the definition to include

> . . . a food shall be deemed to be adulterated if it has been prepared, packed, or held under insanitary conditions whereby it may have been contaminated with filth or whereby it may have been rendered injurious to health.

In 1979, the Federal FD&C Act was amended to make it illegal to receive contaminated food. Any company involved with foods sold in interstate commerce, except for meat and poultry products, falls under FDA jurisdiction. Meat and poultry products are under the United States Department of Agriculture (USDA) jurisdiction. Appendix D lists the principal government agencies involved with food safety regulation and provides a brief explanation of their roles.

The procurement department is the first line of defense against unsafe food products entering a company's facility. Verifying that suppliers can provide safe products requires both time and effort early in negotiations, but can prevent unsafe product from ever being shipped to your facility. Relying on inspectors or lab analyses to identify and reject unsafe product after it has entered your facility is not only risky, but is a costly way to assure a safe food product.

The process of selecting a supplier of a food product includes food safety issues. At a minimum, a supplier should demonstrate a management commitment to food safety by

1. Being aware of, and complying with, applicable government regulations.
2. Following good manufacturing practices.
3. Having a product identification and a traceability system.
4. Having a process in place to control and prevent food
   contamination.

How does one determine a management commitment to these
basic food safety practices? Initially, ask, then follow up with a visit
to verify that what was said actually is being practiced.

Determining if a company complies with the appropriate government regulations requires a basic knowledge of the regulations pertaining to the product that is being procured. If you are uncertain of
the regulations, good places to start inquiring are food industry associations (Appendix C) and government agency offices (Appendix D).
After becoming familiar with the regulations pertaining to the product you are procuring, specific questions can be asked to ascertain if
the supplier is complying with the law. Suppliers who do not comply
with food laws are a risk to do business with, both from a safety
standpoint and the possibility of being implicated with them in the
event of legal action.

To prevent the possibility of being criminally implicated with a
supplier, a general requirement to do business is to obtain a Continuing
Food and Drug Guaranty. The guaranty is designed to exempt the buyer
from criminal prosecution provided the buyer does not do anything to
the product. This is a guaranty by the seller/supplier of a product subject
to the FD&C Act that the product is not adulterated or misbranded
within the meaning of the act. The guaranty should clearly state that it is
the supplier's responsibility to assure that products are in conformance
with all the requirements of the applicable laws.

For all practical purposes, a request for a Continuing Food and
Drug Guaranty should cause a supplier to evaluate food safety practices to verify compliance with the FD&C Act. By having a signed
Guaranty on file, you have taken the first steps to establish that your
supplier is in compliance with federal regulations.

Good manufacturing practices (GMPs) are FDA regulations. The intent of GMP regulations is to interpret Section 402(a)(4) of the FD&C Act and establish criteria to aid industries in complying with the law. The GMPs summarize the correct procedures on how things should be accomplished in a food production or processing facility. For this reason, FDA's GMPs are important in maintaining safe food products. They are contained in the Code of Federal Regulations, Title 21, Part 110 (21 CFR 110), which can be obtained from the Superintendent of Documents, U.S. Government Printing Office, Washington, DC 20402. Any food supplier should have an internal set of rules that address every element of the GMPs, and every employee of the supplier should be following those rules. Ask a potential supplier to provide a copy of the company's GMPs and inquire how they inform the employees of their roles in producing a safe food product.

A food supplier should have a coding system in place that identifies product by lot or batch, and records the ingredients used by their individual lot identities. A system of this nature is necessary in the event that an individual ingredient is found to be unsafe. Traceability of ingredients into products and through distribution allows questionable product to be rapidly identified and completely quarantined or retrieved. A coding system should be reliable and understandable. Coding on product must contain the required information and it must be legible. Verification of product identification and traceability is typically done at the supplier's facility by reverse tracing. This is conducted by choosing one lot of your product and tracing back through the manufacturing process records to determine exactly what lots or batches of ingredients were used in the manufacture of your product. A well-documented paper trail indicates that the supplier maintains good control of the identity of the product and its components during the manufacturing process.

To provide a safe food product, a supplier must fundamentally prevent dangerous microorganisms and hazardous foreign matter from reaching the customer. The most cost-effective way to accomplish this is by preventing the occurrence of adulteration or contamination.

Prevention focuses on identifying and controlling the numerous variables that affect food product safety. These include the building, both interior and exterior, pest control, ingredients, packaging material, employees, equipment, operating procedures, sanitation procedures, storage, and shipping. To control the myriad of variables that affect the safety of food, a systematic and comprehensive approach is required by the supplier.

Hazard analysis critical control point (HACCP, typically pronounced *has-sip*) is a system that identifies and monitors safety criteria in a process to prevent hazards from occurring. HACCP is regarded as the most effective and economical way to prevent microbial, chemical, and physical contamination of food products. HACCP originated in the chemical processing industry over 40 years ago. In the 1950s, the Atomic Energy Commission began using HACCP principles to design nuclear power plants. The National Aeronautics and Space Administration suggested that the HACCP approach be used in the production of space rations, to minimize the possibility of foodborne illness among space crews. At that time, one of the contractors manufacturing space food was the Pillsbury Company. Pillsbury realized that by applying HACCP principles to the manufacture of food, they would minimize their liability. In 1971, Pillsbury adopted a HACCP process to maintain food safety.

A HACCP system

- Identifies those control points in the food processing operation that are important in the prevention of adulteration
- Identifies the hazards associated with each control point
- Establishes adequate controls at each control point
- Establishes adequate monitoring of the controls at each control point
- Establishes corrective actions with documentation

The hazard analysis begins by flowcharting the entire manufacturing process—from raw material procurement to consumption by the ultimate customer. With the entire process diagramed, the critical control points can be identified. Critical control points are those variables that (if not maintained) can result in the production of an unsafe food product. Once identified, the control limits, monitoring procedures and frequencies, and corrective actions are determined.

Several food safety regulatory agencies recognize the benefits of the HACCP approach and are recommending that food manufacturers adopt this approach. A HACCP program is voluntary, the regulatory agencies are only recommending it. However, if you are responsible for procuring safe food products for your company, it is up to you to mandate that your suppliers have a hazard prevention and control system in place. Without a system, your supplier's problems become yours.

Procuring quality products at the best value is the objective of any company's procurement department. This chapter has attempted to discuss some unique aspects of procurement in the food industry. Terminology differs slightly as it does between most industries. Managing bulk materials presents some unique problems. Additional problems are encountered in the analysis of food products. Most methods of analysis are destructive tests and many methods are qualitative. Similar problems often are encountered in the cosmetic, drug, and chemical processing industries. Food products are highly sensitive compounds that are affected by almost every variable in our natural and imposed environments. Once harvested or produced, food is subject to physical, chemical, and biological deterioration. Procuring safe, high-quality food products requires a basic knowledge of the food product, its industry, and the government agencies that regulate its safety.

Appendix A

Procurement Quality Definitions

Acceptance sampling–Sampling inspection in which decisions are made to accept or not accept product or service; the methodology that deals with procedures by which decisions to accept or not accept are based on the results of the inspection of samples.

Appraisal cost–Cost associated with measuring, evaluating, or auditing products, components, and purchased material to assure conformance with quality standards and performance requirements.

Attribute measurement–Qualitative measurement that typically shows only the number of parts or the number of defects per part failing to conform to specified criteria.

Audits–Systematic examination of the acts and decisions with respect to quality to verify or evaluate compliance to the operational requirements of the quality program or the specifications or contract requirements of the product or service. Audits of a supplier's quality system or process must be performed at the supplier's facility. Audits of a supplier's product may be performed either at the supplier's facility or in-house.

Bilateral tolerance–Splitting of a tolerance by a median axis so that each side is identical.

Calibration–Standardization by determining the deviation from a standard to ascertain the proper correction factors.

Capability ratio (CR)–Measurement of the proportion of specification width that is consumed by process variation.

Common cause–Source of variation that is random and affects all the individual values of the process output being studied.

Continuous improvement–Operational philosophy that produces products of increasing quality for customers in an increasingly efficient way and improves the return on investment on an ongoing basis.

Control chart–Graphic method for evaluating whether a process is or is not in a state of statistical control.

Control plan–Plan that establishes and maintains adequate written procedures covering all critical characteristics and key processes to ensure a consistent and acceptable quality product.

Corrective action–Resolution of problems between user and producer arising due to product nonconformance.

Customer complaint–Formal or informal allegation by the customer due to failure in meeting previously agreed on requirements by the supplier.

Design of experiments–Planned test that is used to determine whether there is a statistical relationship between variables.

Deviation–Process through which a producer is authorized to ship nonconforming products to the user with the user's concurrence.

Disposition–Final arrangement or settlement of nonconforming product in an orderly way.

Distributor–Nonmanufacturing source of product. Usually where no transformation of product takes place.

Drawing (blueprint)–Sketch of the product being produced with specified tolerances of each characteristic.

Engineering support–Essential part of a good quality system that encompasses product design and development, as well as reliability testing of new or revised products.

External failure cost–Cost generated by defective products in the field after having been shipped to customers.

Final inspection–Examination of a product to ensure that it conforms to all applicable specifications and requirements before it is packaged and shipped to the customer.

Flowchart–Diagram that shows step-by-step progression of a product through a manufacturing system showing all factors that could adversely affect quality at the point where they occur.

Frequency distribution–Tabulation of the number of times a given outcome has occurred within the sample of products being checked.

Gage repeatability–Measurement of the consistency obtained with one gage when used several times by one operator while measuring the identical characteristic on the same parts.

Gage reproducibility–Measurement of the consistency of different operators using the same gage while measuring the identical characteristic on the same parts.

Gage variability–Measurement of the consistency of at least two sets of measurements obtained with a gage on the same parts as a result of time.

Incoming inspection–Inspection of purchased parts at the customer's facility after the shipment of parts from the supplier to ensure supplier compliance with specifications and contractual agreements.

Inspection–Process of measuring, examining, testing, gaging, or otherwise comparing the unit with the applicable requirements.

Inspection (100 percent)–The inspection of all parts in a lot for all characteristics to ensure compliance to specifications.

Internal failure costs–Costs generated by a producer in making defective and nonconforming materials and products that do not meet company quality specifications.

Key process characteristics–Manufacturing processes deemed crucial in producing a product to its design intent.

Key product characteristics–Properties deemed crucial by the user to satisfy the design intent.

Lot control–System that provides the means to trace pertinent information about the materials and/or components comprising a given product.

Material certification–Process through which documented evidence establishes that a product is in compliance with designated specifications.

Measuring and testing devices–Equipment used to evaluate a product's conformance to its specifications.

Nonconforming material–Material that is not in compliance with specifications.

Normal (Gaussian) distribution–Condition where measured variation is symmetric about a central value and has a bell-shaped form.

Prevention cost–Cost of strategies directing actions and analysis toward continuous improvement of process management.

Process–Combination of people, equipment, materials, methods, and environment that produce output to a planned effect.

Process audit–Analysis of elements of a process and appraisal of completeness, correctness, or conditions.

Process capability–Limits within which a tool or process operates based on minimum variability as governed by the prevailing circumstances.

Process capability index (PCI)–Ratio that measures the inherent variability of a process in relation to specification limits.

Process capability ratio (CPK)–Ratio that measures the centering and variability of a process in relation to specification limits.

Process survey–Survey used to evaluate whether a supplier has process controls in place to ensure that the supplier's process will manufacture quality products. Process controls include proper tooling, equipment, inspection, and so forth.

Procurement quality–Any and all aspects dealing with the purchasing of products.

Product audit–Quantitative assessment of conformance to required product characteristics.

Product/process characteristic–Any given attribute of a product or process.

Rating method–Quantitative method of evaluating systems and performance.

Ship-to-stock (STS)–Program in which the supplier and customer work together for improved quality and conformance of manufactured parts to eliminate the need for incoming or source inspection of purchased parts or products. Under this program, individual products or processes are qualified as opposed to an overall supplier certification. Also, maintenance of this program is provided through audits.

Skip-lot–Plan in acceptance sampling in which some lots in a series are accepted without inspection when the sampling results for a stated number of immediately preceding lots meet stated criteria.

Special cause–Source of variation that is not inherent in the system and can be prevented.

Source inspection–Inspection of purchased parts at the supplier's facility by a customer representative to ensure supplier compliance with specifications and contractual agreements.

Specification–Specific limits or parameters that are required to assure the success of a product to perform as designed.

Standard deviation/sigma–Measurement of the spread of dispersion of a set or values about their average value.

Statistical control–Process considered to be in a state of statistical control if variations among the observed sampling results can be attributed to a constant system of chance causes.

Statistical process control (SPC)–Use of statistical techniques to analyze a process or its output to take required actions to achieve and maintain a state of statistical control and improve the process capability.

Supplier certification–Program aimed at qualifying suppliers already on an approved status to a higher level of approval called certification. This usually encompasses review of the supplier's past delivered product history, and an in-depth quality system survey. Certification of a supplier usually is all-encompassing and covers all products. Once certification is granted to a supplier, the customer institutes a reduced sampling at incoming inspection.

Survey–Broad overview of a supplier's system or process used to evaluate the adequacy of that system or process to produce quality products.

System audit–Documented activity performed to verify, by examination and evaluation of objective evidence, that applicable elements of the quality system are suitable and have been developed, documented, and effectively implemented in accordance with specified requirements.

System survey–Survey conducted to assess whether the supplier has appropriately controlled systems that will adequately prevent the manufacture of nonconforming products.

Variable measurement–Quantitative data in which physical properties are measured, such as hole diameters or coating thickness.

Variation–Inevitable differences among individual outputs of a process that are grouped into common causes and special causes.

Vendor rating–System of measurement of vendor or supplier performance against set goals or standards.

Verification–Physical confirmation of a stated condition.

See also:

1. ANSI/ASQC Standard A1-1978. *Definitions, Symbols, Formulas, and Tables for Control Charts.* Milwaukee, Wis.: American Society for Quality Control.
2. ANSI/ASQC Standard A2-1978. *Terms, Symbols, and Definitions for Acceptance Sampling.* Milwaukee, Wis.: American Society for Quality Control.
3. ANSI/ASQC Standard A3-1978. *Quality Systems Terminology.* Milwaukee, Wis.: American Society for Quality Control.
4. ANSI/ASQC Standard C1-1968 (ANSI 21.8-1971). *Specifications of General Requirements for a Quality Program.* Milwaukee, Wis.: American Society for Quality Control.
5. American Society for Quality Control Statistics Division. *Glossary and Tables for Statistical Quality Control,* 2d ed., Milwaukee, Wis.: American Society for Quality Control, 1983.
6. American Society for Testing Materials Committee on Terminology. *Compilation of ASTM Standard Definitions,* 6th ed. Philadelphia, Penn.: American Society for Testing Materials, 1986.

Appendix B

Audit Guidelines

Auditing is a necessary part of the ship-to-stock (STS) program to ensure the continued quality of products that are shipped directly to stock. Audits are different from the STS supplier surveys in that, while surveys are a preliminary evaluation of possible STS candidates, audits are evaluations based on the criteria which were agreed to during qualification of the supplier quality system. Another way of looking at surveys and audits is to say that a survey is a review for system and process adequacy where an audit is a review for compliance to documented system, process, and product requirements. It is my belief that these professionally conducted audits will be of benefit to both the customer and the supplier.

This appendix has been divided into the following sections:

Section 1 Introduction

STS audits will help ensure that the quality of products purchased through the STS program is maintained. You and your supplier must agree to criteria relevant to three audit areas: system, process, and product. Auditors will then verify, report, and assure a supplier's compliance with these criteria. This appendix will define the responsibilities for auditing and provide general information for the auditing of STS products.

Section 2 Ship-to-Stock Audit Organization

The customer representatives should handle all daily interactions with each supplier. Their auditing responsibilities should include

- Serving as a liaison between the supplier and the customer
- Conducting audits based on frequencies specified in the STS agreement
- Monitoring all necessary in-house audits on STS parts
- Documenting all audit results
- Issuing corrective action requests when required and ensuring that they are implemented
- Discussing audit and survey results with the supplier
- Notifying the supplier of changes to the audit schedule

The supplier representative should be responsible for the following:

- Periodically auditing his or her own company and product as specified in the STS agreement
- Serving as a liaison between the supplier and the customer

Scheduling and Criteria
System and process audits are based on the supplier's documentation for the system or process used to manufacture the qualified part.

Product audits are based on the product's specifications for manufacture and fitness for use.

The following principles apply to all STS quality audits:

- Audits should be conducted in a professional manner; nonconformances should be handled immediately in a constructive manner.
- Auditors should have a thorough knowledge of quality and auditing principles.
- Audits should be conducted where the action is.
- The auditor should maintain control and not be led by the supplier.
- Auditors should verify all verbal information.
- Auditors should prepare an appropriate checklist before each audit emphasizing product quality and reliability. (You and your suppliers should reach a consensus on the criteria included.)
- The auditor should verify facts by informally discussing audit results with the supplier representative before the closing conference.
- Top management, for both the supplier and the customer, must be involved in the closing conference when the results require their attention.
- To be effective, corrective action must be followed up.
- Auditors should continually modify their checklists for successive audits to ensure the most effective audit.
- Auditors must be realistic, firm, and fair.
- All audit reports should be kept on file.

Reports, including corrective action plans, should be prepared after each audit and submitted to both supplier and customer management. Formal corrective action must be taken on any critical deficiencies found during an audit. Minor deficiencies may be resolved on an informal basis, but the deficiency should be documented and corrective action verified during follow-up audits.

Ship-to-Stock Audits

System Audits

A system audit should include all phases of the supplier's system and contain six major categories.

- Drawings and specifications
- Purchased material
- Measuring and testing equipment
- Process control and product acceptance
- Storage, packing, shipping, and record retention
- Quality program management

Process Audits

Process audits should be conducted periodically at the supplier's facility to ensure adherence to documentation. Usually audits are conducted quarterly to semiannually.

Some examples of process audit frequencies are

- Critical products—quarterly
- Complex, key, or high-volume products—quarterly
- Minor or supplier-controlled products—semiannually or annually

The customer representative who performs process audits should establish an auditing plan that includes all phases of the supplier's process for manufacturing a particular product. The following is a list of major types of process audits shown as examples in this work.

- Machine supplier
- Injection molding supplier
- Casting supplier
- Sheet metal or stamping supplier
- Special process audit

Product Audits

An STS product audit is a review of a part to determine if it duplicates the criteria of the first-article inspection. A supplier's inspection documents also may be audited during a product audit. Product audits may be conducted at the supplier's facility by either the supplier or customer representative, or the audit may take place at the customer site and be performed by the customer representative. When the audit occurs at the supplier site and is performed by the supplier representative, the customer representative should witness or verify the process and review the results. If the audit occurs at the customer site, the auditor should use the customer's inspection areas, equipment, and laboratories as needed. The supplier representative may be allowed to witness this process. If the audit uncovers deficiencies, the supplier representative should be shown the method used. This will ensure that inspection of product is consistent regardless of where and by whom it is performed.

Section 3   Ship-to-Stock System Audit

An STS system audit is an in-depth review of a supplier's system to ensure that it is in compliance with documentation. It is based on supplier standards, such as the supplier's quality manual.

System audits usually will be performed once a year or completed in sections throughout the course of the year. They will include a follow-up on corrective action areas when necessary.

System Auditing Plan

The system auditing plan is intended to include all phases of the supplier's system and contains six major categories.

1. Drawings and specifications
2. Purchased material
3. Measuring and testing equipment

4. Process control and product acceptance
5. Storage, packing, shipping, and record retention
6. Quality program management

The survey format shown may be used as a base from which the system audit checklists may be developed. These lists should be tailored to the supplier's system and include references to the supplier's policies and procedures where applicable.

STS is considered a cooperative approach to quality. When a supplier performs an internal self audit, there is no reason why the customer auditor cannot piggyback on the information. In essence, the customer auditor can tailor the checklist to coincide with the supplier's internal audit.

The customer's auditor should complete an appropriate summary report after each audit. The auditor and the supplier's management should review the audit results and ensure that any corrective actions are implemented.

The auditor should bear in mind that the purpose of the entire audit is to evaluate a supplier's system on its ability to yield products that will not require incoming inspection at the customer's facility. Above all, everyone must remember that the audit is to *evaluate* and *improve* the audited elements if deficiency is found. The audit must be a win–win experience, not a gotcha experience.

Section 4   Ship-to-Stock Process Audit

An STS process audit is a periodic review of the supplier's method of production and documentation of inspections to ensure that points agreed to in the characteristic accountability report have been maintained. Usually process audits are conducted quarterly to semiannually.

Some examples of process audit frequency are

- Critical products—quarterly
- Complex or high-volume products—quarterly
- Minor or supplier-controlled products—semiannually or annually

> *Note:* A breakdown indicating the frequency of audits for specific areas within each process category precedes the auditing checklist in this appendix.

The customer representative who performs process audits should establish an auditing plan that includes all phases of the supplier's process for manufacturing a particular product. The following pages are examples of process audits for four different supplier categories. Five special process audit checklists also are included. These checklists should be used as guidelines and may be modified to properly meet the needs of the process audit. It is important that auditors record any conditions found which are, or could be, detrimental to product quality, even if such conditions are not included on the prepared checklist.

The auditor also should complete a summary report. If necessary, the auditor and the supplier's management should review the audit results and ensure that corrective actions are implemented.

Ship-to-Stock Process Audit Examples

Major Supplier Categories
- Machine
- Injection molding
- Casting
- Sheet metal or stamping

Special Process Audit Checklists
- Painting
- Certification review (heat treat, plating, nondestructive testing)
- Heat treat
- Plating
- Nondestructive testing
    - –X ray
    - –Penetrant

Machine Supplier Audit Example

Schedule

Audit Areas	Suggested Audit Frequency
A. Stock (release, traceability, and storage of raw material)	Quarterly
B. Manufacturing operations (jig boring, milling, drilling, turning, grinding, deburring, etc.)	Quarterly
C. Heat treat and plating (certification review)	Semiannually
D. Marking	Quarterly
E. Final inspection and gage calibration	Quarterly
F. Nondestructive testing	Quarterly
G. Plate layout	As required for first-article/product audit
H. Packaging and shipping	Quarterly

Machine Supplier Process Audit

Supplier_____

Auditor_____

Date completed_____

A. Stock area	Yes	No
1. Proper paperwork is required for storage.	_____	_____
2. Use of stockroom is controlled.	_____	_____
3. Material is properly coded when going into stock.	_____	_____
4. Stock area is organized.	_____	_____
5. Material waiting testing is segregated and controlled.	_____	_____
6. Verification for proper alloy (lab test of certification review) occurs.	_____	_____
7. Material is properly coded for checkout and removed by authorized personnel only.	_____	_____
8. Purchase order identifies specification, part number, and revision.	_____	_____
9. Dimensions are verified when material is removed.	_____	_____

Notes

_____
_____
_____
_____
_____
_____
_____
_____
_____
_____
_____
_____
_____
_____
_____

Machine Supplier Process Audit

Supplier_____

Auditor_____

Date completed_____

B. Manufacturing operations	<u>Yes</u>	<u>No</u>
1. Area is organized.	_____	_____
2. Measuring devices are properly calibrated.	_____	_____
3. Received parts are properly identified.	_____	_____
4. Drawing revisions are current.	_____	_____
5. Detailed instructions are on or near machines.	_____	_____
6. Operator follows instructions.	_____	_____
7. Proper measuring equipment is available. (Refer to characteristic accountability report.)	_____	_____
8. Measurement of one randomly selected part corresponds to dimensions on the operation sheets or engineering drawings.	_____	_____
9. Dimensions generated at this station are inspected per the frequency of the characteristic accountability report.	_____	_____
10. Discrepant parts are adequately identified and separated.	_____	_____
11. Parts sent from area are properly identified.	_____	_____

Notes

_____

_____

_____

_____

_____

_____

_____

_____

_____

_____

_____

_____

_____

_____

_____

Machine Supplier Process Audit

Supplier_____

Auditor_____

Date completed_____

C. Certification review (heat treat and plating)	Yes	No
1. Requirements are specified on purchase order.	_____	_____
2. Proper documents are sent with part.	_____	_____
3. Part is properly identified.	_____	_____
4. Part is returned with proper identification.	_____	_____
5. Part is certified to comply with specification.	_____	_____
6. Part is tested to ensure compliance with specification.	_____	_____

Test description:_____

_____

_____

_____

_____

Notes

_____

_____

_____

_____

_____

_____

_____

_____

_____

_____

_____

_____

_____

Machine Supplier Process Audit

Supplier_____

Auditor_____

Date completed_____

		Yes	No
D.	Marking		
	1. Items routed to marking area are properly identified.	_____	_____
	2. Marking conforms with specified method and format.	_____	_____
	3. Specific marking instructions are available.	_____	_____
	4. Examine four part numbers for marking (size, legibility, etc.)	_____	_____

Notes

_____

_____

_____

_____

_____

_____

_____

_____

_____

_____

_____

_____

_____

_____

Machine Supplier Process Audit

Supplier_____
Auditor_____
Date completed_____

E. Finish inspection and gage calibration   <u>Yes</u>   <u>No</u>

1. Variable dimension data are recorded and _____ _____
   retained when required.
2. Dimensions and surface finish meet require- _____ _____
   ments of control drawing. (Spot-check parts.)
3. Proper measuring equipment is available in _____ _____
   area per characteristic accountability report.
4. Equipment is calibrated per quality control _____ _____
   manual. (Check records on a gage being used.)
5. Inspection process sheets contain _____ _____
   a. Characteristics to be inspected.
   b. Frequency of inspection.
   c. Gages and fixtures to be used, if any.
6. Frequency of dimensional inspections meets _____ _____
   minimum specified per characteristic
   accountability report.
7. Inspection forms are completed properly. _____ _____
8. Acceptable parts and paperwork are identified _____ _____
   by inspector.
9. Rejected parts are tagged to distinguish them _____ _____
   from accepted products.
10. Rejected parts are segregated pending _____ _____
    disposition.
11. Rejected parts are reviewed at team meetings _____ _____
    and corrective action is taken.

Notes

_____
_____
_____
_____
_____
_____
_____
_____
_____
_____
_____

Machine Supplier Process Audit

Supplier_____

Auditor_____

Date completed_____

		Yes	No
F.	Nondestructive testing		

X ray

1. Parts that have passed X-ray inspection are marked.   _____ _____

2. Parts are adequately deburred and cleaned to prevent false X-ray indications.   _____ _____

3. Parts are visually inspected prior to X ray.   _____ _____

4. X-ray viewers are clean and located properly to ensure proper reading of film.   _____ _____

5. X-ray technique procedure is available.   _____ _____

6. X rays are taken per the approved technique.   _____ _____

7. Operator complies with the specifications of the process sheets.   _____ _____

8. The current revision of the specification or process sheet is available.   _____ _____

9. Proper acceptance criteria are available.   _____ _____

10. Defects are clearly identified on parts.   _____ _____

11. Defects are clearly identified on film.   _____ _____

12. Records of parts inspected by X ray are available and accurate.   _____ _____

13. Records show accept or reject reason.   _____ _____

14. Records are signed by the inspector.   _____ _____

15. Discrepant parts are segregated.   _____ _____

16. Rework parts are reviewed by engineer and routed to ensure heat treat and re-X ray.   _____ _____

17. Scrap material is disposed of properly.   _____ _____

18. Film is identified with lot, part number, serial number, etc.   _____ _____

19. Film envelope is identified.   _____ _____

20. 2T sensitivity acceptable.   _____ _____

21. Density of film is per specification.   _____ _____

22. Number of lots audited is per specification.   _____ _____

23. Densitometer is available, calibrated, and traceable to NIST.   _____ _____

24. The density strip is available, calibrated, and traceable to NIST.   _____ _____

F. Nondestructive testing	Yes	No
X ray (continued)		

25. Level II/III radiographers do all acceptance reading.

26. Eye examinations are current.

27. Written examinations are current.

28. Records of inspector's exams are available.

29. Automatic processor is controlled.
   a. Density strips are run daily and logged.
   b. Temperature is checked daily.
   c. Replenishing rate is checked and logged periodically.

30. Radiographers are audited and results logged.

31. Parts are available for review on questionable indications.

32. Questionable parts are re-X rayed.

33. Film is punched with inspector identification.

34. Certifications are properly completed.

35. Certification identifies serial number, etc., of rejects.

36. Film envelope or copy of certification in envelope identifies serial number of rejects.

Penetrant

1. Inspectors stamp parts that have passed penetrant inspection.

2. Location of defect is clearly identified on part.

3. Inspector signs records.

4. Parts are adequately cleaned prior to penetrant inspection (scale, water, oil, and grease removed).

5. Penetrant inspection process sheet is available.

6. The operator uses process sheet or specification.

7. Correct revision of process sheet or specification is used.

8. Discrepant parts are segregated.

9. Inspectors meet eyesight requirements.

10. Eye examinations are current.

11. Records and test reports verify that examiners are current in certification.

F. Nondestructive testing   <u>Yes</u>   <u>No</u>
    Penetrant (continued)

    12. Parts are serialized prior to inspection.   _____   _____

    13. A test sample with known defects is checked   _____   _____
         to verify process.

    14. Checks for contaminations are made on   _____   _____
         penetrant, emulsifier, and developer baths
         or powders.

    15. Operator processing parts adheres to time   _____   _____
         cycles.

                                Notes

_____
_____
_____
_____
_____
_____
_____
_____
_____
_____
_____
_____
_____

Machine Supplier Process Audit

Supplier_____

Auditor_____

Date completed_____

G. <u>Plate layout, first piece</u>	<u>Yes</u>	<u>No</u>
1. Proper data are utilized and all characteristics are accounted for.	_____	_____
2. Proper tools are used.	_____	_____
3. All dimensions are controlled/monitored periodically.	_____	_____

Notes

_____

_____

_____

_____

_____

_____

_____

_____

_____

_____

_____

_____

_____

_____

Machine Supplier Process Audit

Supplier_____

Auditor_____

Date completed_____

	Yes	No
H. Packaging and shipping		
1. Boxes are properly labeled.	_____	_____
2. Parts are packaged to prevent damage.	_____	_____
3. Parts are protected against corrosion.	_____	_____
4. X rays are included and properly labeled when necessary.	_____	_____
5. Packing list specifies the number of parts, test bars, and certifications enclosed.	_____	_____
6. Release forms and certifications are enclosed as required.	_____	_____

Notes

_____

_____

_____

_____

_____

_____

_____

_____

_____

_____

_____

_____

_____

_____

Machine Supplier Process Audit Summary

A. Stock area comments: _____

_____

B. Manufacturing operations comments: _____

_____

C. Certification review comments:_____

_____

D. Marking comments:_____

_____

E. Final inspection comments: _____

_____

F. Nondestructive testing comments:_____

_____

G. Plate layout, first piece comments: _____

_____

H. Packaging and shipping comments: _____

_____

General comments:_____

_____

_____

_____

_____

_____

_____

_____

Use additional pages as necessary.

Injection Molding Process Audit Example

Schedule

Audit Areas	Suggested Audit Frequency
A. Stock area (release and storage of raw material)	Quarterly
B. Molding operations	Quarterly
C. Marking	Quarterly
D. Painting	Quarterly
E. Final inspection and gage calibration	Quarterly
F. Packaging and shipping	Quarterly

Injection Molding Process Audit

Supplier_____

Auditor_____

Date completed_____

A. Stock area	Yes	No
1. Proper coding of stock in storage.	_____	_____
2. Organized stock area.	_____	_____
3. Proper paperwork is used for stock and stock release.	_____	_____
4. Use is controlled.	_____	_____
5. Material awaiting testing is segregated and controlled.	_____	_____
6. Proper formulation certification from supplier is verified.	_____	_____
7. Each batch or container leaving area is coded.	_____	_____
8. Lab that performs accept or on-site testing for uniformity of granules and chemical analysis is certified.	_____	_____

Notes

_____
_____
_____
_____
_____
_____
_____
_____
_____
_____
_____
_____
_____
_____

Injection Molding Process Audit

Supplier_____

Auditor_____

Date completed_____

B. Molding operations	Yes	No
1. Drawing in use is current revision.	_____	_____
2. Detailed instructions are on or near machines for heat, time, pressure, ram speed, etc.	_____	_____
3. Operator follows instructions.	_____	_____
4. Proper measuring equipment is available per the characteristic accountability report.	_____	_____
5. Measuring devices are properly calibrated.	_____	_____
6. Parts periodically sampled during production run.	_____	_____
7. Measurement of randomly selected parts or components corresponds to dimensions on operations sheets or drawings.	_____	_____
8. Dimensions generated are being inspected per the frequency of characteristic accountability report.	_____	_____
9. Discrepant parts are identified and segregated.	_____	_____
10. Parts are protected to prevent damage.	_____	_____
11. System is in place to prevent deviations from post-molding stress relief.	_____	_____
12. Parts leaving area are properly identified.	_____	_____
13. Area is organized.	_____	_____

Notes

_____

_____

_____

_____

_____

_____

_____

_____

_____

_____

_____

_____

_____

_____

Injection Molding Process Audit

Supplier_____

Auditor_____

Date completed_____

C. <u>Marking</u>   <u>Yes</u>   <u>No</u>

    1.   Material routed to area is properly identified.   _____   _____

    2.   Specified marking method and format is used.   _____   _____

    3.   Specific marking instructions are available.   _____   _____

    4.   Parts are identified for batch, material, or date   _____   _____
        of molding as required.

Notes

_____

_____

_____

_____

_____

_____

_____

_____

_____

_____

_____

_____

_____

_____

Injection Molding Process Audit

Supplier_____

Auditor_____

Date completed_____

		Yes	No
D.	<u>Painting</u>		
	1. Paint batch has approval number.	_____	_____
	2. A current usable paint chip is available.	_____	_____
	3. The paint cycle is posted in paint area, including paint solvent mix gun pressures, bake time, temperature, etc.	_____	_____
	4. Equipment is in working order. Check pressure gages, spray guns, oven charts, spray booths.	_____	_____
	5. Work is inspected for color, gloss, and thickness.	_____	_____
	6. Work is packaged when fully dry and cool.	_____	_____

Notes

_____

_____

_____

_____

_____

_____

_____

_____

_____

_____

_____

_____

_____

_____

Injection Molding Process Audit

Supplier_____
Auditor_____
Date completed_____

E. Final inspection and gage calibration	Yes	No
1. Variable dimension data ar recorded and retained when required.	_____	_____
2. Dimensions and surface finish meet requirements of control drawing. (Spot-check parts.)	_____	_____
3. Proper measuring equipment is available in area per characteristic accountability report.	_____	_____
4. Equipment is calibrated per quality control manual. (Check records on a gage being used.)	_____	_____
5. Inspection process sheet contains a. Characteristics to be inspected. b. Frequency of inspection. c. Gages and fixtures to be used, if any.	_____	_____
6. Frequency of dimensional inspections meets minimum specified per characteristic accountability report.	_____	_____
7. Finished inspection forms are completed properly.	_____	_____
8. Accepted parts and paperwork are identified by inspector.	_____	_____
9. Rejected parts are tagged and segregated pending disposition.	_____	_____
10. Rejected parts are reviewed at team meetings and corrective action is initiated.	_____	_____
11. Serial numbers or lot identification of products is inspected/recorded.	_____	_____
12. Accountability is possible for all products.	_____	_____
13. Physical tests such as impact and tensile are performed as required.	_____	_____
14. U/L flammability tests are performed as required.	_____	_____

Notes

_____
_____
_____
_____
_____
_____

Injection Molding Process Audit

Supplier_____

Auditor_____

Date completed_____

		Yes	No
F.	Packaging and shipping		
1.	Boxes are properly labeled.	_____	_____
2.	Parts are packaged to prevent damage in transit.	_____	_____
3.	Packing list specifies number of products, test results, certifications enclosed.	_____	_____
4.	Release forms and certifications are enclosed, as required.	_____	_____

Notes

_____

_____

_____

_____

_____

_____

_____

_____

_____

_____

_____

_____

_____

_____

_____

Injection Molding Process Audit Summary

A. Stock area comments: _____
_____

B. Molding operations comments: _____
_____

C. Marking comments: _____
_____

D. Painting comments: _____
_____

E. Final inspection comments: _____
_____

F. Packaging and shipping comments: _____
_____

General comments: _____
_____
_____
_____
_____
_____
_____
_____
_____
_____

Use additional pages as necessary.

Casting Audit Example

Schedule

Audit Areas	Suggested Audit Frequency
A. Stock (release and storage of raw material)	Quarterly
B. Molding control	Quarterly
Investment castings (wax, assembly)	Twice Quarterly
Sand castings (pattern and mold assembly)	Twice Quarterly
C. Casting (melting and pouring)	Twice Quarterly
D. Heat treat	Twice Quarterly
E. Material testing (tensile, chemistry)	Quarterly
F. Marking	Quarterly
G. Final inspection and gage calibration	Quarterly
H. Nondestructive testing (FPI, X ray)	Quarterly
I. Finish and straighten	Quarterly
J. Packaging and shipping	Quarterly

Casting Process Audit

Supplier_____

Auditor_____

Date completed_____

A. Stock (release and storage of raw material)	Yes	No
1. Proper paperwork is required for storage.		
2. Use of stockroom is controlled.		
3. Material is properly coded.		
4. Stock area is organized.		
5. Material waiting test is segregated and controlled.		
6. Verification for proper alloy (lab test of certification review) occurs.		
7. Material is properly coded for checkout and removed by authorized personnel only.		
8. Purchase order identifies specification, part number, and revision.		
9. Dimensions are verified when material is removed.		

Notes

_____

_____

_____

_____

_____

_____

_____

_____

_____

_____

_____

_____

_____

Casting Process Audit

Supplier_____

Auditor_____

Date completed_____

		Yes	No
B.	Mold control—Investment casting		
1.	Proper identification of dies.	_____	_____
2.	Dies stored to prevent damage.	_____	_____
3.	Dimensional inspection is performed periodically on waxes to verify die.	_____	_____
4.	Detailed instructions are on or near injection mold machine, including heat, time, etc.	_____	_____
5.	Operator follows instructions.	_____	_____
6.	First wax inspection records are on file.	_____	_____
7.	Assembly procedure is documented.	_____	_____
8.	Photos, drawings, or models of assembly are available.	_____	_____
9.	Waxes are properly stored.	_____	_____
10.	Temperature of wax area is controlled.	_____	_____
11.	Wax inspection is performed.	_____	_____
12.	Shell process instructions are in area and followed, including number of dips, shell backup, dewax pressure/temperature, and cure time.	_____	_____

Notes

_____

_____

_____

_____

_____

_____

_____

_____

_____

_____

_____

_____

_____

_____

_____

Casting Process Audit

Supplier_____

Auditor_____

Date completed_____

B. Mold control—Sand casting	Yes	No
1. Proper identification of pattern.	_____	_____
2. Patterns stored to prevent damage.	_____	_____
3. Periodic inspection to verify pattern wear.	_____	_____
4. First part inspection from pattern on file.	_____	_____
5. Mold procedure documented (type and condition of sand).	_____	_____
6. Core procedure is documented.	_____	_____
7. Mold buildup documented by photos or models showing locations of cores, chills, etc.	_____	_____
8. Bake procedure is documented.	_____	_____
9. Operators are following procedures.	_____	_____

Notes

_____

_____

_____

_____

_____

_____

_____

_____

_____

_____

_____

_____

_____

_____

Casting Process Audit

Supplier_____
Auditor_____
Date completed_____

C. Casting (melting and pouring)	Yes	No
1. Melting instructions are in area (time, temperature, alloy additions, etc.)	_____	_____
2. Pouring instructions are in area.	_____	_____
3. Molders follow procedure.	_____	_____
4. Quality person is in area during pour.	_____	_____
5. Castings leaving area are properly identified.	_____	_____
6. Raw stock received in area is properly identified.	_____	_____
7. Furnace is calibrated.	_____	_____
8. Area is organized.	_____	_____
9. Scrap is properly identified.	_____	_____
10. Discrepant parts are segregated.	_____	_____

Notes

_____
_____
_____
_____
_____
_____
_____
_____
_____
_____
_____
_____
_____
_____
_____

Casting Process Audit

Supplier_____
Auditor_____
Date completed_____

D. Heat treat	Yes	No
1. Parts are received with proper identification.	_____	_____
2. Furnace is calibrated.	_____	_____
3. Cycle is controlled.	_____	_____
4. Heat treat procedures are available.	_____	_____
5. Procedure is being followed.	_____	_____
6. Furnace charts are retained.	_____	_____
7. Hardness is tested and recorded.	_____	_____
8. Area is organized.	_____	_____
9. Parts leaving area are properly identified.	_____	_____

Notes

_____
_____
_____
_____
_____
_____
_____
_____
_____
_____
_____
_____
_____
_____

Casting Process Audit

Supplier_____

Auditor_____

Date completed_____

E. Material testing (tensile and chemistry)	Yes	No
1. Specimen material is properly received and identified.	_____	_____
2. Specimen is properly prepared.	_____	_____
3. Specimen finish is proper.	_____	_____
4. Test equipment is calibrated.	_____	_____
5. Test is conducted per specification.	_____	_____
6. Results are properly interpreted.	_____	_____
7. Test results are properly documented.	_____	_____

Notes

_____

_____

_____

_____

_____

_____

_____

_____

_____

_____

_____

_____

_____

_____

Casting Process Audit

Supplier_____

Auditor_____

Date completed_____

F. Marking	Yes	No
1. Items routed to marking area are properly identified.	_____	_____
2. Marking conforms with specified method and format.	_____	_____
3. Specific marking instructions are available.	_____	_____
4. Four part numbers are used for marking (size, legibility, etc.).	_____	_____

Notes

_____

_____

_____

_____

_____

_____

_____

_____

_____

_____

_____

_____

_____

Casting Process Audit

Supplier_____
Auditor_____
Date completed_____

G. Final inspection and gage calibration	<u>Yes</u>	<u>No</u>
1. Variable dimension data are recorded and retained when required.	_____	_____
2. Dimensions and surface finish meet requirements of control drawing. (Spot-check parts.)	_____	_____
3. Proper measuring equipment is available in area per characteristic accountability report.	_____	_____
4. Equipment is calibrated per quality control manual. (Check records on a gage being used.)	_____	_____
5. Inspection process sheets contain a. Characteristics to be inspected. b. Frequency of inspection. c. Gages and fixtures to be used, if any.	_____	_____
6. Frequency of dimensional inspections meets minimum specified per characteristic accountability report.	_____	_____
7. Inspection forms are properly completed.	_____	_____
8. Acceptable parts and paperwork are identified by inspector.	_____	_____
9. Rejected products are tagged to distinguish them from accepted products.	_____	_____
10. Rejected products are segregated pending disposition.	_____	_____
11. Rejected products are reviewed at team meetings and corrective action is taken.	_____	_____

Notes

_____
_____
_____
_____
_____
_____
_____
_____
_____
_____
_____
_____
_____

Casting Process Audit

Supplier_____

Auditor_____

Date completed_____

H. Nondestructive testing	Yes	No
X ray		
1. Parts that have passed X-ray inspection are marked.		
2. Parts are adequately deburred and cleaned to prevent false X-ray indications.		
3. Parts are visually inspected prior to X ray.		
4. X-ray viewers are clean and located properly to ensure proper reading of film.		
5. X-ray technique procedure is available.		
6. X rays are taken per the technique.		
7. Operator complies with the specifications of the process sheets.		
8. The current revision of the specification or process sheet is available.		
9. Proper acceptance criteria are available.		
10. Defects are clearly identified on parts.		
11. Defects are clearly identified on film.		
12. Records of parts that are X-ray inspected are available and accurate.		
13. Records show accept or reject reason.		
14. Records are signed by the inspector.		
15. Discrepant parts are segregated.		
16. Rework parts are reviewed by engineer and routed to ensure heat treat and re-X ray.		
17. Scrap material is disposed of properly.		
18. Film is identified with lot, part number, serial number, etc.		
19. Film envelope is identified.		
20. 2T sensitivity acceptable.		
21. Density of film is per specification.		
22. Number of lots audited is per specification.		
23. Densitometer is available, calibrated, and traceable to NIST.		

H. Nondestructive testing   Yes   No
    X ray (continued)

24. The density strip is available, calibrated, and   _____   _____
     traceable to NIST.

25. Level II/III radiographers do all acceptance   _____   _____
     reading.

26. Eye examinations are current.   _____   _____

27. Written examinations are current.   _____   _____

28. Records of inspector's exams are available.   _____   _____

29. Automatic processor is controlled.   _____   _____
     a. Density strips are run daily and logged.
     b. Temperature is checked daily.
     c. Replenishing rate is checked and logged
         periodically.

30. Radiographers are audited and results logged.   _____   _____

31. Parts are available for review on questionable   _____   _____
     indications.

32. Questionable parts are re-X rayed.   _____   _____

33. Film is punched with inspector identification.   _____   _____

34. Certifications are properly completed.   _____   _____

35. Certification identifies serial number, etc., of   _____   _____
     rejects.

36. Film envelope or copy of certification in   _____   _____
     envelope identifies serial number of rejects.

Penetrant

1. Inspectors stamp parts that have passed   _____   _____
    penetrant inspection.

2. Location of defect is clearly identified on part.   _____   _____

3. Inspector signs records.   _____   _____

4. Parts are adequately cleaned prior to penetrant   _____   _____
    inspection (scale, water, oil, and grease
    removed).

5. Penetrant inspection process sheet is available.   _____   _____

6. The operator uses process sheet or specification.   _____   _____

7. Correct revision of process sheet or   _____   _____
    specification is used.

8. Discrepant parts are segregated.   _____   _____

9. Inspectors meet eyesight requirements.   _____   _____

10. Eye examinations are current.   _____   _____

H. Nondestructive testing	Yes	No
Penetrant (continued)		

11. Records and test reports verify that examiners are current in certification.   _____   _____

12. Parts are serialized prior to inspection.   _____   _____

13. A test sample with known defects is checked to verify process.   _____   _____

14. Checks for contaminations are made on penetrant, emulsifier, and developer baths or powders.   _____   _____

15. Operator processing parts adheres to time cycles.   _____   _____

Notes

_____

_____

_____

_____

_____

_____

_____

_____

_____

_____

_____

_____

_____

_____

Casting Process Audit

Supplier_____
Auditor_____
Date completed_____

		Yes	No
I.	Finish and straighten		
1.	Instructions are documented.	_____	_____
2.	Fixtures used for final acceptance are calibrated.	_____	_____
3.	Nondestructive testing is verified after straightening.	_____	_____

Notes

_____

_____

_____

_____

_____

_____

_____

_____

_____

_____

_____

_____

_____

_____

_____

_____

Casting Process Audit

Supplier_____

Auditor_____

Date completed_____

J. Packaging and shipping	<u>Yes</u>	<u>No</u>
1. Boxes are properly labeled.	_____	_____
2. Parts are packaged to prevent damage.	_____	_____
3. Parts are protected against corrosion.	_____	_____
4. X rays are included and properly labeled when necessary.	_____	_____
5. Packing list specifies the number of products, test bars, and certifications enclosed.	_____	_____
6. Release forms and certifications are enclosed as required.	_____	_____

Notes

_____

_____

_____

_____

_____

_____

_____

_____

_____

_____

_____

_____

_____

_____

Casting Process Audit Summary

A. Stock area comments: _____
_____

B. Mold control comments: _____
_____

C. Casting comments:_____
_____

D. Heat treat comments: _____
_____

E. Material testing comments: _____
_____

F. Marking comments:_____
_____

G. Final Inspection comments:_____
_____

H. Nondestructive testing comments:_____
_____

I. Finish and straighten comments: _____
_____

J. Packaging and shipping comments: _____
_____

General comments:_____
_____
_____
_____
_____
_____
_____
_____
_____

Use additional pages as necessary.

Sheet Metal or Stampings Audit Example

Schedule

Audit Areas	Suggested Audit Frequency
A. Stock (release traceability and storage of raw material)	Quarterly
B. Manufacturing operations (stamping, shearing, forming, welding, assembly)	Quarterly
C. Heat treat and plating (certification review)	Semiannually
D. Marking	Quarterly
E. Finish inspection and gage calibration	Quarterly
F. Painting	Quarterly
G. Packaging and shipping	Quarterly

Sheet Metal or Stampings Process Audit

Supplier_____
Auditor_____
Date completed_____

	Yes	No
A. Stock area		
1. Proper paperwork is required for storage.	_____	_____
2. Use of stockroom is controlled.	_____	_____
3. Material is properly coded.	_____	_____
4. Stock area is organized.	_____	_____
5. Material waiting test is segregated and controlled.	_____	_____
6. Verification for proper alloy (lab test of certification review) occurs.	_____	_____
7. Material is properly coded for checkout and removed by authorized personnel only.	_____	_____
8. Purchase order identifies specification, part number, and revision.	_____	_____
9. Dimensions are verified when material is removed.	_____	_____

Notes

_____
_____
_____
_____
_____
_____
_____
_____
_____
_____
_____
_____
_____
_____
_____
_____

Sheet Metal or Stampings Process Audit

Supplier_____
Auditor_____
Date completed_____

B. Manufacturing operations	Yes	No
1. Parts are received with proper identification.	_____	_____
2. Current revision of drawing or process sheet is used.	_____	_____
3. Detailed instructions for operation are available.	_____	_____
4. Operator follows instructions.	_____	_____
5. Proper measuring equipment is available. (Reference the characteristic accountability report.)	_____	_____
6. Measuring devices are properly calibrated.	_____	_____
7. Randomly selected part dimensions correspond to those found on the operation sheets or engineering drawings.	_____	_____
8. Dimensions generated at this station are inspected per the frequency of the characteristic accountability report.	_____	_____
9. First piece from setup was approved by QC.	_____	_____
10. In-process inspections are being performed per the supplier plan.	_____	_____
11. If punch, etc., was repaired during run, repair was verified by QC prior to restart.	_____	_____
12. Discrepant parts are adequately identified and segregated.	_____	_____
13. Parts leaving area are properly identified.	_____	_____
14. Area is organized.	_____	_____

Notes

_____
_____
_____
_____
_____
_____
_____
_____
_____
_____

Sheet Metal or Stampings Process Audit

Supplier_____
Auditor_____
Date completed_____

		Yes	No
C.	Heat treat and plating (certification review)		
1.	Requirements are specified on purchase order.	_____	_____
2.	Proper documents are sent with part.	_____	_____
3.	Part is properly identified.	_____	_____
4.	Part is returned with proper identification.	_____	_____
5.	Part is certified to comply with specification.	_____	_____
6.	Part is tested to ensure compliance with specification.	_____	_____

Test description:_____

_____
_____
_____
_____

Notes

_____
_____
_____
_____
_____
_____
_____
_____
_____

Sheet Metal or Stampings Process Audit

Supplier_____

Auditor_____

Date completed_____

D. <u>Marking</u>   <u>Yes</u>   <u>No</u>

   1.   Items routed to marking area are properly   _____   _____
identified.

   2.   Marking conforms with specified method and   _____   _____
format.

   3.   Specific marking instructions are available.   _____   _____

   4.   Four part numbers are used for marking (size, _____   _____
legibility, etc.)

Notes

_____

_____

_____

_____

_____

_____

_____

_____

_____

Sheet Metal or Stampings Process Audit

Supplier_____
Auditor_____
Date completed_____

E. Final inspection and gage calibration	Yes	No
1. Variable dimensions data are recorded and retained when required.	_____	_____
2. Dimensions and surface finish meet requirements of control drawing. (Spot-check parts.)	_____	_____
3. Proper measuring equipment is available in area per characteristic accountability report.	_____	_____
4. Equipment is calibrated per quality control manual. (Check records on a gage being used.)	_____	_____
5. Inspection process sheets contain a. Characteristics to be inspected. b. Frequency of inspection. c. Gages and fixtures to be used, if any.	_____	_____
6. Frequency of dimensional inspections meets minimum specified per characteristic accountability report.	_____	_____
7. Inspection forms are completed properly.	_____	_____
8. Acceptable parts and paperwork are identified by inspector.	_____	_____
9. Rejected products are tagged to distinguish them from accepted products.	_____	_____
10. Rejected products are segregated pending disposition.	_____	_____
11. Rejected products are reviewed at team meetings and corrective action is taken.	_____	_____

Notes

_____
_____
_____
_____
_____
_____
_____
_____
_____
_____
_____

Sheet Metal or Stampings Process Audit

Supplier_____

Auditor_____

Date completed_____

F.	Painting	Yes	No
1.	Paint batch has approval number.	_____	_____
2.	A current usable paint chip is available.	_____	_____
3.	The paint cycle is posted in paint area, including paint solvent mix gun pressures, bake time, temperature, etc.	_____	_____
4.	Equipment is in working order. Check pressure gages, spray guns, oven charts, spray booths.	_____	_____
5.	Work is inspected for color, gloss, and thickness.	_____	_____
6.	Work is packaged when fully dry and cool.	_____	_____

Notes

_____

_____

_____

_____

_____

_____

_____

_____

_____

_____

_____

_____

_____

Sheet Metal or Stampings Process Audit

Supplier_____

Auditor_____

Date completed_____

G. Packaging and Shipping	<u>Yes</u>	<u>No</u>
1. Boxes are properly labeled.	_____	_____
2. Parts are packaged to prevent damage.	_____	_____
3. Parts are protected against corrosion.	_____	_____
4. X rays are included and properly labeled when necessary.	_____	_____
5. Packing list specifies the number of products, test bars, and certifications enclosed.	_____	_____
6. Release forms and certifications are enclosed as required.	_____	_____

Notes

_____

_____

_____

_____

_____

_____

_____

_____

_____

_____

_____

_____

_____

_____

Sheet Metal or Stamping Process Audit Summary

A. Stock area comments: _____

_____

B. Manufacturing operations comments: _____

_____

C. Heat treat and plating comments: _____

_____

D. Marking comments:_____

_____

E. Final inspection comments: _____

_____

F. Painting comments: _____

_____

G. Packaging and shipping comments: _____

_____

General comments:_____

_____

_____

_____

_____

_____

_____

_____

_____

Use additional pages as necessary.

Special Process Audit

Schedule

Audit Areas	Suggested Audit Frequency
A. Painting	Quarterly
B. Certification review	Semiannually
C. Heat treat	Semiannually
D. Plating	Semiannually
E. Nondestructive testing	Quarterly
–X ray	
–Penetrant	

Special Process Audit

Supplier_____

Auditor_____

Date completed_____

A. <u>Painting</u>	<u>Yes</u>	<u>No</u>
1. Paint batch has approval number.	_____	_____
2. A current usable paint chip is available.	_____	_____
3. The paint cycle is posted in paint area, including paint solvent mix gun pressures, bake time, temperature, etc.	_____	_____
4. Equipment is in working order. Check pressure gages, spray guns, oven charts, spray booths.	_____	_____
5. Work is inspected for color, gloss, and thickness.	_____	_____
6. Work is packaged when fully dry and cool.	_____	_____

Notes

_____

_____

_____

_____

_____

_____

_____

_____

_____

_____

_____

_____

_____

_____

Special Process Audit

Supplier_____
Auditor_____
Date completed_____

		Yes	No
B.	Certification review		
1.	Requirements are specified on purchase order.	_____	_____
2.	Proper documents are sent with part.	_____	_____
3.	Part is properly identified.	_____	_____
4.	Part is returned with proper identification.	_____	_____
5.	Part is certified to comply with specification.	_____	_____
6.	Part is tested to ensure compliance with specification.	_____	_____

Test description:_____

_____
_____
_____
_____

Notes

_____
_____
_____
_____
_____
_____
_____
_____
_____
_____

Special Process Audit

Supplier_____
Auditor_____
Date completed_____

C. Heat treat	Yes	No
1. Proper documents are sent with parts.	_____	_____
2. Parts are properly identified.	_____	_____
3. Returned parts are properly identified.	_____	_____
4. The area is organized.	_____	_____
5. The flow of material is controlled.	_____	_____
6. Check the furnace control and calibration.	_____	_____
7. Heat treat instructions are available and identify the following:		
a. Furnace type	_____	_____
b. Load pattern	_____	_____
c. Preheat treat cleaning	_____	_____
d. Preheat time and temperature	_____	_____
e. Solution time and temperature	_____	_____
f. Quench medium	_____	_____
g. Quench medium temperature	_____	_____
h. Age time and temperature	_____	_____
i. Cleaning method	_____	_____
j. Special instructions	_____	_____
k. Hardness test, etc., is recorded	_____	_____
l. Furnace charts are retained	_____	_____

Notes

_____
_____
_____
_____
_____
_____
_____
_____
_____
_____

Special Process Audit

Supplier_____
Auditor_____
Date completed_____

D. Plating		Yes	No
1.	Parts are received with proper identification.	_____	_____
2.	The cleaning process is being followed.	_____	_____
3.	The cleaning process is under control.	_____	_____
4.	The plating process cycle is available in the area.	_____	_____
5.	The plating process is being followed.	_____	_____
6.	Accept/reject criteria establish specifications, thickness, sampling, etc.	_____	_____
7.	Temperature instruments are calibrated.	_____	_____
8.	Solutions are checked periodically and recorded.	_____	_____
9.	Solutions are reanalyzed after additions of chemicals.	_____	_____
10.	Materials used for solutions are certified or a chemical analysis is performed.	_____	_____
11.	Plated parts are baked after plate to relieve hydrogen embattlement as required.	_____	_____
12.	Finished parts inspection record is available.	_____	_____
13.	Parts are protected to prevent handling damage.	_____	_____
14.	Defective parts are segregated and removed for material review.	_____	_____
15.	Certification is provided and traceable to lot or batch.	_____	_____
16.	Area is organized.	_____	_____

Notes

_____
_____
_____
_____
_____
_____
_____
_____
_____
_____

Special Process Audit

Supplier_____
Auditor_____
Date completed_____

E. Nondestructive testing	Yes	No
X ray		
1. Parts that have passed X-ray inspection are marked.	_____	_____
2. Parts are adequately deburred and cleaned to prevent false X-ray indications.	_____	_____
3. Parts are visually inspected prior to X ray.	_____	_____
4. X-ray viewers are clean and located properly to ensure proper reading of film.	_____	_____
5. X-ray technique procedure is available.	_____	_____
6. X rays are taken per the approved technique.	_____	_____
7. Operator complies with the specifications of the process sheets.	_____	_____
8. The current revision of the specification or process sheet is available.	_____	_____
9. Proper acceptance criteria are available.	_____	_____
10. Defects are clearly identified on parts.	_____	_____
11. Defects are clearly identified on film.	_____	_____
12. Records of parts inspected by X ray are available and accurate.	_____	_____
13. Records show accept or reject reason.	_____	_____
14. Records are signed by the inspector.	_____	_____
15. Discrepant parts are segregated.	_____	_____
16. Rework parts are reviewed by engineer and routed to ensure heat treat and re-X ray.	_____	_____
17. Scrap material is disposed of properly.	_____	_____
18. Film is identified with lot, part number, serial number, etc.	_____	_____
19. Film envelope is identified.	_____	_____
20. 2T sensitivity acceptable.	_____	_____
21. Density of film is per specification.	_____	_____
22. Number of lots audited is per specification.	_____	_____
23. Densitometer is available, calibrated, and traceable to NIST.	_____	_____

E. Nondestructive testing   Yes   No
X ray (continued)

24. The density strip is available, calibrated, and   _____   _____
    traceable to NIST.

25. Level II/III radiographers do all acceptance   _____   _____
    reading.

26. Eye examinations are current.   _____   _____

27. Written examinations are current.   _____   _____

28. Records of inspector's exams are available.   _____   _____

29. Automatic processor is controlled.   _____   _____
    a. Density strips are run daily and logged.
    b. Temperature is checked daily.
    c. Replenishing rate is checked and logged
       periodically.

30. Radiographers are audited and results logged.   _____   _____

31. Parts are available for review on questionable   _____   _____
    indications.

32. Questionable parts are re-X rayed.   _____   _____

33. Film is punched with inspector identification.   _____   _____

34. Certifications are properly completed.   _____   _____

35. Certification identifies serial number, etc., of   _____   _____
    rejects.

36. Film envelope or copy of certification in   _____   _____
    envelope identifies serial number of rejects.

Penetrant

1. Inspectors stamp parts that have passed   _____   _____
   penetrant inspection.

2. Location of defect is clearly identified on part.   _____   _____

3. Inspector signs records.   _____   _____

4. Parts are adequately cleaned prior to penetrant   _____   _____
   inspection (scale, water, oil, and grease
   removed).

5. Penetrant inspection process sheet is available.   _____   _____

6. The operator uses process sheet or specification.   _____   _____

7. Correct revision of process sheet or   _____   _____
   specification is used.

8. Discrepant parts are segregated.   _____   _____

9. Inspectors meet eyesight requirements.   _____   _____

10. Eye examinations are current.   _____   _____

E. <u>Nondestructive testing</u>	<u>Yes</u>	<u>No</u>

Penetrant (continued)

11. Records and test reports verify that examiners   _____   _____
     are current in certification.

12. Parts are serialized prior to inspection.   _____   _____

13. A test sample with known defects is checked   _____   _____
     to verify process.

14. Checks for contaminations are made on   _____   _____
     penetrant, emulsifier, and developer baths
     or powders.

15. Operator processing parts adheres to time   _____   _____
     cycles.

Notes

_____

_____

_____

_____

_____

_____

_____

_____

_____

_____

_____

_____

_____

_____

Special Process Audit Summary

A. Painting comments: _____

_____

B. Certification review comments: _____

_____

C. Heat treat comments: _____

_____

D. Plating comments: _____

_____

E. Nondestructive testing comments: _____

_____

General comments: _____

_____

_____

_____

_____

_____

_____

_____

_____

_____

Use additional pages as necessary.

Ship-to-Stock Product Audit

An STS product audit is a review of a part to determine if it meets the criteria of the specification much in the same way as was done with the first-article inspection or qualification. Product audits may be conducted at the supplier's site by either the supplier or customer representative, or the audit may take place at the customer site and be performed by the customer representative. When the audit is performed by the supplier at the supplier's site, the customer representative should witness or verify the process and review the data collected. If the audit occurs at the customer site, the auditor should use the customer's inspection areas, equipment, and laboratories as required. The supplier representative may choose to witness this process.

Product Auditing Plan

A product audit should be conducted after all processes and inspections have been completed. Because the purpose is to determine if the supplier's process manufactures a product that meets established specifications, the audit should consist of checking all parameters, including dimensions, material certifications, and, where applicable, certifications of nondestructive or reliability tests. Using product standards, drawings, and specification listings, the auditor should list all of the elements of the part that must be audited. In essence, a product audit is like doing another first-article inspection. The results of the audit will verify that the previously agreed to process still produces product that meets specification.

The auditor should complete a summary report for every product audit that will be kept on file. The auditor and the supplier's management should review the audit results and, if necessary, ensure that corrective action is imlpemented.

Product Audit Scheduling

Product audits are conducted based on time or on quantity. For example, the audit could be conducted monthly or quarterly, or for every

20,000 pieces shipped. The frequency must be agreed to in the STS agreement. If a part is scheduled to be audited, but will not be shipped during a particular month, the very next shipment should be audited. If a supplier has many similar parts in the program, a randomly chosen part from a family of parts should be audited.

Appendix C

Food Industry Associations

American Association of Candy Technologists, Glenrock, New
    Jersey
American Association of Cereal Chemists,* St. Paul, Minnesota
American Association of Meat Processors, Elizabethtown,
    Pennsylvania
American Bakers Association, Washington, D.C.
American Bottlers of Carbonated Beverage, Washington, D.C.
American Butter Institute, Washington, D.C.
American Catfish Marketing Association, Indianola, Mississippi
American Chemical Society,* Washington, D.C.
American Corn Millers Federation, Washington, D.C.
American Dairy Association, St. Paul, Minnesota
American Dairy Products Institute, Chicago, Illinois
American Egg Board, Park Ridge, Illinois
American Feed Industry Association, Arlington, Virginia
American Frozen Food Institute, McLean, Virginia
American Institute of Baking, Manhattan, Kansas

American Institute of Wine and Food, San Francisco, California
American Meat Institute, Washington, D.C.
American Mushroom Institute, Washington, D.C.
American National Standards Institute,* Philadelphia, Pennsylvania
American Public Health Association,* New York, New York
American Seed Trade Association, Washington, D.C.
American Society of Brewing Chemists,* St. Paul, Minnesota
American Society for Testing and Materials,* Philadelphia,
    Pennsylvania
American Spice Trade Association, Englewood Cliffs, New Jersey
Apple Processors Association, Washington, D.C.
Association for Dressings and Sauces, Atlanta, Georgia
Association of Official Analytical Chemists,* Washington, D.C.
The Beer Institute, Washington, D.C.
Biscuit and Cracker Manufacturers' Association, Washington, D.C.
Chemical Manufacturers Association, Washington, D.C.
Chocolate Manufacturers Association, McLean, Virginia
Corn Refiners Association, Washington, D.C.
Flexible Packaging Association, Washington, D.C.
Food and Drug Law Institute, Washington, D.C.
Food Processors Institute, Berkeley, California
Independent Bakers Association, Washington, D.C.
Institute of Food Technologists, Chicago, Illinois
Institute of Shortening and Edible Oils, Inc., Washington, D.C.
International Association of Milk, Food, and Environmental
    Sanitarians, Ames, Iowa
International Banana Association, Washington, D.C.
International Bottled Water Association, Alexandria, Virginia
International Dairy-Deli-Bakery Association, Madison, Wisconsin
International Dairy Food Association, Washington, D.C.
International Dairy Federation,* Brussels, Belgium
International Ice Cream Association, Washington, D.C.
Milk Industry Foundation, Washington, D.C.
National Broiler Council, Washington, D.C.

National Center for Food Safety and Technology, Summit-Argo, Illinois

National Cheese Institute, Washington, D.C.

National Confectioners Association, McLean, Virginia

National Feed Ingredients Association, West Des Moines, Iowa

National Fisheries Institute, Arlington, Virginia

National Food Processors Association, Washington, D.C.

National Frozen Food Association, Harrisburg, Pennsylvania

National Grain and Feed Association, Washington, D.C.

National Ice Cream and Yogurt Retailers Association, Columbus, Ohio

National Live Stock and Meat Board, Chicago, Illinois

National Meat Canners Association, Washington, D.C.

National Oilseed Processors Association, Washington, D.C.

National Pasta Association, Arlington, Virginia

National Peanut Council, Alexandria, Virginia

National Pork Board, Des Moines, Iowa

National Pork Producers Council, Washington, D.C.

National Soft Drink Association, Washington, D.C.

National Turkey Federation, Reston, Virginia

Organic Food Production Association of North America, Greenfield, Massachusetts

Pacific Egg and Poultry Association, Modesto, California

Paperboard Packaging Council, Washington, D.C.

Peanut Butter and Nut Processors Association, Potomac, Maryland

Pickle Packers International, St. Charles, Illinois

Produce Marketing Association, Newark, Delaware

Protein Grain Products International, Washington, D.C.

The Rice Millers Association, Arlington, Virginia

Snack Food Association, Alexandria, Virginia

Southeastern Poultry and Egg Association, Decatur, Georgia

The Sugar Association, Washington, D.C.

Sweetener Users Association, Washington, D.C.

United Egg Producers, Decatur, Georgia

United Fresh Fruit and Vegetable Association, Alexandria, Virginia
United States Cane Sugar Refiners' Association, Washington, D.C.
United States Tuna Foundation, Washington, D.C.
Western States Meat Association, Oakland, California

*Denotes associations that publish analytical methods.

Appendix D

Federal Government Agencies Involved with Food Safety

The federal food safety and quality regulatory system consists of as many as 35 different laws and involves 12 federal agencies. Six of the 12 agencies have the major roles in carrying out food safety and quality activities. They are the Food and Drug Administration (FDA), which is part of the United States Department of Health and Human Services (HHS); the United States Department of Agriculture's (USDA) Agricultural Marketing Service (AMS), Federal Grain Inspection Service (FGIS), and Food Safety and Inspection Service (FSIS); the Environmental Protection Agency (EPA); and the National Marine Fisheries Service (NMFS), which is part of the United States Department of Commerce. Collectively, these agencies are responsible for assuring that consumer foods are pure and wholesome, safe to eat, and produced under sanitary conditions.

The six agencies perform a broad array of activities relating to food regulation. Their programs

- Set standards for what processed foods should contain
- Approve facilities, equipment, and processes used in preparing foods

- Approve additives, animal drugs, or pesticides before their marketing or use
- Set tolerances for acceptable amounts of pesticides and other chemical residues in food
- Inspect food and food processing facilities, including testing food for illegal residues
- Determine what information labels should contain and what packaging is acceptable
- Monitor state and local inspection programs for food retail and service establishments

Food and Drug Administration

The FDA is responsible for ensuring that domestic and imported food products (except meat and poultry products) are safe, sanitary, nutritious, wholesome, and honestly labeled. The FDA shares responsibility for egg products with AMS.

The Federal Food, Drug, and Cosmetic Act also authorizes FDA to establish standards of identity, quality, and fill of container for food products. FDA is required to review and approve food and color additives before they can be marketed.

FDA also is responsible for preapproval and surveillance of all animal drugs and food additives in feeds marketed in interstate commerce.

FDA is headquartered in Washington, D.C. Three main offices carry out food safety and quality activities—the Center for Food Safety and Applied Nutrition, the Center for Veterinary Medicine, and the Office of Regulatory Affairs.

Agricultural Marketing Service

USDA's AMS ensures the safety of shell eggs moving in consumer channels and egg products produced by processing plants involved in intrastate, interstate, and foreign commerce. The agency's only food safety regulatory responsibilities are in the egg products and shell egg surveillance programs. The other AMS programs focus primarily on food-quality services, such as commodity standardization, inspection, and grading services for dairy, egg, fruit, meat, poultry, and vegetable products.

The AMS is headquartered in Washington, D.C.

Federal Grain Inspection Service

The primary mission of USDA's FGIS is to facilitate the marketing of grain, oilseeds, pulses, rice, and related commodities. This is accomplished by establishing standards, accurately and consistently certifying quality, and providing for uniform official inspection and weighing.

Their major food safety and quality activities include

- Inspection of corn, sorghum, and rice for aflatoxin, a natural contaminant considered to be carcinogenic
- Developing and disseminating information about chemical residues in grain which is used by other agencies to establish permissible levels of pesticides in grain
- Helping ensure food quality by inspecting domestic and imported grain

FGIS carries out its inspection and weighing services through headquarters in Kansas City, Missouri, and Washington, D.C. Four units of FGIS are involved directly with food safety and quality activities. They are the Quality Assurance and Research Division, Field Management Division, International Monitoring Staff, and Compliance Division.

Food Safety and Inspection Service

USDA's FSIS administers a system of inspection laws to ensure that meat and poultry products moving in interstate and foreign commerce for use as human food are safe, wholesome, and correctly marked, labeled, and packaged.

Headquartered in Washington, D.C., four major FSIS organizational units are directly involved with inspection and supportive activities. These units are Inspection Operations, Regulatory Programs, International Programs, and Science and Technology.

Environmental Protection Agency

EPA is responsible for regulating all pesticide products sold or distributed in the United States and for establishing tolerances (maximum legal limits) for pesticide residues in or on food commodities, water, and animal feed. FDA, USDA, and state enforcement agencies are responsible for enforcing tolerances established by EPA.

The EPA is headquartered in Arlington, Virginia.

National Marine Fisheries Service

The National Marine Fisheries Service conducts a voluntary seafood inspection and grading program and performs research on seafood safety.

The NMFS is headquartered in Silver Spring, Maryland. The Inspection Services Division and the Utilization Research and Services Division are the two divisions primarily responsible for executing the food safety and quality programs.

In addition to the six major agencies, a number of other federal agencies carry out important, but less significant, food safety and quality activities.

- USDA's Agricultural Research Service (ARS) is headquartered in Washington, D.C. ARS performs food safety research to help ensure an abundance of high-quality agricultural commodities.
- USDA's Animal and Plant Health Inspection Service (APHIS) protects the nation's animal and plant resources from diseases and pests that indirectly affect food safety. APHIS is headquartered in Washington, D.C.
- The Treasury Department's Bureau of Alcohol, Tobacco, and Firearms (ATF) is responsible for administering and enforcing laws covering the production, distribution, and labeling of

alcoholic beverages and tobacco products. However, wine beverages that contain less than 7 percent alcohol are the responsibility of the FDA. ATF is headquartered in Washington, D.C.

- The Centers for Disease Control and Prevention are a branch of the Department of Health and Human Services. They are charged with protecting the nation's public health by providing leadership and direction in preventing and controlling diseases. CDCP is responsible for researching, monitoring, and controlling outbreaks of foodborne disease. They are headquartered in Atlanta, Georgia.
- The Treasury Department's Customs Service assists other federal food safety and quality agencies in carrying out their responsibilities related to imported foods. The U.S. Customs Service is headquartered in Washington, D.C.

The information contained herein is a summary of a Congressional Report compiled by the United States General Accounting Office. The entire report, entitled "Food Safety and Quality: Who Does What in the Federal Government" (GAO/RCED-91-19B), can be obtained from the U.S. General Accounting Office, P.O. Box 6015, Gaithersburg, MD 20887.

Appendix E

Prior Contributors

1983 VVTC

Dave Field	Abbott Laboratories
Alfred Geiser	National Qual-Tek Service Company
H. D. Greiner	Management Systems Analysis
Terry Hoffhines	3M
Robert E. Jouppi	Transmation
Richard J. Laford	Wang Laboratories
William Anderson	Consultant
Andrew B. Andreasen	Infrared Industries
Arthur R. Blank	Fiat-Allis North America
Dr. C. L. Carter	Rath & Strong
Robert C. Cloutier	DCAS-Navy
John Deutikom	Canadian General Standards Board
J. Dol	Fokker B. V. The Netherlands
Roger G. Langevin	Argyle Associates
Barry Lawrimore	The Audichron Company
Charles V. Leach	Westinghouse Electric Corporation

Richard A. Maass	Abbott Laboratories
John A. Malatesta	Didak Corporation
Don McNeil	Transport Canada
Charles E. Meadows	Lorillard
Meril Monashkin	Burndy Corporation
August P. Mundel	Consultant
Paul E. Ruhling	Westinghouse Electric Corporation
Ben Silver	Babcock & Wilcox
Harvey Shock	Product Assurances
Walter Uhorchak	Lockheed Georgia Company
Marvin Weir	VMX
James C. Wilson	Didak Corporation
Howard N. Wilson	Consultant
Quitman White, Jr	UNC Naval Products

First Edition Prepared by

William H. Anderson	General Electric Company
Thomas L. Blair	Texas Instruments
J. J. Brennan	Sylvania Electric
Paul E. Bruce	Lockheed
C. L. Carter Jr	C. L. Carter, Jr. & Associates
R. M. Christie	Starline
Arvine F. Cone	Sandia Corporation
J. B. Connors	Atlantic Research
O. K. Crouch	R. J. Reynolds Tobacco Co.
R. L. Cutright	C. L. Carter Jr. & Associates
A. Davis	Ogden Tech. Labs
Eugene W. Ellis	Pratt & Whitney Aircraft
J. B. English Sr.	Autonetics, North American Rockwell
H. Farrar	NASA

David L. Field	AVCO Lycoming Division
Jack B. Foster	Electra-Scientific Division Gulton Industries
C. H. Garrod Jr.	Rel-Qual Associates
Bailey Gee	Ragen Precision Industries
J. Goldfarb	Ogden Tech Labs
Harry D. Greiner	Radio Corporation of America
Rainey Greiner	Edwards Company
F. W. Hayden	Autonetics, North American Rockwell
William Hemminghaus	Lenkurt
L. J. Knight	Northrup, Nortronics Space Division
Neil M. Leary	AVCO Missile Systems Division
Isador Levin	Machlett Laboratories
Stanley Lopata	Ragen Precision Industries
S. R. Luboyeski	Amphenol Corporation
Richard A. Maass	Hitchcock Publishing Company
R. McArthur	Hughes Aircraft
J. H. McCreight	Ampex Corporation
J. R. Megliola	Plastic Coating Corporation
Mario M. Minardi	Autonetics, North American Rockwell
Meril R. Monashkin	Burndy Corporation
J. S. Mule	Pratt & Whitney Aircraft
Richard B. Mulock	Lockheed
Reed Pennell	Motorola
Paul Plepis	Perkin Elmer Corporation
Thomas G. Ragona	Diamond Shamrock Chemical Corporation
Robert H. Rahiser	Westinghouse Atomic Power Division
M. R. Seldon	General Dynamics
Richard K. Smith	North American Van Lines

Lawrence A. Swaton	Martin Marietta
G. A. Thomas	Autonetics, North American Rockwell
T. M. Vining	Defense Supply Agency
W. W. Wagner	IBM
W. D. Walker	C. L. Carter, Jr. & Associates
A. L. Wilson	Hewlett-Packard
Howard N. Wilson	Bendix Corporation

Second Edition Prepared by

William H. Anderson	General Electric
Thomas L. Blair	Texas Instruments
Thomas H. Breedlove	Martin Marietta Corporation
C. L. Carter, Jr.	C. L. Carter Jr. & Associates
Everett H. Dale	Fingerhut Corporation
Harry G. Dinackus	General Electric Company
Eugene W. Ellis	Pratt & Whitney Aircraft
David L. Field	Abbott Laboratories
Anthony W. Forchielli	Western Electric Company
Jack B. Foster	Electra-Scientific Division Gulton Industries
Kermit J. Kalna	Western Electric Company
Paul O. Marti	United Technical Center
David F. Roberts	Mack Trucks
Harley G. Selkregg Jr.	General Electric Company
Lou Simon	Avon Products
Loren M. Walsh	Hitchcock Publishing Company
A. L. Wilson	Hewlett-Packard
Howard N. Wilson	Bendix Corporation

Third Edition Editorial Review Board

W. Anderson
W. Adam
D. Field
R. Laford
R. Maass
R. von Osinski

Fourth Edition Editorial Review Board

James L. Bossert	Eastman Kodak
Arthur Blank	Admiral Company
David S. Files	Eastman Kodak
Richard J. Laford	Stevens-Arnold Division
Barry S. Lawrimore	Audichron
Brian Margetson	Northern Telecom (Canada)
John O. Brown III	Cummins Engine Company

Appendix F

Bibliography and Suggested Reading

Bibliography

Aquino, Michael A. "Improving Purchased Material Quality." *Purchasing World* 29, 5 (May 1985): 100–102.

Bain, William Jr. "Total-Value Management: The New Road to Competitive Advantage." *Chief Executive,* 33 (Autumn 1985): 46–49.

Barks, Joseph V. "Holland: More Strategies for International Distribution." *Distribution* 85, 5 (May 1985): 64–72.

Beels, Gregory. "Strategy for Survival." *Quality* 24, 4 (April 1985): 16.

Berry, Bryan H. "Now Chrysler Wants to Take on the World." *Iron Age* 229, 22 (November 1986): 45–48.

Bertrand, Kate. "Crafting 'Win-Win' Situations in Buyer-Supplier Relations." *Business Marketing* 76, 6 (June 1986): 42–50.

Boyer, Edward. "Are Japanese Managers Biased Against Americans?" *Fortune* 114, No. 5 (September 1986): 72–75.

Bridges, Linda. "LAN Leasing." *PC Week* 3 (January 1986): 51.

Brooks, Sandra. "Defiance Is Termed 'World Class'." *Production* 3, 2 (February 1986): 13.

Brush, Gary G., Thomas C. Hsiang, William McKeown, and Thomas Rogers. "After the Bell System Break Up: Bellcore Supplier Quality." *Quality Progress* 17, 11 (November 1984): 16–18.

Burgess, John A. "Developing a Supplier Certification Program." *Quality*, 1 (January 1987): 36.

———. "RIP: A Rejection Improvement Program." *Quality Progress* 17, 11 (November 1984): 70–72.

Burke, Jane. "Changing Systems: Who Is Abandoning Whom?" *Library Journal* 111 (February 1986): 55.

Cherry, Joseph V. "Vendor's Viewpoint: Quality, Response, and Delivery." *Quality Progress* 17, 11 (November 1984): 40–42.

Cloer, W. C. "Objective: Zero Defects Suppliers." *Quality Progress* 17, 11 (November 1984): 20–22.

Debacco, Tom. "Integrate to Sell." *Systems International* 14, 11 (November 1986): 119–120.

Derose, Louis J. "Assuring Supplier Quality." *Purchasing World* 27, 11 (November 1983): 40.

Devlin, James M. "Weaker $ Turns Nordic Customers to U.S. Suppliers." *Business America* 9 (March 1986): 13.

Ealey, Lance. "World-Class Suppliers: How They make the Grade." *Automotive Industries* (January 1987): 1–87.

Ergas, Henry. "Information Technology Standards: The Issues." *Telecommunications* 20, 9 (September 1986): 127–33.

Faillace, Joseph N. "Managing the QA Database." *Quality Progress* 19, 11 (November 1986): 13–16.

Farrell, Paul V. "Is There a Role for Purchasing in Improving U.S. Productivity?" *Purchasing World* 29, 9 (September 1985): 42.

Feldman, Allen W. "Vendor Quality Rating and Customer Perception." *Quality Progress* 17, 11 (November 1984): 64–66.

"Glossary of Selected Terms Related to Testing and Inspection." *1983 Buyer's Guide and Directory* 1. Metals Park, Ohio: American Society for Metals (1983).

Goodman, Jeffrey S. "Future Resistance: Setting Standards for Software Vendors." *Credit and Financial Management* 88, 5 (May 1986): 17–18, 21.

Gordon, Howard. "The Multivendor Muddle." *Network World* 3, 35 (November 1986): 43–44.

Greenburg, Harold, and Paul Huppenbaur. "Ship to Stock—A Quality Partnership Success Story." *ASQC 38th Annual Quality Congress Transactions*. Milwaukee: American Society for Quality Control, May 1984. 46–51.

Grenier, Robert. "Total Quality Assurance, Part V." *Quality* 25, 4 (April 1986): 38–41.

Hagan, John T. "The Management of Quality: Preparing for a Competitive Future." *Quality Progress* 17, 11 (November 1984): 12–15.

Harbour, Jim. "Is New-Tech Really the Answer?" *Automotive Industries* (July 1986): 9.

Harper, Doug. "Value Added, the Key to Distributor Survival." *Industrial Distribution* 75, 11 (November 1986): 58.

Hart, Robert F. "Letter . . . To All Single Source Suppliers." *Quality* 25, 4 (April 1986): 64–65.

Hayes, Glenn E. "World-Class Vendor Quality." *Quality* 25, 6 (June 1986): 14–18.

Hoeffer, E. "How Ford Makes Quality Happen." *Purchasing* 90, 5 (March 1981): 51, 53.

Holmes, Donald. "A Quality Portfolio Management Chart." *Quality* 25, 12 (December 1986): 67.

Houston, Jerry. "Torque Auditing for SPC." *Quality* 25, 11 (November 1986): 29–33.

Huber, Robert F. "Assembly Gives a Perspective on Costs." *Production Week* 95, 5 (May 1985): 34–38.

Hunt, Robert O. "Quality from the Source." *Quality* 21, 4 (April 1982): 54–56.

Karabatsos, Nancy A. "World-Class Quality." *Quality* 23, 1 (January 1986): 14–18.

Kimber, Raymond J. "Chrysler's Renaissance." *Quality* 23, 6 (June 1984): 80–81.

Kirland, Carl. "JIT Manufacturing—What You Need to Know." *Plastics Technology* (August 1984): 63–68.

Krepchin, Ira P. "How MRP II and JIT Work Together at DuPont." *Modern Material Handling* 41, 15 (December 1986): 73–76.

Laford, Richard. "Cut Inspection Costs and Improve Quality with Ship-to-Stock." *Bureau of Business Practice Production Bulletin* 606 (March 1986): 1–4.

———. "Ship-to-Stock." *Quality Progress* 17, 11 (November 1984): 52–54.

———. "Ship-to-Stock." *30th EOQC Annual Conference Proceedings.* Stockholm: European Organization for Quality Control (June 1986) 147–54.

———. *Ship-to-Stock: An Alternative to Incoming Inspection.* Milwaukee: ASQC Quality Press, 1986.

Laford, Richard, and Robert Steers. "Receiving Inspection Ship to Stock, Part 1 and Part 2." *33rd ASQC Annual Quality Congress Transactions.* Milwaukee: American Society for Quality Control, May 1979. 68–72.

Lindenmuth, Richard. "Stabilizing Volatile Telephone Instrument Market." *Telephony* 208, 6 (February 1985): 126–32.

Maass, Richard A. *For Goodness' Sake, Help.* Milwaukee: ASQC Quality Press, 1986.

———. *Supplier Certification: A Continuous Improvement Strategy.* Milwaukee: ASQC Quality Press, 1990.

———. "World Class Quality—An Innovative Rx for Survival." *ASQC 39th Annual Quality Congress Transactions.* Milwaukee: American Society for Quality Control, May 1985. 258–74.

MacDonald, Roger, Paul Saacke, and Gary Brush. "The Bottom Line on Quality: Training Reaches Beyond QA Personnel." *Quality Progress* 18, 11 (November 1985): 59–61.

Maraschiello, Bill. "JIT and the Receiving Room." *Handling Shipping and Management* 27, 8 (August 1986): 36–38.

Matthews, Joseph R. "Boy Scouts from Missouri." *Library Journal* 111 (February 1986): 51.

McBryde, Vernon E. "In Today's Market, Quality Best Focus for Upper Management." *IE* (July 1986): 51–55.

McCasland, Charles. "JIT + SPC = Q(uality)." *Manufacturing Systems* 3, 7 (July 1985): 47–48.

Moskal, B. S. "Just-in-Time—Putting the Squeeze on Suppliers." *Industry Week* 222, 1 (July 1984): 59–60, 62.

O'Neal, Charles. "New Operating Philosophy Means Smart Supplier Selection Is a Must." *Marketing News* 20, 23 (November 1986): 31.

Palda, Kristina S. "Technological Insensitivity: Concept and Measurement." *Netherlands Research Policy* 15, 4 (August 1986): 187–98.

Pantases, Angeline. "Vendors Hunt for the Key to Success." *Datamation* 32 (May 1986): 82.

Pelchat, Raymond. "Quest—Quality Enhanced Supplier Test." *ASQC 39th Annual Quality Congress Transactions.* Milwaukee: American Society for Quality Control, May 1985. 41–46.

Pennucci, Nicholas. "Assuring Vendor Process Control to Reduce Incoming Sampling." *Quality Progress* 17, 11 (November 1984): 56–57.

Schonberger, Richard J. *Japanese Manufacturing Techniques.* New York: The Free Press 1982.

————. *World Class Manufacturing.* New York: The Free Press, 1986.

Sehnert, Tim. "Getting Suppliers Involved in Purchasing Quality Improvement." *Purchasing World* 30, 3 (March 1986): 68–69.

Serchuk, Alan. "Rate Supplier Quality Openly." *Purchasing* 74, 1 (January 1973): 53–54.

Shaw, Donald R. "Determining Package Quotient-Supplier Quality: User Needs." *Data Management* 17, 3 (March 1979): 16–19.

Shortell, Ann. "The Auditors." *Canadian Business* 59, 11 (November 1986): 38–44.

Shrabek, Quentin R. "Process Diagnostics—Seven Steps for Problem Solving." *Quality Progress* 19, 11 (November 1986): 40–44.

Stone, Robert B. "What Major Companies Expect from a Supplier and His Product." *Production* 91, 5 (May 1983): 29, 31.

"Supplier Quality Improvement Today." *Quality Progress* 17, 11 (November 1984): 48–51.

"Supplier Quality Improvement Today—Part II." *Quality Progress* 17, 12 (December 1984): 35–38.

Sullivan, Kristina. "Users Turn to LAN Vendors for Multiuser Databases." *PC Week* 3 (February 1986): 127.

Talley, Dorsey J. "Cost Cutting with the Lone Ranger Concept." *Manage* 34, 4 (October 1982): 12–14.

Teja, Edward. "PC Board Vendors Rush to Fill EGA Standards." *Mini-Micro Systems* 19, 9 (July 1986): 69–81.

Temkin, Robert H. "Automating Auditing: Auditing Will Never Be the Same." *Corporate Accounting* 4, 4 (Fall 1986): 56–59.

Tolan, Thomas. "Provider Quality: Long Distance Inspection Services." *Quality Progress* 17, 11 (November 1984): 74–75.

Unger, Harlow. "Car Makers Force Steel Industry Turnaround." *Industrial Management* 9, 10 (November 1985): 11.

Wortham, William A. "Problem-Solving in the QC Area Creates a 'Ripple Effect.'" *Industrial Engineering* 18, 7 (July 1986): 78–82

Suggested Reading

Algian, G.W., ed. *Purchasing Handbook.* 5th ed. New York: McGraw-Hill, 1993.

Bhote, K. R. *Strategic Supply Management.* New York: AMACOM, 1989.

Feigenbaum, A. V. *Total Quality Control.* 3d ed. New York: McGraw-Hill, 1991.

Juran, J. M. *Juran's Quality Control Handbook*. 4th ed. New York: McGraw-Hill, 1988.

Juran, J. M., and F. M. Gryna. *Quality Planning and Analysis*. 3d ed. New York: McGraw-Hill, 1993.

Kane, V. E. *Defect Prevention*. New York: Marcel Dekker, 1989.

Maass, R. A., J. O. Brown, and J. L. Bossert. *Supplier Certification: A Continuous Improvement Strategy*. Milwaukee, Wis.: ASQC Quality Press, 1990.

Weber, R.T., and R. H. Johnson. *Buying and Supplying Quality*. Milwaukee, Wis.: ASQC Quality Press, 1993.

Index